Rites and Myths of Seduction

Other books by Aldo Carotenuto

To Love, To Betray: Life as Betrayal
A Secret Symmetry: Sabina Spielrein Between Jung and Freud
The Vertical Labyrinth: Individuation in Jungian Psychology
The Spiral Way: A Woman's Healing Journey
Eros and Pathos: Shades of Love and Suffering
Kant's Dove: The History of Transference in Psychoanalysis
The Difficult Art: A Critical Discourse on Psychotherapy
*The Call of the Daimon: Love and Truth in the Writings of
 Franz Kafka—The Trial and the Castle*

Rites and Myths of Seduction

Aldo Carotenuto

Translated by
Joan Tambureno

Chiron Publications • Wilmette, Illinois

Originally published in Italian in 1994 as *Riti e miti della seduzione.*
© 1994, R.C.S. Libri, Bompiani, S.p.A. Milan.

English translation prepared for Aldo Carotenuto by Joan Tambureno.

Library of Congress Catalog Card Number: 2001007822

Printed in the United States of America.
Copyedited by Linda Conheady.
Book design by Ellen Scanlon.
Cover design by D. J. Hyde.

Library of Congress Cataloging-in-Publication Data:

Carotenuto, Aldo.
    Rites and myths of seduction / Aldo Carotenuto ; translated by Joan Tambureno.
        p. cm.
Includes bibliographical references and index.
    ISBN 1-888602-19-8
    1. Psychoanalysis. 2. Seduction–Psychological aspects. 3. Jungian psychology. I. Title.
BF173 .C412 2002
150.19'54–dc21

2001007822
CIP

Contents

Introduction

Man is continuously seduced by life, in the sense that he is invited to become involved, to look inside himself in order to know himself through the recollection of things, forms, and emotions. The act of seduction has been a constant in the lives of men (and women) from Biblical times on up to the present—it has been the flame lighting the way to discovery, creation, and love, but also to perdition.

The act of seduction is defined here as "carrying elsewhere," the sweeping of the subject outside and beyond usual experience. *Rites and Myths of Seduction* takes us on a fascinating exploration of the myths, rites, and occasions of seduction—not only the seduction of love, but also the seduction of any *ignotum* that captures the individual, causing him to start down an unfamiliar path. This book describes a voyage in search not only of those affective roots that determine the various forms of involvement, but also of the exorcisms and fears that fascination inevitably activates, eventually becoming the underlying causes of loss and betrayal.

In the context of the psychoanalytical model of those object relationships that propose once more, and confirm, the perpetual and essential role of the relationship, the author examines the unconscious motivations at play in the game of seduction, focusing on those areas of observation most closely related to his experience as psychoanalyst: seduction in infancy, seduction in the couple relationship, and seduction in the analytical relationship.

One

Being Elsewhere

One loves only when in what is pursued there is some-
thing inaccessible, something not possessed.
                                    —M. Proust, *The Prisoner*

Seduction is something more than an occasional event in our
sentimental lives—it is a constant presence. It also represents the
very trauma of our entering into contact, tuned with the world.

Man is perpetually seduced; as a child, in wonderment at each
new acquisition, it is the seduction of sounds, colors, smells,
anything that activates his fantasy; as an adolescent, it is the
force of dreams and the attraction of utopia that "leads him elsewhere," in the gratifying sensation of omnipotence, when he
feels capable of conquering the world, realizing any ambition. In
an adult, seduction takes on the many hues of desire—through
the manifold figures with which man animates his imaginary in
order to overcome his being one, his existential solitude, molding forms and symbols to create a personal universe, identity,
and roots. Thus, seduction can be considered not only in the
context of love but also of ideas, the spirit, evil, or images.
Wherever there is the slightest hint of possible reparation or
gratification, of reassembling our tensions, of feeling that we
participate fully in life, through the challenging experience of
losing oneself and finding oneself once more, seduction exists.

Of course, the word *seduction* in the strictest sense inevitably
conjures up the most famous and exemplary figure of the seducers, the mythical Don Juan. The fame of this master of seduction
is so widespread that his name has become synonymous for that
multitude of obscure imitators inspired by him. But our intention

here is to examine some of the less-hackneyed aspects of this mythical personage, providing perhaps new material for psychological reflection on the less explicit, less literal significance of the mysterious seduction impulse—in both seducer and seduced. Other personages and other myths will be examined in the attempt to shed additional light on the relationship between seduction and other aspects of human experience, such as the experiences of evil or loss. Seduction designates a particular circular space, where the Me is placed in relation to the Other. It is marching to another rhythm, other drums, an alternation of approach and withdrawal, presence and absence, order and confusion. It is the distortion of all meaning before the unknown, which is incarnated by the other who enchants and disorients us—that which enchants is just that capacity of the other to disorient us, to distract us from our present and set us down violently in a rare and troubling elsewhere, as any experience that solicits the emergence of deep complexes must. Keeping in mind the many-faceted aspects of seduction, we will begin with an etymological analysis of the term *seduction* (its derivatives and cognates) in an attempt to penetrate the stratification of meanings that time and experience have crystallized into a verbal figure *telling* us what seduction is.

Once more, the term *seduction* originally meant *carrying off.* *Seduce* derives from the Latin *sed,* combined with *ducerem,* where the morpheme *sed* stands for "a part." In German the word *seduction* (*Verfuhrung*) has a similar composition: the morpheme *-fuhrung* in fact comes from *fugren* = *ducere* (that is, conduct), and the prefix *ver-* has an analogous meaning to that of the Latin prefix *sed.* What comes to mind is "divert" or "turn aside." *Seducere* means therefore "to conduct away." Thus, the seduced individual is captured, seized by an irresistible force, removed from a precise order of meanings, and conducted "elsewhere."

Love, in fact, always inflicts violence on the individual, if by "individual" we intend a subject who maintains a "trading" relation with reality, under the banner of profit and in the interests of his own personal balance sheet; that is, his own needs. Love upsets this balance by introducing a new element: the needs of the other. This process remains for the most part concealed from us and, consequently, on the conscious level we can still delude ourselves that the desire aroused by the other has not set us off balance, that it is no more than one more need to be satisfied, one more of *our* needs. And yet, on some level, we are aware that something has radically changed, that a novelty has been introduced that will not be easy to deal with. Desiring another means entering another world, one that also includes dreams, needs, and desires *that are not our own.*

> Desire . . . in the search of its objects (fantastic or real) decentralizes the subject, challenging his narcissistic aspiration for oneness, and in this sense the object is an object-trauma. (Masciangelo 1988, 414)

Love, then, requires breaking out of the "narcissistic shell." It is a common mistake to believe that loving is easy, that for the human being falling in love is the most obvious and most spontaneous interior impulse, requiring no particular knowledge or instruction. It is not, however, quite that simple. If we consider the antagonism that is created between narcissism and love—that is, between the request (depending to some extent on needs generated by the instinct of self-preservation) for the libidinal equilibrium and the energetic activation that the object relationship requires—it will become clear how the incapacity to love, to be seduced—that is, conducted "to a different place," even temporarily—is created.

Thus, although the vocation of Eros is clearly one of diverting, of wounding, of altering, those alterations are functional, at least potentially, to the reorganization of a new psychological order. This capacity to transform is also created during the long period of incubation in which fantasies that animate (*love*) remain confined to the unconscious (David 1971, 37), where they are subject to the contrasting dynamics of psychic opposites. What can suddenly appear on the horizon is the person who seemingly incarnates them: our seducer. But it is not always possible to let ourselves be "led away," as regards our own internal images and a deep encounter with the other. Otto F. Kernberg (1976) observed that falling in love necessitated having positively completed two fundamental phases of psychological development: the integration of oral eroticism in the reciprocity of the object relationship with the mother, and a full genital satisfaction in the sphere of a mature object relationship. Definitively, the capacity to fall in love depends on the development of positive, interiorized object relationships. Very often, where there is a problem connected to early narcissistic wounds, there is also a substantial difficulty in making a commitment to a mature relationship, in going beyond the occasional encounter that leaves no trace nor introduces any particular requests. These are encounters that make it possible to maintain defensive barriers against what appears to be the most serious threat to equilibrium: intimate involvement. Sexual promiscuity—which we will consider more closely in the context of the figure of Don Juan—can also be interpreted as flight from relationship. In fact, it can indicate an incapacity to either go beyond the phase of superficial, immediate contact or establish a total and stable object involvement. In the hysterical personality, promiscuous comportment often implies an unconscious sense of guilt before mature and satisfying relationships that, unconsciously, would represent a "forbidden Oedipal fulfillment" (ibid., 488).

The sexual promiscuity of the narcissistic personality is instead connected to the desire for objects that are easily idealized: women who are either beautiful or considered precious for some reason, or "impossible" men who, because they resist, must be conquered at all costs. What is the real unconscious experience as regards these much sought-after preys? Kernberg speaks of greed and unconscious envy, of the need to possess in order to devalue:

> Insofar as sexual excitement temporarily heightens the illusion of beauty . . . withheld, a temporary enthusiasm for the desired sexual object may imitate the state of falling in love. Soon, however, sexual fulfillment gratifies the need for conquest, coinciding with the unconscious process of devaluating the desired object, and resulting in a speedy disappearance of both excitement and interest (ibid., 489).

The unconscious game, however, does not end here, given that these personalities project their envy and unconscious greed onto the other, who—as they incarnate persecutory phantasms—

4

inspires in them the fear of being "imprisoned," "castrated," "forced," to the point of causing rupture, as their need for freedom has not been comprehended by the other. Certainly, the urge to flee, attempts to manipulate, and the projection of unbearable emotions onto the other conceal the deep, ungratified hope of finding the response to a profound need of human love, "as if it were magically bound up with corporeal surfaces— breasts, penises, buttocks or vaginas" (ibid., 489). The possibility of these personalities developing a more authentic pattern of relationship lies—as clinical experience has proved—in the capacity to make contact with their depressive experiences connected to an early sense of guilt and the interest for the object onto which the attention is centered. Obviously, the fact of having fallen in love is not alone sufficient proof that one is capable of sustaining a deep relationship, even though it does indicate a potential willingness to abandon defenses in the interests of a temporary fusional regression; that is, once more, the willingness to be conducted elsewhere.

In the process of falling in love, that form of reciprocal seduction, the two protagonists lead each other away, offstage, beyond the rules and conventions of the social game. They become allies and even accomplices in their attempt to elude observation—as though belonging to some secret cult—in order to abandon themselves freely to psychic movements of an exceptional intensity. It is this moving away from generally accepted norms that renders the love experience literally *indescribable,* comprehensible only to those experiencing it. Roland Barthes (1977, 191–192) described it this way:

> A difficult paradox; I can be understood by all (love derives from all, its idiom is a current one), but at the same time I can be heard only by one who *shares, precisely* and *at a particular moment,* my language . . . Society deals me an unusual punishment, openly: no prohibition; I am only suspended *a humanis,* distant from human things with a tacit decree of insignificance: I am part of no repertory, no sanctuary shelters me.

Apropos of the deviation that seduction implies, Jean Baudrillard wrote that "seduction is never linear . . . it is oblique"

(1979, 147). Cupid's darts always arrive from hidden places: the identity of the seduced is one conjugated in the passive voice, but the past tense as well in the sense that we find ourselves seduced, caught in the trap, realizing always *after* the fact that we have been wounded. It would be difficult to speak of seduction without ever having been involved personally: it is an inadvertent action, a question of delayed action. And, in a certain sense, it *occurs in spite of ourselves.* And yet, as we shall see, we can be struck only because we have already been *exposed,* even *disposed;* that is, inhabited by an unconscious desire that rendered us vulnerable to the piercing of Eros. But how does this happen?

As psychoanalysts, in our investigation of the phenomenology of seduction, we must be extremely attentive in the areas of subterranean movements, unconscious motivations, and above all the secret, transforming processes apparently made possible by the love experience. The intensity of an emotion is in fact always indicative of an unconscious complex. We know that complexes represent those autonomous and powerful affective contents of the unconscious (Animus, Anima, etc.).

We enter into contact with the complex with—or better still, the complex is manifested by—each intense emotional experience. The more intense the emotion, the more evident the force of the complex in action. The love fascination is the *via regia* to facing our own unconscious components; it is that space in which, thanks to the painful game of Eros, we can best gain access to the realm of our image-affect, that dynamic sedimentation of our earliest introjections (of primitive love objects), tacitly guiding our choices as adults. The dynamic of the complex is manifested in our relationships with those we love or will love. Suggesting that the seduced subject can be considered a more or less conscious accomplice in the seductive game of the other implies that the one seduced is already well disposed toward an activation of unconscious components pressing in the direction of consciousness, in order to be assimilated. In fact, what is characteristic of any unconscious image is previous contact by the subject through projections onto persons or objects in the external world (Perry 1976).

Unconscious components inevitably emerge in the emotional field in the form of involvement with someone or something.

Consequently, through the other, we are captured and fascinated by internal contents clamoring for attention, and thus, given the vast quantity of unconscious material, the ends and objects of desire will be infinite. Obviously, this does not diminish in any way the significance of the relationship, the truth of or love for the other. In fact—as Jung stated—it is proof that the soul of man "live(s) only in and by human relationships" and that "without the conscious recognition and acceptance of our fellowship with those around us there can be no synthesis of personality" (Jung 1946, 233). We might then agree with J. P. Perry (1976) that the emotional life is the activity of the unconscious, the instrument through which new contents emerge to consciousness.

The figure of Don Juan will be considered as the superlative figure of the male seducer. And yet, a consideration of the forms and suggestions that have emerged from the universal imaginary—from myth to art—could suggest that the quality of the seducer is a *feminine* quality. In fact, the art of seduction belongs to the realm of woman. Is it possible, then, that Don Juan possesses a "female" soul? In his reference to the constituent "obliqueness" of eroticism, Baudrillard maintains that the secret of female strength lies in being (and having always been) *elsewhere:* "The female seduces because she is never there where she is thought to be" (1979, 15).

This brings us back to the irresistible quality of the immovable love object, the doubly seductive and elusive quality of love when it appears as obscure and incomprehensible.

In a relationship, the other's indifference, perceived as an unyielding affect and an "affirmation of a negation," activates the search for a secret to justify that absence of desire (Bucelli 1993, 269): it is impossible to conceive of that absence, which is the other's withdrawal from our desire, without conjecturing explanations that in any case only intensify the attraction we feel. With the absence of the other, desire emerges—and at that point, seduction has occurred.

We might here analyze the etymological—but also semantic—proximity of the terms *seduction* and *sedition*. Both share the morpheme "sed." It is this "proximity" that renders fascinating Jean Baudrillard's thesis, according to which seduction is fundamentally the subversion of order. This means subversion of the internal order and the spatial-temporal fabric of our existence, the upsetting of the daily quality and the regularity of private affects. Seducer or seduced—more or less profoundly—is transformed by this experience and rendered unrecognizable to himself.

Describing seduction as "oblique" and "subversive" implies placing that experience in a "sinister" or evil light. *Our* perspective is slightly different, but for the moment we will limit ourselves to registering and analyzing how experience perceives and describes seduction. Thus, perceived as being somewhat akin to evil, seduction has always been attributed a negative aura. The patient's narration of himself will often describe someone at the mercy of the perverse game of the other, as someone relegated to the realm of evil and aggressiveness. The other has the power to fling him into the deepest depths, diabolically trampling his dignity and destroying his will. Some of you will be familiar with Heinrich Mann's story *The Blue Angel* (1905), and certainly most of you with the film it inspired, directed by Joseph Sternberg. The theme is the perdition of Professor Unrat, a severe and irreproachable schoolmaster, who becomes caught up in a fatal and all-consuming passion for Rosa Frolich, a cafè-concert performer whose seductive arts captivate him totally, leading him to perform certain actions that cost him his career, his reputation, and the very perception of his own dignity. From a dignified man of letters, he becomes a cunning corrupter and gambler, consumed by a passion that is actually his fascination for death and degradation, the vertiginous abyss, annihilation.

In the Christian tradition—which we must constantly take into consideration, as it is one of the bases of our *Weltanschauung,* our concept of the world—the great seducer is Satan. In the religious view, the destiny of man was sealed in a primordial act of seduction: Satan's seduction of Eve; Eve's seduction of Adam. Original Sin, therefore, is the result of a double seduction. This alone would be ample reason to explain the central role seduction plays in human existence.

Another observation on the negative acceptation of the term *seductive* as compared to *seducing* is provided by Gianna Marina Petronio Andreatta, who also points out how we describe as seductive a "person who manipulates the other in the desperate need to control him" (1989, 191).

Renata De Benedetti Gaddini, on the other hand, assimilates to the semantic field of *to seduce* subjugating, trapping, deceiving, and disillusioning (1989, 160).

An observation of children reveals how their seductive quality, their perception of their own powerlessness and the fear of being annihilated, is compensated by a series of behavioral sequences, or signals, which neutralize the aggressiveness of the adult and activate responses of solicitude and caring. The facial morphology, crying, and smiles of the child arouse the mother's tenderness; we might even say seduce her. As adults we perform the same propitiatory rituals when we dress in a certain way, take pains with our appearance, aiming—unconsciously or consciously—to seduce or neutralize the aggressiveness of others. Just as in interpersonal communication, the rules of interaction (looks, words, and pauses) create a system of reciprocal seduction, a protected circuit in which both individuals take part in a game of seductive maneuvering, in the attempt to *control* the other. The game of seduction would therefore actually be one of counter-seduction, aimed at holding in check the potential seductive power of the other: he who seduces is temporarily safe from seduction. Is seduction, then, no more than a power game? As we will see further on, making a distinction between "instrumental" seduction and seduction "with a purpose" involves running the risk of reducing seduction to a situation in which the power plane is confused with and dominates the love plane.

Two

Countenance/Mask

It is the eternal law of love that beings are born for one another only at the first instant of love.
— S. Kierkegaard, *The Diary of a Seducer*

Establishing a typology for seduction, setting down its various components, would be more complex than it might seem. And this is precisely because not only does seduction occur at a particular point in the love relationship, but also it is present throughout all human existence. Organizing the vast range of material this subject involves would also require a circumscription of those particular *spheres* in which seduction operates.

Subsequently, identifying power and love as the focal points of the phenomenology of seduction would involve establishing the various *types* of seduction, in the context of both the *need for power* and the *need for love*.

Another problem—inherent in the *modes* of seduction—is determining the instruments—conscious or unconscious—utilized to satisfy desire.

And, ultimately, there is the question as to the *typology of the seducer:* is it possible, by observing an individual and analyzing his conduct, to establish that we are in the presence of a seducer? Although we may describe a person as being "seductive," it is less simple to explain why we do; we are at a loss to describe what impressions these individuals create or what images they arouse to lead us to consider them seducers or seductresses. The fascination of seduction is oblique, mysterious, made up of gestures or allusion rather than explicit messages, of consciously evasive movements as regards the other's desire. It is something bordering on an art, a fascinating ambivalence that can come very close to perversion. The French director Louis Malle, in one of his films, *Damage* (1992), presents us with a certain sexual seduction in which the most ambiguous and troubling aspects of this phenomenon converge. The leading female character, loved at the same time by her young fiancé and his father, perfectly incarnates the type of woman-Anima described by Jung—a woman able to impersonate the projections of the man she seduces so perfectly that she appears as genuinely reliable and tender to her young lover as she does dark, shrewd, and enigmatic to the mature one. She is perceived by the one as vulnerable and in need of affection, and by the other as inscrutable and elusive. This confirms the analytical assumption that the other—above and beyond *his own* reality—assumes the countenance of *our* fantasies, becoming the shadow onto which we project the internal image of *our* sexual counterpart.

The question here as regards seduction is, In what spheres does seduction operate? The answer would be actually a great many. In any case, we will limit ourselves here to enucleating three: seduction within the love relationship, seduction in the analytical relationship, and the Oedipus seduction (or seduction in infancy). We might nonetheless consider the different meanings of seduction, referring to some basic coordinates of the analytical discourse. Seduction, at least as regards its psychological references, which do not in any case exhaust its portent or presume to be the final word on meaning, is deeply rooted in the area of the *repression* of the loss of the love object and its "recovery" through symbolic activity that emancipates the subject from the immediate satisfaction compulsion.

The mother, according to Freud, is the first seductress. Her body and her love remain etched in our memory as the absolute and prohibited space of desire:

> When Freud stated that *love is nostalgia* (1919, 106), the *nostalgia of the mother* (1938b, 615), he was alluding to the nostalgic attraction of the mnestic traces of experiences of satisfaction and sensuality with the mother and her body (Masciangelo 1988, 399).

The reciprocal possession in the fusion with the mother characterizes the child's very "being":

> Children like expressing an object-relation by an identification: 'I am the object'. 'Having' is the later of the two; after loss of the object it relapses into 'being'. Example: the breast. 'The breast is a part of me, I am the other breast.' Only later: 'I have it' . . . that is, 'I am not it'. (Freud 1938a, 299)

But the child's desire for his mother is limited and frustrated; the maternal presence is inevitably discontinuous, and her absence can be experienced by the child as a wound, a mournful separation. It is a physical separation that he must bear, and that is intensified by the introduction of a "third" party, the father, who—while at a certain level of infantile fantasies can be experienced as the violent separator—actually represents a primary and fundamental significance of the limit, an "other" presence that loosens the fusional embrace, becoming guarantor of a relational rhythm of the mother-child couple, "capable of checking the prolongation of the experience of absence, or excessive presence of the mother, in a destructive experience of annihilation" (Masciangelo 1988, 402). It is this distance that renders the maternal seductive.

The paternal figure has therefore an organizing function in the child's processes of separation and differentiation, which lead to the passage from fusion to inter-subjectivity and the transformation of loss into absence and desire. If the child succeeds in elaborating the mother's "being elsewhere" as a going toward a third (the father, but also all that which does not coincide with the maternal role, his entire desiring dimension), which does not, however, cheat him or deprive him of love, the experience of that absence can be transformed into a creative intra-psychic experience and the lost object will be "retrieved" in a new form. It will be initially an epiphany of the symbol and a fecund tending toward the other, the seductive power of whom he will recognize; that is, the evocation of a lack that yearns to be filled through eros. The fusional quality, on the other hand, negates desire, which is a straining toward what is other than oneself, since distance—as it is distinction and expectation—is not tolerated. Where there is fusion, eros is incestuous and uroboric, eternally locked onto itself, and any "third" is experienced as an intruder. It is a third unable to activate his seduction—that is, separate the subject from the fusional embrace with the maternal, because that very presence is a threat of annihilation, the danger of a symbiotic rupture that would mean the end of the subject.

The erotic experience instead implies the recognition of the alterity; the acceptance of the other as a free being who seduces, first of all, precisely by virtue of his being "elsewhere." What do we mean by this? That giving in to seduction is more complicated than it might seem. It is easier to identify with the role of the seducer, and his resources, than abandon oneself to that intimate torment of being at the mercy of desire, the presence/absence of the other, which inevitably creates constellations of other longings and the desire for completeness and union. Above all, behind the seduction of the other, there is the fear of exposure, of the wounds that love inevitably inflicts—if by loving we intend venturing beyond the dominion of one's own ego, to a foreign dimension that places us before what is extraneousness, the stranger, within us—our Double, our Shadow.

Before the appearance of that stranger, we are overwhelmed by apprehension; we offer strong resistance, and rightly so, as James Hillman (1972b, 80–81) states, given the fact that fear "is the beginning of psychology":

> Love and fear go together, forming a kin of awe, transforming the psyche's awareness, giving it a religious sense that it must tread with care, fearfully . . . Such denial . . . arouses the anima to differentiate its psychological needs . . . Love stirs fear. We are afraid to love and afraid in love, magically propitiating, looking for signs, asking for protection and guidance.

The fear of exposure to the temptation of seduction signifies the unconscious comprehension of the initiatory voyage which, thanks to the other, we will undertake. However, what is the route and destination of eros? It is by now clear that love follows the dream of recomposing the divided parts and reunification at the very instant of the embrace. Plato and his vision of Eros is

13

often referred to: the mythical androgyne or hermaphrodite, the ancient fable of Love and Psyche. Mystic doctrine informs us that love in its highest expressions expands the spaces of the soul, obscures the Ego, placing it at the service of a vaster totality, or the divine that subtends all creation.

The idea underlying all concepts of the erotic experience is its connection to the problem of contraries and therefore its tendency to revive an experience of reconciliation. An example of one of the more suggestive versions of the androgyne myth is the ancient cult of Shiva, which has survived in India as a metaphysical and esoteric doctrine, the basis of a profound religious and philosophical speculation. Although the god Shiva in his non-manifest-being is without physical substance, he contains within him all the powers and all the contraries of sexes and all forms. The instant Shiva doubles, the force of desire takes form, which is the attraction of opposites, and it is of desire that worlds are born. The manifestation of Shiva is represented by the goddess Sakti, and the eternal coupling of the two produces the androgyne, the perfect representation of the divine.

Jung, following Freud, retraces in the psyche the foundation of an original bisexuality and a tendency to recuperate psychic completeness through contact with unconscious heterosexual components. Noting in his own unconscious the presence of a complementary feminine figure, which he called *Anima* (*Animus* being the woman's unconscious male figure), a sort of alter ego we carry within us, he associated it with the problem of opposites and the necessity that the individual integrate rather than resist them. This complementary, unconscious image of a sexual alter ego can be projected by the individual onto a real person. Through the erotic experience and its internal elaboration, the individual integrates counter-sexual aspects, and thus enriches his own personality.

Assuming our own latent femininity or virility, and consequently rendering ourselves complete, signifies assuming the totality of our own psychism in the form of a true bisexuality. The androgyne is thus a myth of reintegration. Jung's attraction for philosophical dualism—illustrated by his great passion for gnosticism—does not in any way lock him onto a Manichaean concept of existence, which in fact is avoided by a deeper consciousness of the identity of opposites and the relativity of their being opposite. The opposition of contraries creates the attraction of opposites, and the discrimination between the sexes the nostalgia for the removal of discrimination. In this world of concatenation, contraries are always connected (Lilar 1963, 170).

The erotic experience, considered in its most complete and profound expression, could be defined as a total and integrating experience—and a far cry from the idealization of love, which—taking its cue from an erroneous understanding of Platonism and an exaggerated body/spirit dualism—was the basis of courtly, disembodied love.

> For some, the sexual act is essentially unforgivably vile, shameful, degrading, and nothing can raise it from this baseness. For others, it must be sanctified as a sacrament. . . . True lovers are equidistant from this confusion. Nothing could be easier than convincing them that love sanctifies. They know: in love . . . everything is sacred if sexuality is assumed with its mystery, in its gravity, in its totality (ibid., 197–198).

The contiguity of the erotic experience to the sphere of the sacred is evident. It involves that area in which the extremes—excess and dispersion, fusion and absolute otherness—meet, and it is common to both to dispel the delimitation of single beings in favor of a unity that in the language of lovers and mystics alike is expressed with the same metaphors and images. The tendency of being overwhelmed, canceled, according to Rudolf Otto (1936), is also extraordinarily similar to the consummation of the sexual act.

Sacred or profane, lovers speak of love as an experience that is at the same time ecstatic and terrifying. It is the revelation of a beauty that, transcending the lover and the beloved, disorients and blinds. Thus Rainer Maria Rilke could write that "beauty is nothing more than the dreadful at its beginning." It is perhaps this symbolic "third" beauty that is created from the union of two individuals, the "spiritual son" conferring duration to the spiritual being of lovers (Jacobi 1944).

Whatever name we give this spiritual filiation, it is proof that the authentic erotic experience is above all an experience of psychic conjunction, because the suffering of the psyche draws together the poles divided by experience, so that sacred and profane, sensuality and spirituality, loss and abundance, Eros and Thanatos can once more exist together in the paradox of love. We say exist together and not coincide, because in human passion there is a vain *straining* toward union. Lovers intuit the dark sense of the apparent dualism in the amorous phenomenon, the tension imposed by passion, and this explains the anxiety that emerges with the realization that the other possesses something that seduces us, which is capable of arousing our desire. It is the same apprehension and anxiety experienced by the infant when he recognizes in the presence/absence of the mother the source of his pleasure and at the same time the threat of unhappiness. And the lover also experiences, through the presence/absence of the other, all the agitation of the body and the soul, when the loved object appears as his only possible nourishment.

The same aspects emerge—as we have had occasion to observe—within the analytical relationship in which the very particular character of the analyst's presence is in itself seductive, stimulating as it does the unconscious fantasies of the patient. This is a controversial situation that, precisely because it can easily lead to serious misunderstanding, must be resolved. As Hillman observes, the transference is not a typically analytical event: it is not created in the setting, nor is it the exclusive prerogative of the therapist-patient relationship. Transference exists whenever a tie of affection or an intimate involvement—any relationship significant for the soul—is formed between two individuals. The peculiar nature of the *analytical transference* is due to the particular structure of the relationship, the particular material with which the two individuals operate, and the force with which it emerges. For a long time the transference was considered as incidental—albeit necessary—to the process, in any case bound to the patient's resistance. Jung intuited that it was necessary to restitute substantial truth to the transference love, which should be considered in any case as an intense involvement that, comprehended and assumed in its symbolic aspects, becomes functional to spiritual growth and self-realization. Of course, there is also a defensive, collusive, and regressive aspect in the experience of transference created by the inequality that exists between therapist and patient from the outset of the treatment. The one considering himself the weaker of the two must absolutely defend himself because, being at a disadvantage inevitably mirrors that infantile condition, that powerlessness, before adults who "can do with us as they will." In the state of regression activated by the setting, seduction becomes a weapon, a means of survival, since certain types of resistance are virtually "physiological"—which I might say is almost positive.

In the very particular circumstances of the analytical relationship, in fact, seduction functions primarily as an attempt to correct a situation of unequal forces that the patient experiences in an ambivalent way. Although, on the one hand, the omnipotence with which the therapist is vested is necessary to the patient who needs to trustingly place himself in the hands of one who, precisely due to that power, can cure him (this is in fact at an initial phase, the request of the analysand), on the other a similar investiture renders the patient extremely vulnerable, defenseless, fearful of the numinous quality with which he himself *has invested* his healer. Seducing the therapist thus becomes for some a means of neutralizing that power and at the same time a strategy to keep their own aggressiveness at bay. However, it is a double-edged sword because the idealization of the therapist can cause the persistence of the patient's resistance; the fantasies of seduction actually conceal an aggressive, and at times intensely destructive, component as the object, seen as a depository of power and plenty, is the obvious target for envious attacks. According to D. Winnicott (1971), the constructive and creative experience provided the patient by the analytic process gives him access to the primary experience of destructiveness. In truth, men do not easily conceive of the fact that, even in its earliest forms, love eros is expressed in ways that appear to our discriminating consciousness as fairly ambivalent—that ambivalence which Freud encountered in the competition of opposing forces that converge in love, which he described as the paradox of an *aggression which aspires to the closest union.*

The idea of destruction seems unbearable, and yet the ability to sustain our own destructive drives is the basis of the capacity to enjoy ideas, the most varied experiences of existence and our

17

own corporeal experience. The purpose of analytical treatment is precisely to make possible a connection, a synthesis between dissociated psychic needs, so that the patient, once free of self-deceit that kept him torn between impossible desires and the incapacity for real adjustment, can reduce the infantile dependence on those internal objects that protect him and at the same time keep him in his neurotic prison.

Eros makes possible the transformation of the psyche through the efforts, trials, and suffering it imposes. These require a patience and courage typically feminine, the patience of long gestation and the courage to give life to new forms of the self, thus giving form to our own desire. Eros seduces in order to render us more human.

Three

Becoming Invisible

If we are consumed by languor or let ourselves be ruined, or if at times we deal ourselves death, it is because a certain sentiment of predilection has warned us of the prodigious dissolution and the explosion which the bestowed embrace will create. For it is in the nature of love to burn rather than acquire, to squander wealth and ruin those who love.
—G. Bataille, *The Love of an Immortal Being*

The erotic experience defines the privileged space in which we can live fully our corporal nature in the abandonment to a desire for the other. It is through the erotic encounter that we become *visible* and that the other is rendered *visible* to us, since desire permits the miracle of a continuously new incarnation, a renewal over time. Obviously, we all possess a body; however, it is only when we encounter desire that we become truly aware of our being a body—a body that, through the sensibility of another, can experience beauty.

Erotic fascination is one of the preferential ways of access to a confrontation with our internal images, those that tacitly guide our choices in love. And as the erotic encounter progressively creates a field of interaction in which our fantasies can take form, the more likely it is that we pass from the simple experience to self-knowledge. Getting to know the other, abandoning ourselves to desire, becomes true erotic expression only on condition that what has been repressed returns; the appearance of an unknown figure of our desire is what transforms us and initiates us to psychic reality. Only rarely during a lifetime do we live so disturbing an experience of seduction, as a "passage into the unknown." It is an experience in which internal activation and fantasy prevail, and in which the subject is shattered into an infinity of possible others who assume all the roles and masks of desire. In that mythical scenario, according to James Hillman, each one is nymph and satyr, maenad and Amazon, god and beast. The subject is freed for an instant of that univocal aspect that renders him a logical and rational being, that Apollonian consciousness responsible for the foundation of the thought that, as Nietzsche stated, would defend itself from internal lacerations using the weapons of intellect and "pretence." If through Apollonian consciousness man controls and attempts to give form, order, and clarity to the chaotic formlessness of the emotions whose emergence he fears, it is clear that seduction, in its Dionysiac aspect, is experienced by the consciousness as a threat of internal destabilization. The more the individual identifies with epic and solar consciousness and the norms of collective moral consciousness, the more dangerous will be the event, in itself extraordinary, of seduction.

The language of ancient Greece provides an interesting insight on the basically ambivalent meaning of the term *seduction* and its semantic bases. Greek mythology, with the wealth and versatility of its images and figures—be they heroes or gods—is, for the psychoanalyst, a precious source of information on the universe of the soul, on how ancient man named his emotions and attempted a recomposition of his internal contradictions by projecting them onto a mythological ambience, on the meanings and mysteries with which he measured himself, and on the initiations to psychic reality, through mythic narration, which sustained him throughout his entire life. In particular, mythological—like oneiric—language is expressed in images, and our continuing fidelity to the image is due to its being an efficient container for various psychic functions, a sort of "snapshot" of the internal state of those producing it. In ancient Greece, seduction had more aspects—as many as the countenances of the personages acting as artifice or victim. Moreover, as the act of seduction was a work of the divinity, as such, it was obviously perceived by the Greeks as numinous. The epithet "seductive" is in fact often attributed to supernatural actions or impersonal forces, in order to stress the demonic aspect and the fact that the subject is seized and rendered object.

The "elsewhere" introduced by Jean Baudrillard could be declined in this case as divine, and in fact the divine is for man essentially elsewhere. Aphrodite seduces with beauty and the arts of her son Eros; Hermes with words, Zeus with power; Pan with abduction and rape . . . Homer, in narrating the voyage of Ulysses in *The Odyssey*, shows us the many faces of seduction encountered by the hero, some of which, for their perverse character, are made to measure for our discourse on seduction as a "negative" art. We refer, for example, to the hero's encounter with the sorceress Circe and the Sirens. Unlike these mythological figures, Ulysses is neither god nor intermediate demon, but a heroic human being who is distinguished from other heroic figures by virtue of his various relationships with many figures— women and goddesses (Hillman 1979)—as the condition to being permitted to continue his voyage and carry out his mission. His aspect of hero, soldier, and navigator is also dependent on his capacity to enter into contact with the versatile nature of the female image, of integrating the *Anima* function. In fact, in the twenty-second book, we read, "he would recognize all these women." Recognition occurs also through the danger of being phagocytized by the overwhelming, seductive requests of castrating female figures, symbols of the terrifying and devouring aspect of the maternal. One example of this is Circe, whose seduction transforms into animals those who yield to her spell, as described in the famous episode in which the imprudent traveling companions of Odysseus are passive protagonists. Another example is the famous encounter of Ulysses with the Sirens and the powerful attraction of their song, as sweet as it is fatal for those allowing themselves to be tempted and ensnared. The seduction of the Sirens, according to the myth, is the exercise of a lethal fascination, the seductiveness of their song dragging to their deaths the hapless sailors who heed it.

This pervasive and fascinating quality of song, or chant, in which two primary elements are combined—word and sound— is also an essential part of the linguistic tradition; that is, when we speak of "enchanting" and "enchantment." We are "enchanted" by a voice or a glance, which succeeds in catalyzing

21

our desire, carrying us away from ourselves. That which enchants—that is, enchains—in the seductive process is its capacity to arouse desire without satisfying it. It is a promise that threatens to reveal itself to the subject who capitulates as merely a mirage. However, it is just that suspension of desire, that expanded time of expectation and promise of infinite gratification, that provides seduction its numinous halo, including it in the realm of eroticism, as

> desire renewed, as pain, nostalgia, forever. Seduction is an enchantment, and must awaken desire and fix it on itself. This is why the sexual invitation must be, at the same time, refusal, and obstacle. The invitation to hastily consume sexual satisfaction is not enchantment. Because it accepts the end, forgetfulness, disinterest. The idea of 'making love and then forgetting about it' is obscene. Enchantment—that is, the erotic—is the opposite of obscene. (Alberoni 1986, 39)

That disturbing quality of Eros, the demonic nature causing us to experience the attraction of the other as a perverse and overwhelming experience, is comprehensible if we consider that it is thus that the intimate structure of our psychic objects and their reciprocal relationships is transformed. And despite—or perhaps precisely due to—our total psychic involvement, the deep affective experience remains for the most part essentially unconscious. In love we suffer, endure, and wait, seized or suspended. In other words, we are passive subjects and it is only with difficulty that, in the duration of a passion, we are able to act reflectively or with discernment. In this sense it is practically impossible to express the essence of the love experience, just as the most intense erotic aspects maintain—even over long periods of time—a sacred aura that removes them from pure contingency. The accumulation of affections, desires, and images that seduction awakens, and the possibility present in the erotic encounter—even if only potentially—of generating psychic transmutations, confers to the experience of seduction (of seducing and *being* seduced) its singular character of promise and infinite potential.

Light is shed on a cardinal theme of the act of seduction, which is its carrying the ensnared subject to a "place" that is not his, with the combination of fear and fascination implicit in that kind of adventure. The actions of the seduced are no longer illuminated by reason (and in common parlance there is the expression "losing one's head"), but governed by the other, or better still, by the internal *daimon,* which takes full possession. We feel robbed, deprived of our capacity to judge, forced to remain in dark, vague, mysterious regions. Painfully, we must recognize that we have placed ourselves entirely in the hands of another. Homer provides us with examples of seduction conjugated with death and perdition: in *The Odyssey* (II, 264), there is the episode of Aegisthus' seduction of Clytemnestra, an event that would have a tragic epilogue, when Clytemnestra kills her husband Agamemnon upon his return from the Trojan War.

According to venerable tradition—which from classic Greek tragedy to decadence has been part of our culture, shaping the very concept of love—seduction and the passion it arouses become irresistible forces, inevitably leading to perdition and death. They evoke excess, going beyond, into the realm of the forbidden, the obscure, causing a blindness that will inevitably create the constellation of radical, irreversible, extreme actions. As opposed to traditional values, the security of institutionalized unions, and the sacred bond of matrimony, passionate love will inevitably appear as an illicit act that threatens to compromise the equilibrium of virtuous existence and group consensus. Seduction is in itself perverse. In India, for example, the love passion is represented by the god Krishna playing his flute by night in the forest of Vrindava. Young brides, upon hearing the sound of his irresistible melody, slip furtively out of their husbands' beds and silently make their way to the moonlit wood, where they dance throughout the night with their splendid god, lost in an otherworldly beatitude (Campbell 1967).

The significance of this Indian parable is that passion transports the individual beyond all temporal law or single relationship because these belong exclusively to the secondary world of separation and manifest multiplicity (ibid.).

However, one need not travel so far to find examples of this association of passion with irrationality and "negative" heroism. One of the most dramatic representations of love as a passion that leads to the annihilation of the lovers is the story, immortal-

23

ized by Dante in Canto V of his *Inferno,* of Paolo and Francesca (Alighieri 1987). What does this parable of love as *passion* and *compassion* teach us, and what is there in the experience of these two creatures from the distant Middle Ages that we post-modernists can share?

Amor, ch'a nullo amato amar perdona: love does not consent to the loved one to refuse to love in return. Paolo and Francesca are brother- and sister-in-law destined to eternal damnation for having yielded to a powerful, mutual attraction. That indulgence led to a double perdition: the death of the body and the priva-tion contemplating God, a true death for the soul created in His image and likeness. Like the tragic tales of Tristan and Iseult and Romeo and Juliet, the thread running through Dante's tale is once more the dual concept of Love and Death. The chronicle of the love and death of Paolo Malatesta and Francesca da Rim-ini, who actually existed in Romagna in the 1200s, was at the time of Dante no more than a crime of passion, an item reported in the local chronicles, the narration of which was passed down orally from 1285 on. Gianciotto Malatesta, the husband of Francesca da Polenta, killed his wife and brother, whom he caught in *flagrante delicto.* The two adulterous lovers—so the story goes—were run through by a single thrust of the sword "that the two might die together." Dante heard this story during the time of his exile in Florence, where he had been taken under the protection of Guido Novello da Polenta, *Signore* of Ravenna and descendant of the unfortunate Francesca. And this was the raw material with which Dante forged Canto V of his *Inferno,* rendering the story of Paolo and Francesca sublime and immortal. By means of a process of transfiguration, the "damned" lovers shed their real connotations to emerge as a uni-versal symbol of the love passion and its relationship with death.

A fundamental assumption of Romantic mythology is that the perturbation of love can lead to the death of the soul seduced. To the anxiety of seduction are ascribed the most intense suffer-ing and an unconditional capitulation to another who "can do with me as he will." The vocabulary of passion is full of terms that vividly describe the condition of the lover: he is a "slave," "succubus," "helpless," "defenseless." It is a matter of a fatal abduction—and it is thus that the perimeter is delineated within which the soul of the lover moves, locked to the desire of the other. But why is there this recurrent conjugation of love and death in cases where the love experience is total?

Plato utilizes the myth of the androgyne to explain amorous predestination: each one of us is incomplete, our whole having been divided, which, in order to be recomposed, seeks our counterpart, the heterosexual pole that would fill this lack. It is a very apt mythical description, which succeeds in fixing in a highly evocative image many intuitions on human nature, on the nature of man's desire and his destiny. The choice of metaphor is also a good one: a body mythically entire, undivided, but "experientially" split, because being defined as "individual" implies being characterized psychologically, becoming an identity. Each of us, born into the world as body, must experience a second birth (the "true" birth of which Neumann speaks, or Mahler's "second birth"), that which is achieved through differentiation from the Body-self of the mother. "True" birth implies a process of separation from the original matrix that is also a process of elaborating loss: only through separation from the maternal body-self can our body acquire a name, a confine, define itself as identity. This is something we might call "psychic-ization."

One of the secret aspirations of the love passion as possible return to the original state is the reconstruction of a nondistinctness, a freedom from any sense of finiteness. In this sense, the orgasmic state—the brief but extremely intense loss of the concept of the ego—is an experience of a loss of confines. This Dionysian aspect is the way of the *orgé,* of the Bacchante and the Maenad, the way of intemperance: it implies an experience of expropriation or demoniac possession favored by the dance, drink, and music.

However, the *divino delirio* of which Plato speaks in *Phaedrus,* the eros of which, although an aspiration to a transindividual union, occurs—in the Jungian sense—not through a regression of the ego, but through its decentralization at the service of a new "center" of psychic totality, the self.

Love, this demonic intermediary between mortal and immortal, is a "divine delirium" which, through the body, fecundates the soul. In this sense, the scope of erotic initiation is something other than the simple loss of confines of the consciousness: it is

25

a disorientation of the ego in favor of a new orientation, that experience of an ego at the service of the self of which Jung (1940–50) spoke. If the spirit is not lost along the way, that which is revealed to the soul-love will be the sacred nature of the Beautiful:

> This erotica is cathartic. From spoliation to spoliation, it goes from the beauty of a single body to dis-individualized beauty and then from beauty freed from a corporal aspect—that is, the beauty of the soul, to that beauty in its turn loosed from the person and flows, beyond any representation to "that which is beautiful for itself alone, . . . in itself, in the truth of its nature, in its boundless purity." (Lilar 1963, 58)

This is the ultimate aim of asceticism, the object of any mystical experience. The lover, Socrates tells us, is he who lends himself to this dominion of the divine, who responds to the invitation of Eros to abandon false identifications and partial objectives, to discover the true object of his desire.

Both the orgiastic way and the way of annulment of the confines of the ego through the Dionysiac "violation," the mystical experience of spoliation of the ego in favor of a new psychic totality, are configured for the ego, which experiences them as something akin to death. And yet, our discriminating consciousness has always considered the Dionysiac experience and the mystic experience as opposites—one being referred to the sphere of the instinct, connected to physical nature and the disinhibition of drives, the other ascribed to the realm of the spirit. But this split inevitably implies falling into the unilateral quality of the consciousness, thus depriving the ego of an experience that, repressed as an aspect of the Shadow, polarizes the libido and isolates complex nuclei, which can then only emerge with the same violence with which they have been repressed. However, this work does not intend to trace the roots and motives of this polarization of Eros and Logos, nature and spirit, or the explanation through feminine/masculine value judgments that identify the material-body-woman as "bad" and the spirit-mind-man as "good." We are all sufficiently familiar with the negative consequences of this accentuated dualism which, acting

on the intra-psychic level—in terms of splitting and repression—
is subsequently transformed into a practice of oppression and
repression of any representation of this gigantic Shadow.
Woman, the corporeal and sensual, has thus ended up representing the incarnation of what is evil, and up until recently was
the victim of an absolute primacy of a religion of "purity" that
was responsible for filling the public squares with human sacrifice and seconding the private violence of bridal chambers and
convents. Modern consciousness—and this is something Jung
had intuited—must confront these by now obsolete identifications if there is to be a leap in quality in the question of what is
good and what is bad for man today. Dante, meditating on the
nature of love and Francesca's conduct, encountered those very
themes that now occupy the consciousness of modern man. But
let us go back to that couple immortalized by Dante: the eternal
damnation of the two lovers unfolds in the circle of the lascivious, in the company of the souls of famous lovers and seductresses, such as Cleopatra, Semiramis, Tristan, and the divine
Helen. The sin of lasciviousness consists of becoming enthralled,
of the soul passively allowing itself to be tempted by the occasions of pleasure, deceiving itself as to the true source of Good.
Becoming enthralled therefore implies less an intentional choice
than a weak ego—*letting oneself be carried away* by instinct, following the enchantments of desire and the mirages of the senses.
However, even the seemingly most insignificant involvement
should not be taken lightly, as even that can set off a chain of reactions in the unconscious that could be potentially destructive.

The lascivious are abandoned in a place without light
(metaphor of an interior blindness, of an internal state lacking
points of reference), swept by strong, alternating currents of air
that create a storm. The souls are continually overwhelmed and
dragged along by the violent tempest, flung one against the
other. It is the inexorable *lex talionis:* just as in life they had allowed themselves to be swept away by the tempest of the
senses and their unbridled desire, after their death they are condemned to remain in the tumult. Thus, as they desired illegiti-
mate union, now they are violently flung one against the other.
They were guilty of distorting the true love relationship, based
on the connection between sentiment and *ratio*. The "talent"—as

27

Dante defines passion—by inflaming the senses, obscures the rational capacity and the instincts, freed from the restraint of the reason, leads man to degradation and renders him similar to the beast, while love and charity kindle in man the flame of divine aspiration.

One group, distinguished from the other souls, is made up of those souls having had an aristocratic concept of love—elaborated in the Provençal school—in particular, those who for love died violently. The concept of *amor cortese,* as we will see, can also shed some light on the phenomenology of seduction. From Francesca's discourse we can deduce those qualities of love that led the two lovers to their tragic destiny. If we were to imagine these to have been blinding and uncontrollable drives to obtain immediate satisfaction of instincts, we would have soon enough had to change our minds; courtly love is quite another thing. Courtly erotica springs from the love that captures the noble, "gentle" spirit; that is, of lofty soul and high morality. It is "Amor ch'al cor gentil ratto s'apprende" (v. 100). Its code is presented to us in various treatises, among which is the famous *De Amore* (1185) of Andrea Cappellano (André le Chapelain), in which the author describes the means, ends, instruments, and gradation of this courtly erotica (Cappellano 1980). Love here is that sung by the troubadours: extramarital love, or at least potentially adulterous, the expression of a rich and intellectually refined society. Unfettered sentiment, it cannot be reconciled with the institution of matrimony since the legal tie is in contrast with the gratuitous freedom of sentiment. For where there is uncontested possession, the trepidation of desire cannot exist. The object of desire is such only if it remains unattainable, so that the smallest concession by the lover becomes cause for delight and a source of poetic inspiration:

> That was bound to the certainty that the success (duration) would have reduced the open revelation of love to the closed horizon of the family world . . . the object had to be freed from those fortuitous elements which subordinate the corporeal being to base reality, and restitute to it that full sovereignty which was revealed for a passing instant in passion only to be negated over time, as the duration brings the tangible thing to the subjugate state: everything over time *serves* something else. (Bataille 1951, 15–16)

Although various and often contrasting concepts of love converge in courtly erotica, it is generally true that the medieval concept develops ideal love on a negative basis, as the dominant motive is impossible love: the unattainable character of the desired object. Also in Classical antiquity love was sung in terms of the suffering and torment of the enamored soul, but there love is ultimately accepted and requited. Only later on would the theme appear of the separation of lovers through death. In courtly ideology, the object is lost from the outset, and the enamored is sick with melancholy—in the Freudian acceptation, the heartbreaking persistence of a tragic sentiment for a love object never truly "past." A phantasm of an object? Ancient medicine actually identified—as the origin of melancholy—a kind of hypertrophy of the imagination. Thus, the quality of courtly erotica and its relationship to amorous melancholy and the phantasm become clearer if we consider that the same theories also made possible the explanation of the genesis of love:

> It is not possible, in particular, to understand the love ceremonial which the lyrics of the troubadours and the *dolce stil n[u]ovo* poets have passed down to modern, Western poetry, without taking into account the fact that it materializes from the outset as a fantastic process. It is not an external body, but an interior image—that is, the phantasm etched, by means of a glance, on the fantastic spirits, is the origin and object of falling in love. (Agamben 1977, 30)

It is also clear that if the love object is an impossible object, if the corporeal aspect is taboo, and if the lady inevitably belongs to someone else, there remains only sublimation, and the incongruity between desire and its frustration must inevitably be translated into erotic melancholy and poetry:

> The lost object is no more than the semblance that desire creates of its courting of the phantasm, and the introjection of the libido is only one of the aspects of a process in which that which is real loses its reality because that which is not real becomes real (ibid., 32).

29

It remains to be ascertained, however, whether it is poetic expression at the service of the phantasm or the phantasm at the service of artistic elaboration—the instrument making possible the epiphany of the creative symbol.

Courtly love ennobles and is a stimulus to achieving perfect virtue. Courtly tradition establishes the gradations of love by means of which the lover—like the religiously inclined through asceticism—perfects himself through devotion to the loved object and the mastery of virtue. The perfect courtly lady gives herself partially to her lover only after having imposed on him a long and difficult amorous discipline constellated by trials of love. Once this discipline has been achieved, the lover is rewarded: a kiss, the permission to embrace the loved one, and eventually the concession of the entire person (carnal union that is not, however, included in all the codices of courtly love; in some of these, absolute chastity remains the rule—ascetic exaltation of privation, or better still the quest for *aesthetic enjoyment* of the woman). One must proceed down this path of devotion with moderation and order, and the true lady never accelerates the rhythm of her concessions. It was veritably a courtly ritual, a religion of love, which codified far more ancient beliefs into ceremonial form (Nelli 1952).

Francesca appears to Dante as the perfect, courtly lady. Her manners, her "courtesy," the language she uses to converse with the poet reveal the high level of her refinement and education. This is not a melodramatic heroine, no Madame Bovary *ante litteram:* while guilty, she conserves the purest of feminine qualities, gentleness, delicacy, and the force of her sentiments. Two famous annotators of the *Divina Commedia*—De Sanctis and Matteini—stress the sensibility and wisdom of this feminine figure to whom, despite the condemnation to the pains of hell, go both the compassion of the poet and the immediate solidarity and heartfelt sympathy of the reader. Francesca is not an incarnation of the "demoniacal woman," moved only by the blind forces of passion, nor is she the incarnation of the fatal seductress utilizing her beauty and charms to nullify the "virtue" of her brother-in-law and cause his ruin. In fact, it is to her that Dante attributes the verses that have rendered famous the doctrine of love and that we have all read and admired in Dante's *Inferno:*

Amor, ch'al cor gentil ratto s'apprende,
rese costui de la bella persona
che mi fu tolta; e 'l modo ancor m'offende.
Amor, ch'a nullo amato amar perdona,
mi prese del costui piacer sì forte,
che, come vedi, ancor non m'abbandona.

(Verses 100–105)

It is in the limpid and courteous manner of the cultured woman that Francesca explains to the poet the nature of her passion for Paolo Malatesta, a passion created by the propensity of the soul for the beauty of all that which is revealed to be kindred to the "gentile" stuff of which the soul itself is made. It is a love that springs forth from the contemplation of the beauty of the other according to what are the courtly canons, the *dolce stil nuovo,* according to which beauty generates love. Also, the nature of this love is such that it is not conceded for the object of desire to remain indifferent—one cannot remain insensible to a similar offer: love is a contagious force that engenders reciprocity.

It is on the basis of the elucidation of the doctrine of courtly love that Francesca attempts to justify her actions, insisting on the authenticity of the sentiments of the lovers and the fatal necessity of their choice. How is it possible to renounce what by its very nature is so kindred to our own souls as to awaken it from the torpor in which it normally lives, inflaming it with the desire for union with the source of so much pleasure? Francesca enunciates a doctrine in justification of the amorous transgression, attempting to remove the love drive from individual responsibility and transfer it to the plane of an irrepressible, transpersonal force. It is a mystical love by nature and by its quality, in its absolute aspect—given the fact that it is possible to die of unrequited love—and in its being the way to perfection and spiritual elevation. The entire lyrical tradition of the troubadours is constellated by religious metaphors, and with the advent of the *dolce stil nuovo* it would become a transcendent experience, the privileged vehicle of which would be woman transfigured into angelic intelligence.

How then was it possible for a doctrine based on such noble aspirations to become so transformed as to become the cause of

31

sin or death? Virgil explains to Dante that those who have died for love have done so because they had submitted reason to the "talent"; overturning the ethic of the guide-reason, they let themselves be directed by their drive to union. The "perverse evil" (v. 93) is therefore the "evil unleashed by perversion, or better still by the guilty deviation from the road of the righteous" (Gargiulo 1990, 136). Love can have a positive value provided that it aids man to purify himself and become divine. Love is possible, but one must not lose oneself for its sake; devotion to the loved one is possible, but that devotion must not be transformed into idolatry. The true love object is God. Madness must not be preferred to wisdom; desire for a human creature must not be given preference over the love of the *sophia*. Love formed by culture and Christian morality must always conserve he who practices it lucidly. Virgil preaches the acquisition of consciousness, while the Eros of the two condemned lovers is loss of consciousness. The beginning of their story is presented as an abandoning of control, the same loss of the "light of reason" described in the love story of Lancelot and Guinevere, the same reciprocal recognition in their glance, the same apprehension and desire.

> All is memory in Eros: the predestination which is nostalgia, beauty which is reminiscence, wisdom which is faithfulness, the love delirium which is grace. While in passion everything is forgetfulness, sleep, falsehood; predestination becomes inexplicable fatality, beauty substituted by sorcery, divine delirium by hallucination . . . passionate love certainly, but which withdraws into the creature rather than opening and flowering beyond the supernatural. (Lilar 1963, 131)

Paolo and Francesca transgressed both against the social norm of marital fidelity and a sacrament, religious matrimony. And yet, although Dante places the two lovers in hell, he neither judges nor condemns them. In fact, the *Canto* contains expressions and images delineating the two lovers as delicate and amiable creatures: Francesca and Paolo are "quei due che insieme vanno e paion sì al vento esser leggieri" (Verses 75–76).

No infernal tempest would succeed in diverting these two "doves from desire called" in all directions; they themselves are made of a light material, resembling the sighs and tears accompanying the memory of their story. Apt in this context are the words of Georges Bataille on the essence of love:

> What the loved one proposes to the lover is an opening to the totality of that which is—only through an opening to his love—a limitless opening, only possible in this fusion, in which object and subject, loved one and lover, cease being in the world isolated, cease being separate from each other and the world, becoming two gusts of a single wind. (Bataille 1951, 9).

Dante also would explain that it is love that leads them ("per quello amor che i mena, ed ei verranno": Verse 78).

The lightness of the two souls which, unlike others, proceed as a couple, and their "anguish"—a term that in the Provençal doctrine of love indicates the sense of torment generated by the unbearable force of desire—their sad story, their terrible, offensive deaths, arouse in Dante feelings of deep compassion. One may, of course, interpret this sentiment—in the acceptation provided by De Sanctis, as the empathetic partaking of the tragedies of others, or that of Sapegno, as anxiety created by the prospect of terrible consequences, or where this pure and exalted force of Love can lead—as one will. What is clear is Dante's shock and his solidarity for the two lovers whom he allows to remain forever united, in an eternal embrace, in eternal damnation.

More troubling is the question of the two brothers—rivals in love—as regards the arrangement beyond the grave. With a harsh and pitiless phase, Gianciotto is condemned and thrust into the icebound realms of Cain for having murdered his brother, while Paolo, despite his having sullied the honor of his brother, is allowed to remain with Francesca.

This is not the only passage in the *Commedia* that reveals how Dante was deeply divided between adhering to the moral standards and culture of his time and a powerful, diametrically opposite impulse. It would suffice to think of the condemnation of the last undertaking of Ulysses, guilty of not having been "contento al quia": a sentence perfectly in line with the Augustinian dispute on the *curiositas* but that strangely resembles an apotheosis. There, to mitigate the digression, was the Promethean dream of and need for knowledge (but in the *Con-*

vivio as well, Dante affirms that "all men naturally desire to know"). In the episode of Paolo and Francesca, as an antithesis to the moral condemnation, doubts emerge generated by the assertion that—mysteriously—even so noble and ennobling a force as Love can precipitate man into irremediable error. How is judgment and condemnation possible if experience proves that there is something in the very nature of Eros that transcends man's will and reason? All courtly literature defines love's seduction as inescapable. We read that Lancelot, *pressed* by Love, kissed Guinevere: in courtly language, "to press" during a tournament means placing the adversary in the absolute impossibility of defending himself. Therefore, the theme of seduction is once more proposed as a force that alienates man from his rational basis. The torment of Dante was that of any creative individual to whom the search for values and standards is internally imposed and that often enough does not coincide with the current moral code of the collective consciousness. The celebrated beauty of *Canto V* of *The Inferno,* combined with the ennoblement of this tragic "passion," is ample proof that Dante, in the process of a poetic elaboration of the love theme, is at odds with a process of integrating his own internal images; consequently, Francesca is also an image of the Anima. This is a feminine image that undoubtedly differs from the incarnation of the ideal of perfection and unattainable purity represented by Beatrice (whose spiritual beauty transcends the expressive capacities of the poet), and that in any case—although in a different way from the woman loved by Dante—leads the poet to sort out the conflict between his own ethical convictions and identification with the culture of his time, obliging him to come to terms with essential matters as to what is good and what evil, what is permissible and what is not, personal and collective standards.

That which initially attracts the attention of one observing the feminine figure described by Dante is the portrait of a psychologically intense and complex woman: Francesca is in a way the Anti-Beatrice, an entirely different feminine type from the courtly "lady" who would be further transfigured by Dante and the *dolce stil nuova.* In fact, analyzing the psychology of the woman whose praises were sung by the courtly poets—from the troubadours on up to the *dolce stil nuova* poets—what is disconcertingly evident is that, if she were to be loved, the woman had to be first submitted to a process of idealization and transfiguration, which removed anything that might express desire or sensuality. To be worthy of courtly love, a woman had to disappear as such and reappear as Lady, as absolute Woman, closed in her distant and inaccessible beauty that rendered her similar to a divinity: as pure and as perfect as an angel. The representation of the courtly ideal is a "fictitious noblewoman," an unattainable object that permits the fulfillment of desire exclusively through aesthetic sublimation. The figure of Francesca da Rimini moves away from this typology. She is a courteous and well-brought-up woman, refined and noble of soul. However, Love renders her fragile before the explosion of desire. Unlike Beatrice and her inaccessible beauty, Francesca appears in all her stature as a woman born to love and weighed down by the burden that a prohibited relationship implies. Unlike the courtly lady, who had the power to "deal death," Francesca—absent and inviolate—is given to death because she has abandoned herself to the call of seduction. The love of Paolo and Francesca is a *total* love; that is, not only elective—singular, exclusive, reciprocal—but open to risk, even total perdition, in order to be realized. It is love assumed up to its extreme consequences, however with nothing of masochistic abjection or libertine *divertissement,* or that kind of challenge to convention that is nothing more than a sham that confirms the rule. No hysteria in the manner of Flaubert, no Romantic effrontery, no adolescent exaltation. The language of Francesca, her dignified and pensive tone, and the silent and prolonged weeping of Paolo, which accompanies the narration of the woman, are proof of a mature love, burdened by the weight of secrecy and ennobled by the extreme test of death. The loved one is indicated by Francesca as he "che mai da me non fia diviso" (v. 135), and the force with which she stresses the indissolubility of the love pact is the proof of a conquest—that of the *duration,* which is certainly not a prerogative of passionate lovers—resulting assuming fully the consequences implicit in total love. The courage of Francesca lies entirely in this capacity to contain the supreme tension that a similar love generates. Bataille (1951, 10) suggests a reason for this:

35

The game of love is so open (authentic, it presents such grave dangers) that, for most of the time, we are afraid. More often than not, we concede only brief instants to unbounded prodigality and excitation. Above all, only timidly do we advance along this truly sacred road which crosses the realm of anguish and fear.

Francesca and Paolo, like Tristan, a companion in misfortune relegated to the same infernal *girone,* entirely accept the risks of "lovesickness," since in it they find new life. Is not a love that Francesca can call at the same time the cause of death and the victory over death—if it is true that neither time nor condemnation by divine law succeeded in separating the two lovers—a prefiguration of that *coincidentia oppositorum* that we find symbolized in other images in which love and death are united? A particularly impressive representation of the mystical tradition of Persia would have Satan the most ardent adorer of God. When God created man, he ordered the angels to kneel before his most noble creature, man. Lucifer disobeyed—such was his love for the Supreme Being—and was for this flung down into Hell and condemned to an eternal privation of the contemplation of God. The Persian poets, when asked what force sustained Satan, responded, the memory of the sound of God's voice when he said: Be gone (Campbell 1967, 29).

The reference to the book that the two lovers were reading when Cupid's arrow reached its mark is in this context significant: Lancelot and Guinevere will succeed in giving themselves completely to each other, but this possibility of union that also contemplates a physical union will mark the condemnation of the lovers, as every transgression implies punishment. Contemplating Paolo and Francesca confronted with this reading, Dante places them before acceding to the only form of love that can aspire to spiritual and carnal completeness, love entirely assumed, and this cannot but condemn them to eternal death. In this, they are faithful to the precepts of Christian morality and the regulating principles of the *ratio* of which the master Virgil is symbol. We should remember that the *Amor* that Francesca inspires is an expression of the first real couple relationship, in the current sense given this experience: an experience of sharing, the total involvement of the individual, an investment experienced as the perception of oneself in a conflicting way, as carried away from oneself and projected into the reality of the other, consigned to a love that is the source not only of one's own pleasure but also of a renewed self-knowledge.

It is in this sacred space of the union that the antinomy between sexuality and spirituality, between pure and impure, between permissible and nonpermissible falls, and in which the ecstatic and the fallen share a common root and a single destiny: the canceling of oneself in love in order to be born again, in a transformed state.

Four

A Troubling Method of Procedure

The primitive mentality does not invent myths, it experiences them. Myths are original revelations of the preconscious psyche, involuntary statements about unconscious psychic happenings, and anything but allegories of physical processes.
　　　　—Jung, *The Psychology of the Child Archetype*

The presence of the image of seduction in the myths of all cultures is proof of the psyche's need to give form to an event that is fundamental for the soul. Tracing in the myth the models of seduction implies examining aspects of our internal dimension in a different and wider perspective, in order to better understand them. It is in this perspective that other interpretations of sexuality, and any other psychic reality for that matter, become possible. Seduction should thus also be considered in light of its archetypal aspects. In the multiplicity of its forms, it represents a means for the psyche to enter into contact with affects, to represent emotions.

Many of the divinities in the Greek imaginary—Zeus, Aphrodite, Eros, Pan, Priapus, Apollo, Dionysus, Hermes, to name but a few—lent form to the various aspects of sexuality. Sexuality, in continual transformation, changes with the phases of life according to which divinity is from time to time activated. Each of these divinities represents a different version of the initiation to sexuality, a different fantastic model with which to live instinct (Hillman 1972b, 76). In this context, López-Pedraza (1977, 99) speaks of a "polytheist sexuality" in which all the gods participate and that consequently—from a psychological perspective—leads the way to all the archetypal constellations. Bound to the Freudian concept of the child as perverse-polymorph, this sexuality is not centered on the primacy of genitalia and the orgasm, or the couple relationship; it is not in the least "monotheistic." It involves identifying the many faces of a polytheistic sexuality, comprehending its manifestations and dynamics and in that perspective focusing attention on seduction, for the soul then signifies looking at all the divinities that represent it, in the Greek imaginary as well as those of other cultures. This effort would be the particular task of modern Western man, as he lacks a divine image with which to represent his sexuality, which would explain in part the perturbation and the repression engendered by sexuality. A return to mythical models would instead open a space in which instinct can be rendered psychic (Hillman 1972b, 76) and transformed into eroticism.

In all archaic cultures, sexuality conserved its sacred aspect. Very precise norms, taboos, and prescriptions regulate the approach to the sexual dimension, necessitating the performance of a series of rituals. The soul is thus protected from the dangers inherent in contact with the numinous aspect of sexuality. Rudolf Otto (1936) defines as numinous the encounter with the sacred. The divine is *mysterium tremendum et fascinans* (ibid.). Any mortal rash enough to attempt to unveil the mystery, and thus incautiously encountering the god with whom there is union, like Semele, risks being consumed by fire, annihilated by the revelation. While Eros requires spaces and rituals if it is to be manifested without risk, the space of the imaginary becomes the *témenos* in which sexuality can be encountered, even before it is experienced in the relationship with the partner. By instructing the soul as to the images inhabiting it, the myths become guides to comportment.

In the Greek imaginary, perhaps more than in others, Eros makes possible a relationship between the human and the divine. This relationship is not established through prayer addressed to an absolute divinity, an arbiter of good and evil, who rewards and punishes humans, demanding total allegiance and obedience, as in the Hebrew imaginary. It is instead a love encounter—not between a god and the human soul—a carnal encounter in which a god or goddess and a human being are united. Thus the function of sexuality here becomes fundamental, the mediator par excellence of the encounter with the divine. The body is not mortified as in the Hebrew and Christian tradition; it is as physical as it is imaginal, an echo of the ancient concept of *corpo sottile*. In this acceptation, the concrete flesh becomes a splendid citadel of metaphors (Hillman 1975, 296). It is in this context that the dividing line between body and soul can disappear, restoring the unity of the two.

Passion, seduction, jealousy, and betrayal permeate the mythical scenes with which the psyche describes the experience of fascination; the capture by numinous, powerful unconscious aspects, imagined as gods. It is a question of a violent irruption, which can lead to madness and death, radically changing the existence of those experiencing it. "It is the rapid and obsessive invasion, which severs the flower of the mind" (Calasso 1988, 69). The image frequently used to represent this event is that of the god who seduces and violently possesses a virgin, be she human or nymph. Attempts by the divine at physical contact with what is human are in any event experienced as rape. The Greeks' relationship with their gods would seem to be divided basically into two types: convivial and rape (ibid.). The gods either visit mortals, teaching them to prepare food and drink (Demeter, bread; Dionysus, wine; Athena, olive oil) and sitting at their tables—for example, the marriage of Cadmus and Harmonia—or else their appearance causes violent upheaval. Seized by sudden passion, the gods possess mortals with little or no concern for their will or the eventual consequences. In this rapid, intense contact, the psyche discovers sexuality bursting into the consciousness, celebrates the kindling of desire, becomes acquainted with the perturbation caused by the relationship with the other.

That sexuality as a *sui generis* function of the psyche—upon which Freud based his theory of the psyche and which Jung utilized to describe the *opus* of *coniunctio*—should be read in its imaginary aspect as recounted in the myths of various cultures. Sexuality is a metaphor that, with its impulses of desire, seduction, attraction, or rejection, echoes the movements of the psyche. The journey into these areas of the imaginary should therefore be in the wake of the myths. The tales of two divinities—Eros (*cf.* Hillman 1972b) and Pan (*cf.* Hillman 1972a)—could be taken as a guide to mythical Greece.

Eros and Pan are expressions of the awakening of desire and its satisfaction. Aroused and seduced by desire, the psyche is forced to emerge from unconsciousness. The love of Psyche for Eros is a voyage toward awareness, the soul's awakening to rediscover its creativity. In the version of the myth recounted by Apuleius in *The Golden Ass,* the result of the encounter of Eros and Psyche, their losing their way and then finding it once more, their tormented love, and their union is in fact *Voluptas*—pleasure. The soul, reawakened and newly conscious of itself, experiences the pleasure provided by generating, pleasure in its own creativity.

But how strewn with obstacles and riddled with torment is the love of Eros and Psyche—as any love between gods and humans is by necessity a risky and often lethal proposition. Seduction in this encounter—never sweet or gentle—is more often than not violent and brutal. It is the hirsute Pan with his caprine, ithyphallic figure and gamy smell who, more than other gods of more refined aspect, represents the violence of this encounter. Pan ensnares the nymphs, menacing their ingenuous virginity, pursuing and possessing them with a frenzy bordering on rape. Thus Pan represents the violence with which the soul experiences the fascinating and disturbing encounter with the god.

In the Greek vision, the terror of sexual fascination, the dark side of desire and seduction, is often represented by Pan. A god of instinct and the natural aspect, Pan dwells in the woods and in the grottos, drinks at springs, and hides in the dark ravines from which he spies and sets upon nymphs. Pan is the "god of nature 'within us'; Pan is our instinct" (Hillman 1972a, 61). He represents that animal life upon which the psyche is founded, constituting the basis of its creative capacity.

It is not surprising, then, with the loss of contact with nature and the subsequent loss of the instinct and sexual imaginary represented by Pan, that in Western culture Pan was transformed from god to demon. The image of Pan has become that of the Christian devil who leads the individual into temptation, to commit the sin of lasciviousness. And the flesh—negated, mortified, and tormented because its voice has been silenced—rebels, populating the imaginary with nightmares and perverse fantasies that are secretly acted out. The confine between real and psychic would apparently then have been lost. Prisoner of Pan, the individual is prey to his own violent desire, of a sexuality that can only act, because it can no longer be represented. Thus, the encounter with the real partner renders concrete a mythical fantasy, capturing the psyche and compelling it to represent its images.

The violent sexuality of Pan is a solitary sexuality, because it is bound to masturbation and because the violence of its satisfaction never leads to the creation of a couple. Pan is alone, continually tormented by his instinct, which he rapidly satisfies, only to return once more to his solitude and the impossibility of real gratification. Pan does not love, he seduces. The end result of his love encounters is abandonment; he abandons the nymphs he has seduced and returns to his solitary life in the woods. His is a damned, nomadic existence in deserted places, which his appetite renders progressively more deserted, and his *canto* "tragedy" (Hillman 1972a, 54). From the song of this solitary goat in fact originates tragedy (the meaning of the Greek word for tragedy is "song of the goat").

Pan is a figure of the compulsion that, in the repetition of acts, longs for the transformation of compulsory comportment (ibid., 63). The compulsion that leads Pan to rape generates panic. His sexuality appears bound to nightmare and anxiety, and contact with it terrifies because it is bound to the violent explosion of instinct—an instinct of bestial semblance, seduction, and violent possession, which, however, represents only one of the faces of sexuality, of seduction. In any case, it would be impossible to do without it. For the soul, in the guise of virgin nymphs, has need of the encounter with Pan, need of his violent and immediate sexuality. Before it can accede to the other levels of Eros, before it can contact the other divinities who regulate sexuality, the encounter with Pan is necessary. That tormented corporeal aspect dominated by the sole intention of satisfying instinct must be first encountered. In this searing contact, the psyche descends into the body, rediscovers it, and gives it expression, subsequently and gradually teaching it other languages represented by new scenes of seduction. In these various horizons, the psyche learns to reunite instinct and love. Thus Pan clears the way for Eros and the other gods of Olympus.

Imprisoned in a body half-goat and half-human, Pan cannot aspire to Olympus. His horizons are earthbound; he is unable to elevate himself heavenward or toward the spirit. Pan is condemned by his very nature, by the impossibility to transcend. In him, the nymph encounters only the chthonic aspect of sexuality, not the celestial one. To Pan, the rising Kundalini—the serpent, tantric image of vital energy—from the genital zone to the head and beyond—remains unknown. Passing through her sex, stomach, heart, and head and then exiting from it, the Sakti-Kundalini, or vital energy, thus encounters Shiva, her husband. While tantric sexuality is the transcendence and rendering spiritual of desire, in which the body serves to facilitate the encounter with the divine, the sexuality of Pan remains bound to the body. Pan teaches the nymphs a corporeal sexuality, the fundamentals of desire and its satisfaction. However, it is precisely because this caprine god cannot accede to Olympus that his desire must be transformed and transcended. This is the encounter with Eros.

Many classical vase and mural paintings depict Eros and Pan as they wrestle to entertain the Dionysiac circle. The contrast between delicate, winged Eros and the wild, goat-hoofed Pan could represent the contrast between two forms of seduction and love. But the psyche cannot do without the game of opposites, and the violence of Pan is as necessary to it as the delicacy of Eros. The death of Pan announced by Plutarch, the death of his tragic horizon and the victory of Eros, extolled in the Christian cult of love, is in fact an impoverishment of the imaginary. The soul has lost the possibility of representing its dark side, of recounting the panic and anxiety generated by the assault of the instinct, an instinct up until that moment unknown and unrelated to the consciousness.

It is certainly no coincidence that Pan and Priapus are considered sons of Hermes—the god who resides in the *hermés,* those phallic stones similar to the Indian *lingam,* which marked paths and around which were celebrated the rites of orgiastic cults. The relationship with Hermes, messenger of the gods, reveals the aspect of communication innate in sexuality. The message of

Pan and Priapus is therefore one that must be heeded and comprehended by the soul.

According to the myths, Pan was the product of the union between Hermes and the nymph Dryope, or with Penelope, the wife of Ulysses, who the god possessed after having changed himself into Aries the Ram (Graves 1955, 89). In this version, Penelope gave herself to Hermes after having lain with all her suitors, and upon his return, Ulysses flees in shame after beholding the monstrous child resulting (ibid.). In another version, Pan is the son of Hermes and the goat Amalthaea. The birth of Pan recounts therefore a tormenting, bestial, and boundless desire, and of this desire, Pan is the incarnation.

In fact, even the mother of the newborn Pan, so ugly, with his horns and goat's hooves, is horrified. The monstrous aspect of Pan mirrors the disturbing character of sexual desire, the fear of the seduced soul. Lazy and indolent, Pan lives in Arcadia, where he tends his flocks and raises bees. On hot summer afternoons he reposes in cool grottos or in the dense woods. To punish those who would disturb his sleep, he lets out frightening howls, terrifying anyone within hearing distance (ibid., 89). The sudden rousing of sexual desire therefore inspires fear in the soul, and the name of Pan is, as we know, closely associated with the manifestation of panic.

Present in all Arcadian fertility rites, which are similar to those of other cultures, Pan is the image of nature's fecundity. He brags of having coupled with all the maenads in the suite of Dionysus. In fact, the preferred lover of the maenads during their orgies on the crests of mountains was a man covered in goatskin, who was killed at the end of the rite. Love and death are bound together in these ancient rituals, the origins of which date back to even earlier fertility cults. In this coupling, Pan demonstrates his ties with the Dionysiac world, its excesses and madness.

One of this god's many conquests was Selena, the moon. In order to deceive her, Pan covered his black fur with a snow-white fleece. Not recognizing him, Selena let herself be seduced, agreeing to climb up on his rump and thus satisfying his desire. The myth is probably an echo of an orgiastic rite celebrated by moonlight in the Kalends of May, during which the May Queen straddles a man before celebrating her nuptials with him (ibid., 90–91). The seduction of Selena could be the narration of the lunar aspects of desire incarnated by Pan. Coupling with Selena, Pan illustrates the cyclical nature of desire and its nocturnal, hidden character. Moreover, the strategy used to possess the goddess reveals a game of opposites. The black caprine fur is covered by white fleece: the obscurity of desire thus succeeds in becoming lighter. To make love to Selena, Pan is forced to modify his nature, to mask it, assuming his own opposite. Only thus can he illuminate his own darkness, his own wild, animal nature. Selena gives to Pan her light: desire, illuminated, reaches the consciousness that, no longer fearing it, can satisfy it. But Selena with her nocturnal light rules over an illusory world, populated by phantasms and shadows. The relationship between Pan and Selena would then evoke the lunar aspect of the psyche, its madness (López-Pedraza 1977, 122). In this the god seems to represent "the ultimate possibility of the psyche, a frontier where the personality either finds a natural self-regulation or else precipitates hopelessly into madness" (ibid., 126).

Among his exploits, Pan boasted of having seduced any number of nymphs. Syrinx, however, succeeded in eluding him and his advances by transforming herself into a reed. In the attempt to possess her, Pan cut many reeds, with which he made the pipe that he subsequently taught Hermes and Apollo to play. But the music of Pan could not rival the celestial melodies produced by Apollo accompanied by the Muses. The sound of instinct would remain, rough and primitive.

Unlike Syrinx, Echo gave herself repeatedly to the god, prior to her unfortunate passion for Narcissus, for which she would be consumed to the point of becoming pure voice. The love of Pan and Echo represents the psychic resonance created by the appearance of the goat god. In this way, "the echoes of Pan reverberate within the soul, and bring the soul to the corporeal level of Pan" (ibid., 122). The emergence of Pan in dreams, in fantasies, as well as in myth, demonstrates the need to reunite with the body (ibid., 118), with all its sexuality and desire. Recognizing Pan, listening to his voice, implies entering into contact with instinct. Thus, Pan initiates the soul, teaching it to relate to sexuality. The seduction by Pan represents the first in a series of stages for exploring the many aspects of the sexual dimension.

Opposite to the obscure and bestial seduction of Pan, but equally disturbing, is the seduction of Eros. Bursting out of the cosmic egg, according to the *Theogony* of Hesiod (1977), Eros was the first of all the gods, without whom none of them would ever have been born. Other versions of the myth consider him the son of Hermes and Aphrodite or of Ares and Aphrodite (Graves 1955, 49). He is described as a rebellious boy and as irreverent, even to his mother. The eternal child, Eros flits about on golden wings, his arrows aimed at gods and mortals alike, inflaming their hearts, which are then overcome by desire. Seduction operated by Eros is therefore imagined as piercing and burning. The desire of love burns and wounds; seduction burns and wounds, with the appearance of the other. Thus Sappho (1958) celebrates the yearning created by the bursting in of Eros:

> Eros moves my soul as the wind upon the mountain bursts upon the oak, loosening its limbs, agitating sweetly and bitterly indomitable beast. To me neither bee nor honey, and I suffer and desire.

From the psychological point of view, the task of Eros is that of "awakening and generating the soul" (Hillman 1972b, 36). It is thanks to Eros that psychological creativity is awakened. This is illustrated by the myth of Eros and Psyche. This procreative function of the soul in any case emerges not only in the phenomenon of falling in love but also in transference. The desire the patient experiences for the analyst and the analyst for the patient is not only the sign of the pathology to be treated—the neurosis or psychosis of transference—but also the sign of the movement of the psyche, recreated through desire. In this movement, Eros stirs up stagnant waters, removing those blocks and obstacles utilized by the soul to avoid living. Eros activated within the relationship can thus treat and educate, rendering possible renewal and transformation. In this sense, Eros is creative. Eros reveals to the soul its imaginal capacity (ibid., 97). Passion, with its perturbations, tensions, anxieties, fears, and impulses, not only permits the soul to rediscover contact with the corporeal dimension but also places it in contact with all its parts. Reawakened by Eros, the soul thus learns to perceive its many countenances, learns to recognize itself.

According to Kerényi and Jung (1940–41), Eros unites the phallic with the psychic and spiritual elements. For the Greek consciousness, Eros would belong to the region of the *metaxy*, that intermediate region between the human and the divine (Hillman 1972b, 82). And in fact, his task is that of binding those two worlds by means of the desire that unites gods and mortals. A son of Hermes, Eros shared with his father the characteristics of messenger and psychopompus. The seduction operated by Eros would therefore on the one hand apparently be related to the function of binding the split psychic parts, and on the other to awakening and transforming the soul.

However, these are only some of the means and ends of seduction recounted by the Greek imaginary. Similar to the seduction of Eros is that of Aphrodite: the seduction of beauty. More beautiful than any other goddess, having been born by sea foam fecundated by the sperm and blood from the genitals of Chronos, who was castrated by his son Zeus, Aphrodite is consecrated to love. This is her main occupation, the task assigned to her by the Moiras, the goddesses of destiny (Graves 1955, 61). In this context, the goddess represents a cosmogonical force, without which life would be impossible. Aphrodite is the personification· of vital energy. Thus myths inevitably describe her as intent on loving and seducing, also the merit of her magic girdle, which no one can resist. In the Hellenistic view, her seduction is never dark and chthonic, as is the seduction of Pan. Only the tie with the pre-Hellenic Great Goddess—of whom, like Demeter and Artemis, she appears the manifestation—renders her the Mistress of Life and Death, respecting that connection between love and death appearing in many cultures. Melaneus ("black"), Scotia ("dark one"), Androphonos ("manslayer"), Epytimbria ("of the tombs") would subsequently become some of her names (ibid., 62), and here we can perceive a return to the obscure and mortal character of seduction.

To the contrary, in the Homeric and post-Homeric world, the seduction of Aphrodite is always as graceful and elegant as the Charities and Graces accompanying her. In this sense, the image of Aphrodite recounts the straining of the soul toward beauty and harmony. Harmony, in fact, is the name of the daughter generated with Ares, the contentious and violent god of war. The love of Aphrodite placates the soul, resolves conflict, generates harmony. Her love and seduction are at the service of a pleasure that is free of guilt. The seduction of Aphrodite, who passes from one love to another, is unadulterated fun. She takes her immortal existence lightly. She is not as industrious or intelligent as Athena, nor is she a lover of nature like Artemis, both of whom were virgin goddesses, and her brand of pleasure does not require the bonds of matrimony, as does that of Hera, the wife of Zeus and goddess of the bridal chamber. Aphrodite represents the eternal game of love and desire, of pleasure enjoyed with any creature to whom she might be attracted. The game of Aphrodite, sweet and heady, is never lethal. Her adventures, her betrayals, never produce violent consequences, as do those of Zeus or the other gods who were wont to kill their mortal lovers. Adonis is the only victim, but he was killed as a result of the jealousy of Ares. Like the Great Goddess who periodically renewed her virginity, Aphrodite, after having betrayed her husband Hephaestus with Ares, recuperated her virginity by bathing in the sea of Paphos, an island consecrated to her. This alternation between a virginal and a mature body persists in the goddess, and she continues to regenerate herself, her charms, her beauty, the novelty of her desire.

Aphrodite gives herself generously, to gods and men alike. Her love for Hermes produces the half-man/half-woman Hermaphroditus; her love for Dionysus produces Priapus, child of the enormous genitals, physical sign of the excessive desire and lasciviousness of his parents. Aphrodite also often loves mortals, unlike the chaste Artemis, who punishes with death those who dare merely look at her. The issue of Aphrodite's love for Anchises is Aeneas, the founder of the Roman *gens*.

The elegance and lightheartedness of the goddess, however, can change into wrathful fury directed at those mortals who fail to honor her, or who are guilty of the sin of *hybris* against her. And her revenge can be terrible. She persecuted at length poor Psyche who, enamored of Eros, was guilty of being considered the most beautiful of all women. She cruelly punished King

Cynyras, who considered his daughter Myrrha more beautiful than her, by rendering him guilty of incest. Driven mad with passion by the goddess, Myrrha lay with her drunken father who, when he realizes what had occurred, kills his daughter by cutting her in two with his sword. This incestuous union produced Adonis, long the object of contention between Aphrodite and Persephone, queen of the underworld.

While Aphrodite represents the elegant lightness of desire, the smiling and benevolent aspect of seduction, Dionysus incarnates its excesses, madness and mortal fascination. The women loved and abandoned by Dionysus move toward inevitable death. Ariadne, Aura, and Erigone all die. Dionysus is an absent god, who tires easily of his lovers, forgets and abandons them, after having possessed them at times with deceit and violence. As Aura sleeps, intoxicated by wine, Dionysus binds and possesses her. He rapes the sleeping Nikaia, virgin warrior, who gives birth to Teletes, the initiation (Calasso 1988, 41–63). The seduction of Dionysus echoes madness and death because it constitutes an initiatory threshold for the soul. Being open to desire and pleasure implies the death of a virginal consciousness that knows no contact or relationship with the other. The seduction of Dionysus should be seen in this context of merging. By abandoning his lovers, the god obliges them to free themselves from a fusional embrace, to return to themselves—something they do not always succeed in doing. Dionysus rules over the threshold of love passion, marking its confines with the madness of unbounded desire, such as that to which the maenads abandon themselves. The orgiastic fury that possesses the Bacchantes in the retinue of the god leads, for example, to Agave tearing Pentheus to pieces, in punishment for having refused to honor the god.

Effeminate and lascivious, inventor of wine and inebriation, Dionysus, the god of women, represents the madness of passion, the loss of reason clouded by the possession of desire. Dionysus himself experiences death and dismemberment. The image of Dionysus torn to pieces and regenerated is a representation of the fragmentation of the soul, lacerated by the pain of love and the intensity of affects and emotions. The connection between Dionysus and the underworld to which he descends to bring back to life his mother Semele brings once more to mind the infernal aspect of seduction, which is also revealed in the myth of Hades and Persephone.

Dionysus and Persephone are both mythical figures bound to mystery cults that celebrate the eternal resurrection of life after death. Here violent seduction verges once more on rape. Hades swallows up Persephone, the inexperienced maiden, as she gathers flowers. The earth opens and Persephone is dragged down into Hell by the god. The seduction of Persephone, who becomes queen of the underworld, recounts the dark, infernal aspect of seduction, its often-mortal absorption. Persephone is kidnapped from life and the light of day. Her seduction appears as a sinking, as entering a shadow dimension terrifying to mortals. Violently wrenched from her maiden's existence, Persephone must move through an unfamiliar, subterranean world. The myth thus becomes a metaphor of the depressive sinking impression that can accompany the feeling of having been seduced and imprisoned by the other, just as Persephone is a prisoner of Hades.

As a maiden, Kore/Persephone is a virgin goddess, but her divine virginity is not as untouched and untouchable as are those of Artemis and Athena, to whom go the appellatives of *Kore* and *Parthenos* (virgin). Persephone is the image of the encounter with the other than oneself. She is the maiden destined to free herself from the embrace of the mother Demeter. While the couple Demeter-Kore represents a continually regenerated feminine dimension, at one and the same time virgin and mother—like the Great Goddess—the couple Persephone-Hades represents the female-male encounter. Persephone represents the passage between two different conditions; living a third of the year in the underworld together with her husband, and the rest with her mother on the earth, she is the image of a condition of eternal liminality. The essence of her existence lies in this living at the confines of Hades, which separates her life as a maiden from that of a bride (Kerényi and Jung 1940–41, 161–162). The nuptials with Hades are for Persephone nuptials of death. At the height of her inviolate life as maiden, Persephone is kidnapped, prey to a seduction that radically transforms her destiny. To fulfill that destiny, Persephone must die to herself; she must descend into Hades—a mythologem that is repeated in the tale of the Sumerian goddess Inanna, the Mesopotamian Ishtar, and the Japanese Amaterasu. Her descent to the underworld, which is followed by a return to the earth, represents an initiatory threshold that places her at the center of the Eleusinian mysteries, mysteries of death and rebirth.

Unlike other mythical seductions, that of Persephone, begun with the violence of the kidnapping, ends with her marriage to her kidnapper. This story is not one of a rapid and episodic exploding of a passing passion, which ends the moment it is satisfied, as with the loves of Zeus, Apollo, or the other gods. The story of Persephone is one of a seduction that opens to encounter, to relationship with the other—a dark other, as different as the shadowy, sad god of the dead could be from a young girl playing happily in a meadow. Faced with the bursting in of an unknown, subterranean eros, Persephone succeeds in integrating it into her own life, changing herself and her condition. Removed from her own unawareness, the goddess learns to master this dark world, becoming its queen. For her, seduction has opened the way to a new consciousness. The sinking of Persephone, her belonging to Hades, living there for four months of the year, does not prevent her from returning to the earth, to enjoy the sun and scale Olympus where the immortals dwell. To the seduced soul, abducted by the love for an unknown god, Persephone teaches how to move between infernal depths and celestial heights, how to transform seduction into relationship.

While Persephone is an image of the seduction that opens to relationship, the virgin goddesses Athena and Artemis represent the impossibility of seduction. As a newborn babe on the knees of her father, Artemis asks for eternal virginity. And Zeus, laughing, satisfies her request. Her savage beauty is destined to remain inviolate. Whoever derided her was destined to a horrible end. Her revenge on Aura, for having questioned her virginity, would be rape by Dionysus and being driven mad, at which point she would murder one of the children born from her union with the god. The fate of Actaeon was no better; seduced by the beauty of the goddess of the hunt, that imprudent mortal spied on her as she bathed, and subsequently bragged about that divine revelation. Implacable and horrible was the punishment inflicted; after having transformed him into a stag, Artemis has him torn to bits by her dogs. Armed with bow and arrows, like her brother Apollo, Artemis has the power both to unleash pestilence and sudden death and to recall them. Her abode is on the woody mountain crests, where she hunts with her virgin companions. As her mother Leto gave birth to her painlessly, she is invoked by pregnant women. The virgin Artemis protects children and small animals, reunifying thus the image of virginity and maternity. In Artemis, the opposites once more touch, without, however, the virginity of the goddess opening to relationship with the male, as is the case with Persephone.

Also a virgin is Athena, born fully armed from the head of her father Zeus, who represents wisdom and industriousness. It is she who teaches women the feminine arts, such as weaving and cooking, and she who invented the vase, the plow, the yoke, the chariot, and the ship (Graves 1955, 845). Goddess of war, unlike Eris (dissention) and the violent and rough Ares, who wins in strategy, she does not love battle and attempts to resolve conflict. Her sense of justice is profound, as is her compassion, and her anger is less terrible than that of the other divinities. When Tiresias surprises her nude as she bathes, she does not kill him as Artemis did Actaeon, but blinds him; however, as though in exchange for his loss of sight, she confers him with futurity (ibid., 86), rendering him an infallible oracle. Threatened by Hephaestus, who attempts to possess her by force, Athena frees herself from his embrace and dries with disgust the sperm the god has ejaculated onto her thigh. However, the discarded, soiled cloth fecundates Gaea, Mother Earth. Kerényi and Jung (1940–41, 159) maintain that, for the Greeks, it is through Athena that the idea of the divine is liberated from its sexual component. Athena represents "pure spiritual force."

Inviolate and sacrosanct, the virgin goddesses represent the feminine force, woman's being "one in herself" (Harding 1953; Bolen 1984); they are the image of an inner refinement. On the other hand, they are also figures of an extreme—almost autistic—detachment. Calasso defines Apollo, Artemis, and Athena as "unnatural, detached gods" (1988, 70). Wrapped in their self-sufficiency, they observe the world with indifference. Their distant gaze seems perennially directed at an invisible mirror in which, undisturbed, they contemplate their own countenances (ibid., 68). The eternal virginity of Athena and Artemis is nothing more than the logical extreme of this detachment, the rejection of any commingling. Although Narcissus fell in love with his own reflected image, it was in any event a figure of seduction, a seduction turned in on itself. Athena and Artemis exit from the stage of seduction. The soul experiences in these figures the necessity of returning to itself, not in narcissistic absorption, but in a re-immersion, individual completeness. That which they introduce is a movement of separation from the other, without which the relationship is merely fusion.

Contrary to Athena and Artemis, in Apollo—the god of the oblique glance, the god of word and prophecy—detachment and passion alternate. Marpessa, Daphne, Cassandra, Dryope, Coronis, Hyacinth, and Admetus capture his senses, obliging him to abandon his divine indifference. Above all, who rendered Apollo mad with love was the young king Admetus, to whom the god had made himself a servant—a punishment inflicted on him by his father Zeus. For love of this mortal, Apollo forgets his divine condition and becomes the most humble and wretched of men. Far different were the results of the other passions of Apollo. While Marpessa remained faithful to her husband, and Daphne in order to elude Apollo is transformed into a laurel, Cassandra's rejection of intercourse with the god is punished with the terrible gift of prophecy perpetually unheeded. Here seduction is related to the acquisition of a deeper view, the acquisition of a more far-reaching knowledge. The soul that opens to Eros learns to see differently, to move through the obscure interior regions like Persephone in the underworld, or to unveil the future like Cassandra. The fate of the Princess of Troy, daughter of Priam, is in this sense emblematic. Her rejecting the love of the god earns her a tragic curse that renders her incapable of communicating what she foresees.

Dryope, Coronis, and Hyacinth, however, yield to Apollo's seduction. Aesculapius, the great healer, born of Hyacinth and struck down by a thunderbolt by Zeus for having restored a dead man to life, will be made divine. Mysterious deaths are in store for many of those who love Apollo. Coronis, who betrayed the god, would be burned alive, while Hyacinth would be accidentally killed by Apollo while being taught to throw the discus. Once more, seduction, as luminous as the sun that Apollo represents, slides into the obscurity of death. The love embrace becomes mortal. Calasso (1988, 33) points out that the Greek verb *jterein* signifies both to seduce and to destroy. Another example of this is the seduction of the enchanted songs of the Sirens, which lead to their deaths those who listen to them.

The violent and destructive aspect of seduction is reflected in the many loves of Zeus. Transformed into a heifer and loved by Zeus in the form of a bull, Io is goaded mercilessly by a horsefly set upon her by Hera, who thus takes her revenge for the faithlessness of her priestess. The love of Zeus for Io results in malediction and ultimately madness. Hera implacably persecutes all the women loved by her husband who, in order to seduce, uses his divine aspect of metamorphosis. Deceit, metamorphosis, and at times rape are constants in the seduction of the king of the gods. To seduce Danaë, Zeus transforms himself into a rain of gold, and to possess Leda he becomes a swan. In the form of a bull, he possesses Europa, who changes into a cow to escape the jealous wrath of Hera. The loves of Zeus, more than those of any other god or goddess, are situated on a metamorphic horizon. The soul experiences thus the mutability and illusory aspects of the forms in which otherness is manifested. The power of seduction is contained in this possibility, in this capacity to assume the form best suited to overcome the resistance of the loved one. Seduction here includes a secret invitation to embrace transformation. The contact of love is in this sense the acceptance of metamorphosis, an openness to change despite the risks and suffering that that implies.

Five

A Particular Relationship

*To be slandered and scorched by the love with which
we operate—such are the perils of our trade, which we
are certainly not going to abandon on their account.*
—S. Freud, *Letter to C. G. Jung of March 9, 1909*

And so, the analytical experience, like the love experience, is another reference to a *passage to death,* a metaphor for a process of transformation by means of which the subject restructures his own personality on the basis of a new inter-psychic dynamic. The relationship between the ego complex and other complexes changes, and consequently also the attitude of the consciousness with the unconscious, of the other than oneself and the world. M. Balint (1932) defines as "new cycle" the renewed psychic order of the patient who, by elaborating the structured defenses in order to love "without anxiety," is finally able to expand his capacity to love and more fully enjoy his own existence.

As the love seduction perceived as a threat of destabilization can arouse defensive reactions, so may the seduction of the soul, with its call to change, generate anxiety and resistance in the ego. Fear of the destruction of the "old" consciousness can block the development of the process because, unconsciously, each patient knows that the healing process occurs through the dissolution of that internal order, those defensive structures upon which—however precariously—his present equilibrium rests. The elements that had up until then dominated the life of the soul must be dissipated if there is to be space for new development.

This process of dissipation in the interests of a still unknown recomposition generates considerable fear; something must die, and with it a part of us. Logically, there would be nothing to lose in rejecting those constructions, mental tendencies, and defenses that have blocked the development of an individual to the point of having necessitated therapeutic intervention. And yet, every identification with the "bad" or "exciting" internal (Fairbairn 1952), albeit pathogenic, object constitutes a model for adapting to the world, for identification: "I suffer, I always trust the wrong person, I am incapable of falling in love, I continue to have the same nightmare . . . *therefore I am*." The repetition compulsion that locks the individual into a Karmic circle of errors, of relapse or "negative destiny," in the end becomes a means of asserting existence, identity. It is a way of remaining true to one's own phantasms, obtaining in exchange benefits of a vicarious kind: the illusion of love, acceptance or completeness. And it is not an easy thing to let go of these illusions.

Passage and death are on center stage during the analytical process. There is a deep affinity between that ritual ceremony which is analysis and the experience of death as it has been described by most religious literature, as the recognition of a destiny that serves to protect the believer from annihilation. However, it is precisely in this "sacred enclosure" that an *affective* relationship will be formed, intended as the activation in the patient of all the erotic forces at the service of the soul to find responses to its needs: love, hate, hunger, anger idealization, abandonment. Erotic pressure and a shared anxiety animate the analytical interaction and—as we will see—the seductiveness of the patient is very often a defensive weapon used to "beat the analyst at his own game," using his own arms—in other words, in order to overcome the fear of being seduced, the patient attempts to *seduce the seducer.*

Thus, the acquisition of a new consciousness and a new knowledge of the self is always accompanied by a sense of guilt or transgression, the fear of "putting to death" the other: the other part of oneself that must die, the old tendencies, but also the invisible other with which one has deeply identified—the internal parent, separation from whom becomes the most tragic of events. It is a "leaving the other to his own destiny," leaving him to "rest in peace"; in other words, for the afflicted and imprisoned consciousness, letting that other die means betrayal. On the other hand, that authentic "descent into the underworld," or immersion in the unconscious that is an essential part of the analytical process, involves the risk of challenging that already precarious, apparent unity of the person at that point where he is forced to confront the stranger inhabiting him, his Shadow. It is then that the conflict begins with that part of him—so difficult to accept—a conflict that can disorient the consciousness and weaken it to the point of obscuring the light—to borrow Jung's very apt metaphor. This passage into the unknown can at times be so darkly preoccupying that the therapist represents the only grasp the patient has on that part of his ego that, involved in the therapeutic alliance, cannot de-structure. In order to avoid the confrontation with the Shadow and the inevitable constellation of depression and guilt, a seduction of the analyst may also be "acted out"—just how, we will see further on. Jung maintained from the outset that the transference, the "eroticized removal," had a sense and a purpose: it can be the result of difficulty encountered in establishing contact and emotional harmony, and therefore an unconscious attempt to cover the distance separating the patient from the analyst. When no common territory is perceived, passionate sentiments or erotic fantasy can emerge in the analysand as a compensatory bridge. This occurs frequently in psychologically isolated patients who, fearing they will not be comprehended even by the analyst, attempt to conciliate the circumstances and their unconscious aversion with a sort of courtship.

The contiguity between transference relationship and defense mechanisms, and in particular that variety of transference that for the most part stimulates the collective imaginary—erotic seduction—is evident in the "original myth" of the analytical couple: Breuer and Anna O. In that relationship, Breuer intuited the reciprocal nature of the involvement and, too upset to reflect, opted for a hasty retreat, leaving his patient in the hands of his young colleague, Sigmund Freud. It was a case of the physician's putting into action a spontaneous and thoughtless self-defense because, convinced that the patient's love was directed at him personally—and thus a case of real love—he took those sentiments at face value. In all probability, he was also defending himself from himself. He failed to maintain that distance that would have helped him perceive, behind that love, the persistence of a once-negated desire to be satisfied.

It was Freud who would discover the "transference"—that is, the typical nature characterizing the analytical relationship; the deep involvement of the patient. The defense from the transference is no longer acted out, and Freud reconsidered the close contiguity between the transference and the defensive strategies in play in the analytical relationship. In fact, he would say that those *amorosi sensi* of the patient as regards the analyst represent a resistance to remembering, a defense against painful memories and frustrated desires that emerge, as a result of the therapist's evident willingness to take care of him. Freud considers the transference as a resistance to memory and the tendency toward repetition as the nucleus of neurosis. Rather than remembering, the patient relives and repeats experiences fundamental to the constitution of his identity, and that is above all a way of relationship crystallized over time, as though nothing new could occur, or that any new questions could arise requiring responses. The patient renders the past present, as memory is not experienced as such, but as a present reality of desire. Sandor Ferenczi (1909) would state even more clearly that neurosis is the passion for transference.

To further explain the concept of transference, Freud used the distinction between a reprint as opposed to a new edition of a literary work: it is evident that the closer the analytical relationship is to a reprinting, the more exiguous will be the space available for a relationship with the analyst as a true and potentially different interlocutor from the patient's imaginary one. However, with a new edition, the author re-consigns his work to history, to time that changes men and their worldview. Thanks to this attention, the work is no longer a simple record of a past that it in some way reduces but instead makes possible a perception of the traces of a stratified genesis, its quality of being alive. The past is never definitively consigned, and memory is always interwoven with the present. However, in a neurotic existence, reality is negated along with the occasions it offers.

Freud, reflecting on the transference, had already intuited the uncertain confine between the space containing the traces of a past never abandoned and the space of a present that, although faded, remains the framework within which the personages and stories of the past are reanimated. This is so because analytical work is in any case also dependent on the quality and the characteristics of the encounter of two personalities, a game that both are called on to play. An analyst-mirror is not only utopian, it is unnecessary. Also, continuously restituting to the patient always his own transference experiences inevitably becomes a source of incomprehension, feeding the patient's resistance and mistrust. Every transference relationship contains elements of reality, just as every real relationship has in it elements of transference.

The patient is in fact delicately balanced between several apparently contradictory requests, for the purpose of maintaining that fragile equilibrium, which the analyst in a certain sense guarantees. The patient is asked to remember rather than repeat and to move away from an ingenuous adhesion to the reality of the transference sentiments; however, at the same time, he is asked to abandon himself. Nurturing burning and often urgent sentiments, the patient only apparently moves away from the recovery of the past, since abandoning himself to the inevitable emergence of real emotions is in reality an opening to the past. Reliving rather than remembering thus renders the work of the analysis precious and essential for the patient. But Freud himself realized soon enough that the transference cannot be interpreted univocally as a defense: for this is a possibility, not a rule, and an interpretation that can be misused by an analyst threatened by a responsibility he finds too heavy. Should that trustful opening with which the patient allows us to enter and populate his internal world be misinterpreted and restituted to him—for example, as a defense against a destructive drive—it will be tantamount to having agreed to recite his past, of having been seduced by the compulsion to confirm neurotic convictions and trapped in the circularity of a self-fulfilling prophecy. The patient has communicated to us his desire to trust and we will have restituted to him the desperation of having that desire frustrated.

It is necessary to establish just what the analyst and the patient are called on to confront, each with the substance of his own experience and the cognition of his existential itinerary, the affects and their laws. What we intend by *affects* is a complex area of the psyche toward which gravitate sensations, emotions, intuitions, and images of sentiment, all related to the image of the individual and the world, the self, and *other* aspects that populate the internal and external scenes of the subject's life. Thus we speak of "affective complexes" to indicate those split nuclei of the psychic experience, emotionally very powerful, forming those particularly vulnerable and receptive, fragile zones of the subject's experience.

Each individual has *complexes,* that is, areas of hypersensitivity to certain constellations of psychological experiences. We speak of "mother complexes" or "inferiority complexes." What the patient brings into analysis is precisely this area, this nucleus of vulnerability, which—although it protects and conceals and inevitably expresses through various forms of resistance—is in fact the gravitational center that attracts all the subject's energies, explaining his attempt at all costs to catalyze the attention of the analyst. The wound, or lack, attracts and seduces, activating drives and images.

Very often—and here we have the core of the problem—the catalyzing of the patient's internal energies made possible by the analysis is translated in the patient into an activation of sentiment, that which is also called *erotized transference*. Further on, we will consider the eventual reading of this transference, the *impasse* it generates, and the ends it conceals. But, at this point, we will limit our discourse to its phenomenology.

The patient finds himself suddenly immerged in a fluctuating perturbation. The figure of the analyst becomes the center around which rotate emotional fantasies of various types but with the same connotation: the ambivalent oscillation between attraction and fear, between interest and detachment, and between adhesion to the nascent fantasies as regards the therapist and a painful sensation of appearing ridiculous. How is it possible? . . . How could this happen? . . . What does it mean? . . . It is ridiculous, or dramatic, or both. The analyst's aspect, his image, has become "uncanny."

Freud used this term (*uncanny*) in reference to the field of aesthetics, pointing out its relationship to repulsive and distressing affects (Freud 1919, 81) such as fear and anxiety; warning, however, that it does not coincide exactly with any of them, although it evoked them. In fact, the real essence of what is uncanny has to do with ambivalence: all that which causes contradictory and contrasting affects, in which fear is combined with fascination, attraction with shame. It would appear therefore to be intrinsic to a particular area of the affect in which there is not only suffering but also pleasure. Another of Freud's specifications could be of interest to us here: *das Unheimlich* (the strange or unfamiliar) and *das Heimlich* (that is, what is known, familiar or, in another acceptation, that which is hidden, secret). Thus, an affective space would be circumscribed, bound to what is concealed in the places of intimacy. At a certain point, something so intimate and close to the subject is revealed as to be alarming, as to generate anxiety. For the male child, Freud rapidly identified the feminine genital apparatus as the "disturbing" element par excellence, the place of repression. But I believe it is not only sex that becomes the source of deep disturbance, of attraction combined with fear. We have said, for example, that the same treatment is perceived at a deeper level by the patient who asks for help both as a possible cause of pleasure and as a threat to his own equilibrium—an opening to the unknown that generates apprehension.

The analyst, as he activates dynamics of transformation, becomes a source of apprehension in that he creates a tension between opposing tendencies, between attraction for revelation and the recognition of the repressed and anxiety in the face of something new. Discovering what is concealed behind unconscious formations, the therapist reveals the strangely troubling element contained in the "familiar"—in other words, the subject's alter ego, his unknown twin, his Shadow. Of course, all this is not exactly clear and logically distinct in the mind of the patient. Instead it is a question of subliminal perceptions, intuition of danger, and attempting to prevent the feared "seduction" from occurring.

In the area of the affects—that is, of desire—fear and fascination are always intimately related. Any patient will suffer from a prohibition of his deepest desires; that is, the conflict between Ego and Super-Ego, or between Self and false-Self; that which is denied the subject is contact with his authentic desire. Despite this, the subject who decides to go into analysis does so in the hope of being liberated of suffering caused by his compulsion and of succeeding in recognizing his real desire.

Fear and attraction are the two poles between which the patient attempts to maintain an equilibrium. However, it is an acquired art. The erotized transference activates both these aspects of sentiment. The patient's fear of the transference is, if we are to be sincere, the same as the analyst's: the fear of the uncontrollable; that is, going beyond the usual limits—which we might also call the fear of madness. This fear could be compared to the *timor sacro*. It is the holy confusion of which Pascal speaks, the anxiety aroused by our being called to that new enlightenment and consciousness inspired by God in the soul He deigns to touch. It is a sacred inhibition, then, and not mere resistance. It is a fear that can be elaborated during analysis and that is comprehensible, even welcome, as it is a sign that something is slowly trying to emerge, something the ego would rather keep under control. Although it is true that transference love is the effect of a transfer of repetition, it is only partially so. For although it is a copy, a repetition of past affective patterns, what is possible using this sole means known to the patient is an affect, a "fire," a charge of energy, which longs to be placed also at the disposition of the soul and its transformations, and not only resistance.

The love tension that the patient experiences—in many ways similar to the urgency of the adolescent "ardor of the first love"— can be dampened by the analyst if, instead of taking advantage of the occasion to comprehend that tension, he limits himself to dismissing it as resistance. Liquidating transference love, or above all liquidating it presumptively, presenting it to the patient as a "necessary loss," would result in a useless waste of energy. The patient attempts to enter into contact with very powerful internal images, those images that the analyst recognizes as phantasms of the past, but at the same time those as yet indistinct forms concealing the patient's real individual essence and future potential. A patient will consider the analyst his guide in the desert, a desert of mirages and shadows that can be deciphered only with him. The patient's difficulty—that is, the requests he directs to the analyst through his erotized communication—is to succeed in bearing the

emotional ferment created by the intuition of novelty and the re-
sultant sentimental ambivalence, for which he asks a container, a
containment.

Eros, as we know, was the son of Poros and Poenia: of plenty
and privation. Where there is exclusively "excitation," eros becomes maniacal, inflated, falsely Promethean. Thus, eros deprived, blocked, prevented from entering into contact is a sign
of blocked energy: a melancholic eros, depressed and in mourning. The dimension of sentiment in analysis must combine both
these aspects: excitation and containment, energy and controlled
energy. It is for this reason that the space of analysis is a
Temenos, a place for the imaginary, a space in which to invent
oneself. It is also for this reason that liquidating the patient's affective involvement as "resistance" can be damaging, even dangerous. I explained previously (Carotenuto 1986) how the repetition compulsion—at least in the psychotherapeutic context—is
of capital importance. It is thanks to this that the patient brings
into the analytical setting the *live* paradigm of his old disturbance, to once more incarnate for and with us the old intro-
jected model. Compulsion in itself has its positive side, as it is
animated by an unconscious project: that of succeeding finally in
sidestepping the impasse blocking it.

What does the analyst become in the eyes of the vulnerable
patient who, because of his deep lacerations, cannot easily
assume—although consciously he does—the conviction that the
person before him is absolutely trustworthy and sincere? The analyst therefore becomes a powerfully attractive figure and a disturbing one: he is the incarnation of the potential of the love
that heals and at the same time reproduces a phantasm, an internal image that generates anxiety. The analyst is the source of all
good, and at the same time a threatening abyss. This powerful
ambivalence emerges during the analytical work, coloring the
transference throughout its various phases. Generally, the appearance of a tumultuous request for love, above all when the
analytical couple is made up of both sexes, marks the initial
phase of a relationship often lasting for a considerable period of
time. The transference at that point apparently flows along,
serenely: the patient is yielding, favorably accepts the analyst's

explanations, appears to have faith in the treatment, and is attentive and open.

Suddenly, however, the music can change: the patient begins to wonder what is in the mind of the analyst, what type of impression he has formed of him or conceals, of how much love he is capable, and above all *what he represents* for the analyst. A common desire among patients is that of being the favorite, the most loved—as though only that position could ensure his healing. It is a narcissistic fantasy, of course, which should be approached and probed as such, giving it the importance that every fantasy deserves, if only for the fact that it could reveal something of the patient's perception of the treatment and healing. Initially, in fact, the one asking to be freed from a symptom imagines that "coming out of a symptom" coincides with the removal of pain or existential discomfort. In the same way that the child experiencing an unpleasant stimulus (hunger, thirst, fatigue) asks its parents to free him of that inconvenience, the patient formulates a total request that demands an equally total response: free me from pain. This request already denotes a regression *in fieri* from the level of the examination of reality (for which the ego becomes capable of bearing frustration, of procrastination in satisfying the demand and channeling the primary compulsions in the direction of more mature adaptive forms) to the level of immediate satisfaction (dictated by intense suffering): it is that of the pleasure principle, of the hallucinatory gratification of desire. The patient hallucinates the analyst as nourishing him (in certain cases we could speak of "amorous delirium"), and thus sets himself up for a first, necessary defeat; the therapist, although he cannot respond to the patient's request, invites him to trust him, despite the fact that his way of offering good nourishment does not correspond to the way the patient may have imagined.

It is at this point that the erotized transference takes on a different tone and the disturbing element emerges: is the analyst to be trusted or isn't he? Does he or doesn't he nourish; does he or doesn't he love; is he present or is he absent; is he lying or is he telling the truth? What the patient cannot initially comprehend is that what he asks is only what his phantasm allows him to imagine he can obtain. He, like the small child, believes that the frustration of his requests is proof of the badness or incapacity of the other. And does this not also prove, the patient wonders, that it is precisely he himself who is "bad" or "inadequate," he who deserves nothing other than this failure?

Both considerations (the analyst is "bad," or I am "bad") are fruit of the neurotic fantasies animating the subject. Loving and being loved are in reality not dependent only on whether or not one is deserving, and as long as the patient believes he must deserve the love of the analyst or that the analyst must provide proof of his capacity to love and accept, he will remain locked in neurotic circularity. However, it would be absurd on the part of the therapist to expect such "maturity" of the patient at the outset of the treatment, since that would exclude the very condition that led the patient to be there in the first place. Certainly, distinctions are essential, and the nucleus of the problem and the type of subject asking for treatment must be ascertained for each individual case. There are in fact cases in which—as Sandor Ferenczi intuited and subsequently M. Balint and D. Winnicott suggested—only a very strong affective "holding" can modify the structure of the subject and set in motion a process of transformation. But we might also add that transformation only occurs when and if the patient becomes capable of operating symbolically, also because no analyst could ever restitute to the suffering subject that which he was deprived of at a very early and absolutely essential stage in his development.

But let us go back to the critical point: the patient finds himself in a state of great confusion and agitation. He seeks proof of the therapist's love, and when faced with the refusal of his request suspects deceit or betrayal. I believe that asking the patient at that moment to censure and sublimate his drives signifies having failed to create empathic contact. I am thoroughly in agreement with Freud's observation in "Observations on transference-love" (1914a, 164):

> To urge the patient to suppress, renounce or sublimate her instincts the moment she has admitted her erotic transference would be, not an analytic way of dealing with them, but a senseless one. It would be just as though, after summoning up a spirit from the underworld by cunning and spells, one were to send

him down again without having asked him a single question. One would have brought the repressed into consciousness, only to repress it once more in a fright. Nor should we deceive ourselves about the success of any such proceeding. As we know, the passions are little affected by sublime speeches. The patient will feel only the humiliation, and she will not fail to take her revenge for it.

The use of the word "fright" by Freud makes explicit the real cause of the therapist's need to hastily block the patient's transport: fright or, better yet, anxiety. In fact, technique clearly does not suffice to exempt the therapist from the necessity of plunging into the deep waters of the unconscious. Particularly in patients at the borderline of psychosis, for whom it is more difficult to immediately understand the complexity of their discomfort, the impact with the unconscious and the resulting reactions of the countertransference can be extremely violent and generate anxiety. But is it possible to avoid the confrontation with the *daimones* of the unconscious? Isn't it just from this confrontation that could be indicated a way to a possible transformation? Jung understood that circumscribing the phenomenon of the love transference as a simple re-edition of infantile psychosexual events, liquidating the question with simplified interpretations, meant that the treatment had failed.

It would be interesting here to cite a long passage from a letter of Jung's, dated 1914, and addressed to Loy:

Accordingly, I cannot regard the transference, merely as a projection of infantile-erotic fantasies. No doubt that is what it is from one standpoint, but I also see in it . . . a process of empathy and adaptation. From this standpoint, the infantile-erotic fantasies, in spite of their undeniable reality, appear rather as a means of comparison or as analogical images for something not yet understood than as independent wishes. (Jung 1914, 306–307)

Thus, according to Jung, in order to express something still not comprehended, the patient searches for a deeper understanding of his destiny. Consequently, the material that emerges during analysis in the form of love and erotic fantasies must be read as material that, although raw and confused, contains the real potential of his project of individuation. By means of this amplification of the reading of transference love, a way is indicated to the patient to overcome his model of interaction with his own internal images, to which the compulsion corresponds, on the relational level; that is, the conquest of love either through the power of seduction or masochistic surrender. Jung briefly points out the "sacred" aspect of the transference: that is, the patient's desire for transformation, which the analyst—as a catalyzing agent—can help decipher and activate; always, however, within the limits of his role as empathic observer.

The analytical relationship can fail for two reasons: (1) the therapist's insufficient empathic capacity, or (2) collusion with the affective requests of the patient, should these be taken literally.

The first of these failures in the treatment is due to the incapacity of the analyst to analyze the emotional material supplied by the patient, or to pass from the level of rationalist interpretation to one of symbolic amplification. In this case, we can in fact see how that to which we analysts tend and to which we would conduct our patients—the level of symbolic comprehension—is precisely the mortified aspect that has remained unexpressed because it has not been recognized. When we restitute to the patient the offer of his "love"—interpreting it as resistance to the analytical work, a reproduction of relationship models from the past, or the consequence of infantile sexual drives—we are sustaining the assumption that the affective charge that emerges is entirely at the service of the neurosis, of incest. But is this the only unconscious aim of the patient's psyche? It is true that the patient's demand is the vehicle for the desire for immediate satisfaction, but this is so because he has not yet developed that subtle capacity for differentiating in relation to his psychic contents and the symbolic representations that we wish to develop. What the patient feels and communicates is that he loves his analyst, but he cannot yet be aware of the nature and result of that love. Of course, what we can inform the patient, without this compromising our therapeutic pact, is that the analytical situation itself induces this *Sehnsucht* ("yearning"), in that—unlike "desire" or "nostalgia"—yearning indicates the double movement, expressed by the German term, the "desire for someone or something which brings into the present the someone or something which is absent." The figure of the analyst is thus invested. But we should remember that, through the analyst, the patient wishes to arrive at a different destination. It is comprehensible that the urgent need for love can be *also* an expression of resistance; what is not comprehensible is liquidating the entire question with this interpretation.

The second form of failure in the treatment—collusion with the patient's requests—results from having fallen prey to the sexual aspect of the analysis. We will not discuss the negative side of this event, which causes the rupture of the therapeutic alliance. There already exists an exhaustive body of literature on this aspect, which includes works by authors such as Stein (1974), Ulanov (1979, 101–110) and Taylor (1982, 47–54), to mention a few—all of whom stress the harm done to the patient *when* this failure occurs.

Our intention here is to limit our discourse to shedding some light on *why* this occurs, availing ourselves of the work of the Jungian psychologist Nathan Schwartz-Salant (1984), whose observations on the dark core of this acting out and the psychic dynamics subtending it are extremely intuitive and to the point.

What is required for an interpretation of the sexual life, which is an impulse of the Shadow, is real comprehension and not black depression. Only then will its elaboration be possible: otherwise, although the drive energy may be repressed, it will remain as a split nucleus, forming a true shadow complex.

An ethical condemnation must be accompanied by an attentive elaboration; otherwise, there is the danger of liquidating the thorny problem by delegating to the capacity of the single individual the task of elaborating or not elaborating the symptom. What is required, then, is an attempt to recuperate a bit of the soul that has been lost in those places (Schwartz-Salant 1984, 36) and to improve our understanding of its nature.

At this point, we might ask whether the sexual acting out is a self-deceit, a roguish trick, or the making literal of an unconscious resolve aimed at achieving or attaining something that is circumscribed only with difficulty—that is, something ambiguous that makes a literal something connected to the area of the symbolic process. This elusive goal is that substance that Jung calls the *parental libido,* and that Schwartz-Salant defines as *communitas.*

The relationship of which Jung spoke, or the *communitas,* is related to the symbolic of the *coniunctio,* that union of opposites that Jung considered as the structural form of the setting. The *coniunctio* produces relationship and *communitas* in that, by realizing the contact with the split psychic contents, unresolved complexes, and the affect-toned images, there is reunion with the consciousness. It is possible that the *coniunctio,* considered an unconscious regulating factor, is conceived of as a shared experience of the imaginary (ibid., 38).

The alchemist symbol for the reunification of opposites, or the self, is the hermaphrodite, the Rebis of the *Rosarium Philosophorum.* The hermaphrodite, as an archetypal image, can make its appearance in both its positive and negative aspects.

In analytical treatment, for example, the hermaphrodite can represent the hybrid combination of parts of the Self of the analyst and parts of the Self of the patient, in cases in which the relation is dominated by strong projective identifications of split affective components in which there is a dominant *participation mistique,* and an unwitting collusion of the unconsciousness of both partners in the relationship. The two persons can easily feel united in an affective body, sharing the same emotions, while each conserves different defenses and attitudes (ibid., 40); in other words, a body with two heads!

When these collusive combinations occur, the analyst can fall into the error of retaining the patient more capable of elaboration than he actually is, and only subsequently becoming painfully aware of the error of countertransference. This image of the hermaphrodite—that is, the unconscious identity of both patient and analyst—provides fertile ground for a sexual resolution of the communication between the components of the analytical couple. It is for this reason that "sexuality apparently maintains the considerable promise of uniting the opposites in a harmonious and meaningful whole, transforming their monstrous hybrid state" (ibid., 40–41).

The error into which the analyst falls, possibly dragging the patient along with him, is that of deceiving himself that the sexual act is an act of the Self, and therefore positive and transforming. The sexual experience in these cases represents an attempt to integrate split, schizoid aspects of the psyche, sectors in which the sexual, pre-Oedipus component is charged with anxious affects and intense frustrations. This negative aspect of the figure of the hermaphrodite represents a considerable aspect of the Shadow of analysis.

Differing from this is the apparition of the figure of the hermaphrodite in its positive aspect, which is related to the activation of the process of individuation. Jung often pointed out that any process of transformation necessitates confrontation, relationship. It would be difficult to think of individuation as a solitary and introverted process, and even when that might seem to be the case (for example, certain mystics), it turns out that significant relationships have always been maintained: meetings with spiritual sons and daughters, an exchange of letters, and spiritual works and poetry all are forms of contact with an interlocutor.

The analytical relationship is the delegated space in which the activation of the individuation process is solicited, initiating the confrontation with the deepest psychic components of both analyst and patient. It is eros, in fact, which gives expression to the aspiration to and the desire for relationship with both the internal and external world, because it reconnects the past to the present and the present to the future, conferring to the Self the sense of its own continuity. The figure of the hermaphrodite as an image of coupling and conjunction is thus by necessity not only an individual figure but also an image of a united self: the *Rebis* represents a psychic reality that can flow forth from two persons who reach the *coniunctio* as an act belonging to the imaginary (Schwartz-Salant, 1984, 41). This means that the Self can be considered not only as individual reality but also as the fruit of a relationship, without this falling into a negative *participation mistique* and without the subjects' losing their identity. In other words, the conjunction of souls, far from leading to the sexual experience, generates this human connection that is the aspiration of the *parental libido* (once more borrowing an expression of Jung's). As Jung suggested (1946, 233–234):

> Kinship libido—which could still engender a satisfying feeling of belonging together, as for instance in the early Christian

communities—has long been deprived of its Object. But, being an instinct, it is not to be satisfied by Any mere substitute such as creed, party, nation or State. It wants the *human* connection. That is the core of the Whole transference phenomenon, and it is impossible to Argue it away.

This unconscious and powerful need for a human relationship to deeply nourish the soul plays a vital role in the sexual aspect of analysis, when it is erroneously sought for in the concrete sexual act. In my opinion, this opening to the analysis of the Rebis, of the *coniunctio* and the parental libido, has aided the comprehension of how the patient's request for love contains a deep—instinctive, according to Jung—aspiration to that soul-nourishing relationship between individuals. A particularly obvious example of this I-You relationship, on an elevated level, is the legendary relationship between St. Francis and St. Chiara of Assisi, which did not end in the search for a gratifying relationship between two persons, but which freed the energies necessary for the creation and propagation of an evangelic message that profoundly renewed the spirit of the medieval Church.

In fact, the *communitas* that is generated produces a "sense of mutual respect, equality and participation at a very deep level, as though there had been a transfusion" (Schwartz-Salant 1984, 43). Thus, Schwartz-Salant postulates that behind the transference event and the sexual acting out and beyond the unresolved narcissistic wounds, this imaginary goal—in that it is confused with literal conjunction, thus generating the misunderstandings with which we are only too familiar—can also play a considerable role.

Also the idealization, on the part of the analysand, of the analyst and the analytical relationship belongs in part to a repetition of the state of fusion, although maintaining the germ of a potential search for communion. Thus, it is up to the analyst to intuit which elements are vehicles for regressive tendencies and the way to activate a creative channeling of these libidinal energies. In fact, we know that, while we must recognize the legitimacy of the love sentiment that the patient brings into the analysis, it is equally true that an adult capacity to love is also the result of the elaboration of the frustration, the obstacles that the libido encounters in its quest for gratification.

It is through renouncing immediate satisfaction and through the elaboration of the loss of the totality of his relationship with the mother that the child becomes capable of acceding to a mature emotional and sexual life—in other words, of turning to the world and creating new, significant relationships.

Let us look more carefully at some of the salient phases of the process called "transference love." We have described the affective scene in which the patient moves, initially confused by an idealizing aura that at times recalls that illusion of omnipotence identified by Winnicott (1971) as the primitive phase of child's— the relationship with the mother. The analytical project, during this phase, is the weight of fantasies of fusion subtended by narcissistic expectations. Nonetheless, it is a necessary phase because it permits the patient to overcome the inevitable, initial mistrust and fear of the treatment.

As in any love situation, this moment passes and the patient encounters disappointment, both because the analyst does not respond as the patient imagined he would and besides the idealization: painful, conflicting situations begin to emerge, which generate anxiety. Although the analyst may abstain from responding collusively, despite the level of frustration imposed on the patient, the security represented by the continuity of the analytical relationship makes it possible for the analysand to support this painful tension. He knows that the analyst has placed at his disposition his time and skills, urging him to have faith despite the fantasies of rejection created by his solitude and isolation.

Actually, a mature way of loving is also the result of a capacity to live the solitary dimension of the experience, the only one that guarantees that love is a free choice and not a compulsive refuge to escape solitude. How many marriages continue exclusively due to the fear of being alone! But it is impossible to grow in a relationship that leaves no space for that industriousness and creative solitude that allows each one to channel his own energies also beyond the restricted domestic space, without that being interpreted by the partner as a subtraction of love from the relationship.

This paradigm of love as confused participation and as a

shield against solitude and distance for reflection pervades the general way of relating to the world and others. It results in becoming dissipated in providing immediate responses to the many requests coming from the environment and ourselves, never finding that way leading us to the center, that intimate orientation created by acting according to the dictates of our own authentic inclinations.

However, as long as we remain chained to a model of fusion in the search for illusory gratification, it will be impossible for us to broaden our existential horizon, because the energies that would invest the world are engaged in maintaining the protected space of ties belonging to the state of fusion, in defense of the Ego's fragility.

The analytical space, therefore, must simultaneously represent the protected space to contain the anxieties of the patient and the space in which, precisely due to the security generated by its being contained, also makes it possible to bear the frustration that is essential to a passage from neurotic requests for love to the maturity of a love freed from the compulsion for seduction, the power of the other, or masochistic renunciation.

The patient may not comprehend this invitation, and it is then that a negative transference can develop, with its fantasies of flight from the relationship, indifference and disappointment. It can also happen that a long and stagnant phase begins, during which the patient lays claim regressively to the right to an affective response that he feels is lacking, a position that conceals the fear of change and transformation. That fear is a reasonable one, which inevitably arises when we are called to abandon the known for the unknown at a point when we are still unaware of our own potential. It should now be obvious that, beyond general descriptions of the analytical space, the analyst must work principally with his own emotional responses to the emotions of the patient. The awareness of his own countertransference is in fact the core of analytical work, because significant communication is not based on the exchange of contents and information but on the reciprocal activation of affective complexes. Internal resonance is so decisive that verbal messages are comprehended or misunderstood according to individual difficulties, both those of the patient and those of the analyst. Consequently, subjective experience functions as a filter, and all analytical work rotates around the analyst's capacity to understand when what he hears is the result of his own projections. Analytical work also depends on the patient's capacity to understand when what he hears is the result of his own projections.

It is then substantially a question of a circular process, of action and reaction, which structures a dynamic situation requiring continual decoding. For this reason we could substitute the word "countertransference" simply for the word "transference." Psychoanalysis coined this term to describe the conscious and unconscious attitudes and reactions of the analyst in response to the patient's projections. The process of countertransference was situated in a dimension in which the analyst was considered as detached and impartial, involved successively in response to the emotional investment of the analysand. We now know that the analyst participates emotionally from the very outset of the analysis and that the progress of the treatment actually depends in great part on his sentiments and expectations as regards the patient.

Analyst and patient, therefore, are reciprocally called on to sustain the tension. In one, this creates the need to balance the empathic stimulus, those immediate responses that can conceal elements that have not been interpreted analytically; in the other, the necessity of maintaining a balance between the request for love and the solitude that inevitably accompanies individuation.

It is only through relevance to the present, the veracity of one's own sentiment, that the interpretation of the transference becomes real and credible for the patient and thus produces change. Up to the conclusion of the therapy, even the most conscious patient lives in a kind of limbo, because analysis not only solicits transference but also necessitates it as its elective instrument. Together with the analyst, in the culminating phase of the analysis, the patient is led to elaborate the transference, considering the story of his life and the analysis as parallel journeys through which he learns to recognize himself. Being the object of the transference and at the same time its interpreter is the therapeutic *opportunity* of the analyst. The patient's initial version of his own life will not necessarily be the same as the one he takes away after the analysis. It is even to be hoped that patient and analyst will together have rewritten it. This is not that manipulation that could be detrimental to the patient, because the "re-edition" of the novel of his life edited by patient and analyst together is a story that has integrated the dimension of time, elaborated by an individual who has decided to learn from experience. The patient who has seen the *new* way the analyst looks at him is surprised to realize that he also *looks at himself* differently.

Once the patient has gradually developed the capacity to encounter the analyst as a real person and no longer as a transference object, the analysis is on its way to its conclusion. The withdrawal of the projections permits the emergence of a relationship with a different basis, one with reciprocal margins of freedom that inserts the patient in the world with all that human potential previously at the service of the transference. If the neurosis of transference is not resolved by the analyst, it becomes a confirmation—which I am inclined to consider definitive—of the old dependence and the subjection of the child to his parents. The analyst takes the place of the parental figures as an idealized image, and the patient the role of the child who, not having succeeded in "humanizing" his own parents, is incapable also of finding the way to his own individuation.

Between 1921 and 1922, Jung defined the sexual dimension of the transference as an initial phase, which is completed upon finding, through empathy, the *via individuationis*. He thus indicated the character of new religiosity of the analytical relationship. In this context, the transference relationship appears as *one* part of an entire analytical treatment consisting of various stages. Jung's reflection on the transforming value of the symbol and the contact with internal, personal, and archetypal images led him to a symbolic reading of the dynamics of transference and countertransference, according to which the relationship between analyst and patient assumes the significance of a quest for re-conjunction between separate polarities, between the male and female components of the psyche, between consciousness and unconscious, and so on. It is in this context that eros becomes, without diverging from the dynamics of any love relationship, the motivating force of the individuation process. The soul *desires,* and its desire—which, according to Plato, is a yearning for what is good and beautiful—is the instrument for our transformation.

When Jung affirms that transference emerges as the attempt to eliminate distance, he indicates the particular nature of the analytical relationship. It is precisely the specific nature of that relationship, in fact, that activates what we call transference love. Analyst and patient constitute a dyad that is truly unique and often compared to the mother-child dyad. In fact, it is similar in consonance to the mother-child relationship, which is what renders it so intense and reciprocally involving: the *exclusive aspect* of the relationship, the *empathic communication* based on processes of unconscious identification which, by favoring the establishment of a deep relationship, make it possible to live the same states of mind in synchrony (Loewenstein 1951) and *interdependence.* Despite these similarities, the analytical relationship maintains its specific quality and does not lend itself to equation with any other form of relationship between two persons. Its unique quality is in fact due to the peculiar nature of investment and interest of the analyst for the patient, an investment that is at the same time strongly empathic and duly "abstinent."

The analytical relationship assumes the form of the place in which the most secret emotions and the most intense experiences can be manifested and relived and find caring acceptance. The analyst assumes empathetically onto himself the suffering manifested by the patient, but his role implies above all the comprehension of the fantasized reality subtending the pathological acting out, and its *interpretation* through the elaboration of the patient. The interpretation, which constitutes the most specific intervention of the psychoanalyst (Bibring 1954; Gill 1954, 771) is essentially the "translation" of the patient's psychic reality into terms accessible to him and that he can then elaborate and metabolize.

This concept, according to which the analyst is the interpreter of an absolutely unique situation, permits the reawakening of latent potential in any patient. Therefore, if hermeneutics is the art of interpreting texts, the logical assumption is that there are in that text "meanings" to be deciphered and these are what are manifested in the analytical relationship. This intervention, by means of which the analyst takes onto himself the unconscious dynamics of the patient and brings them to maturity to then restitute them to him in a form that gradually anticipates sense and objective, is something the individual will have experienced in the relationship with the mother. According to Winnicott (1971), the mother offers the world to her child rendering herself available as the indispensable container of his still unformed, instinctive experience, which, without the horizon of comprehension provided by the mother, would precipitate the child into boundless anxiety. Thus the analyst can symbolically nourish his patient, within the same empathic consonance that enabled the mother to prevent the child from experiencing disintegration.

So intense an affective and analytical investment on the patient has on the analyst a "seductive" effect, as regards some of the structural characteristics of the setting (Bouhour 1986; Flournoy 1986; Stein 1986):

> Where and when can we situate the trauma of seduction for that which concerns the analytical experience? At the beginning, certainly. The reclining position which encourages passivity and the relinquishing of corporeal defenses is comparable to that of the young girl seduced by her father in *Studies on Hysteria*. More often than not, the analisand yields without difficulty, at times he rebels, at times is distressed, but all the while submitting to it, or refusing to. That situation is in most cases a reciprocal seduction: the analyst establishes, the analisand accepts, and the agreement is tacit. Despite the apparent technique, this first resolution subtends a minimum of accord, if not complicity . . . There is seduction on the part of both, and what is more, it is transformed into phantasm. (Flournoy 1986, 84)

The patient, on the other hand, would like to recognize in the attentive investment the availability and, in the exclusive nature of the relationship, the premise (and the promise) of easy, narcissistic gratification, given that each of us nurtures the desire for total acceptance, state of fusion sharing, and absolute reciprocity. The analytical experience itself facilitates the emergence of "areas empty" of affect (all painful experiences bound to emotional frustration, to experiences of solitude, to absence, and to anxiety) that the patient once more experiences intensely, and in relation to which the analyst could become the object of desire. Ferenczi (1909) states that, in his work with neurotics, the transference inevitably indicates regressive components bound to a sort of primary avidity, of boundless desire, present in the transference from the very beginning of the treatment:

> The first sentiments of love and hate are a transference of the auto-erotic sentiments of pleasure and pain onto the object arousing those sentiments. The first object love and the first object hatred are, if you will, *original transference.*

Prior to the symbolic elaboration of the phantasm, the analyst literally incarnates this first object, present and absent precisely due to his particular way of *being present* in the relationship. His availability and empathy, which draw the patient closer and inspire his trust and the awareness of an acceptance that he has rarely known, render him a privileged object of desire. At the same time, the abstention from personal communication and an extremely sparing use of words, which often lapses into silence, favor the projective activity of the patient, who will transfer onto the analyst the phantasms of his own past. The therapist thus becomes the Other par excellence, who "seduces and abandons," the absent other, a love object who has always withdrawn, and by whom the patient has wished to be loved. The analyst becomes an internal figure of the psychic life of the patient, constantly inhabited by this presence, even outside the analysis. On the other hand, the analyst must recognize—as far as this is possible—those countertransference reactions that will decide, in the final analysis, the nature and quality of the relationship. In other words, he must be constantly aware of how he "lives" the patient, beginning with the first telephone conversation; from the way in which the patient presents himself, the analyst will already be predisposed in a certain way toward him (Hillman 1972b, 120). The circular character of the relationship (any relationship) implies that one orientates the other and seduces him; that is, activates in him certain countertransference reactions, reactivating a phantasm. The analyst's greater familiarity with his own unconscious contents should be obvious, but the unconscious is incommensurable, and any patient can activate in the therapist aspects that have remained unanalyzed. In light of this, the concept of "countertransference" would thus appear quite different (Carotenuto 1986) from those that the manuals would have us believe are the total sum of influences that *can* be exercised by the patient on the unconscious sphere of the analyst. In our perspective, the *countertransference* is the entire unconscious psychological world of the analyst that is continually activated within an authentic interpersonal relationship.

The force of the constellation of internal images created in the analyst by the patient and the activation of deep affects on the part of the patient are mutually seductive. Thus, seduction enters forcefully onto the analytical scene, molding it and vivifying it— at least as a "first act"—according to Jung. In the ensuing communication, the patient will in some way inevitably plumb the psyche of the other, identifying its most fragile zones, thus unconsciously putting to the test the capacities of the therapist before undertaking alongside him his own journey. Greenson (1967) suggested the following:

> In adults all relationships consist of a varying mixture of transference and reality. There is no transference reaction, no matter how fantastic, without a germ of truth and there is no realistic relationship without some trace of transference fantasy. All patients in psychoanalytical treatment have realistic, objective perceptions and reactions to their analyst, and, alongside their transference reactions and their working alliance.

But *who* seduces *whom?* That is a question that has permeated the entire history of psychoanalysis, from Freud on up to the present. In his work with patients, Freud became quickly aware of how present and active the element of seduction was, both at the fantastic level and at the level of real comportment, which led him to maintain that the basis of hysterical and neurotic pathology was precisely a seduction, the adult seduction of a child. We will see in another chapter how the first aetiological model of neurosis was based on a "theory of seduction." Here we will examine how the analytical scene has appeared, from the very dawn of psychoanalysis, as a scene of seduction.

Seduce the patient, seduce the phantasm, seduce the analyst: the memory of the patient is charged with traces and signs of seduction, his dreams are representations of the desire for seduction— up until the arrival of the Freudian "child," the little Oedipus, a being whose identity is defined beginning with a drive request beyond his capacity for psychosexual integration, and which for that reason had to be inhibited and sublimated: the desire to seduce the mother.

As Freud was the first to "discover" transference, he was also the first to intuit the existence of a countertransference, and also in this case his first elaboration was a defensive expression. He defined it, in fact, as the deep emotional response of the analyst's unconscious to the unconscious conflict presented by the patient. It would therefore be a case of a *reaction* to the other, the patient. Similar to the transference, the first image through which the countertransference is considered is that of an obstacle. Freud recommends a strict vigilance on the part of the analyst as regards his own experiences, to be submitted to the careful scrutiny of the conscious through a self-analysis. Later on—above all thanks to the influence of Jung—he would recognize the intrinsic limits of self-observation and would suggest aspiring analysts to undergo didactic analysis. This was a revolution that required time to mature: abandoning the ascetic and reassuring image of the physician, the analyst discovered in the countertransference (a term to which not a few today prefer "the transference of the analyst") both an exceptional instrument for viewing the patient's unconscious and a threat to his own position.

Seduction sweeps into the analytical setting like a *prima donna,* in the spectacular and worldly guise of the hysterical, theatrical woman: "a prosperous girl of intelligent and engaging looks" (Freud 1901, 318) who falls ill in order "to entice her parents' love" (ibid., 336*).* The symptom is a strategy of seduction learned, by chance, in a distant infancy (ibid., 44):

> A little girl in her greed for love does not enjoy having to share the affection of her parents with her brothers and sisters; and she notices that the whole of their affection is lavished on her once more whenever she arouses their anxiety by falling ill. She has

now discovered a means of enticing out her parents' love, and will make use of that means as soon as she has the necessary psychical material at her disposal for producing an illness.

Precisely like the protagonist of Flaubert's masterpiece, Emma Bovary, the patient in early analytical treatments who "countered, owing to her marriage with an inconsiderate husband, who may subjugate her will . . . and lavish neither his affection nor his money upon her" (ibid., 336), by making of her illness a "weapon for maintaining her position, a weapon with which to force her husband to make pecuniary sacrifices for her and to show her consideration, as he would never have done while she was well" (ibid., 336).

Illness seduces and induces the other to bind himself to the one who is ill by caring for her. Is this not the same situation as that of the analytical treatment? I would say it is. But I might add that, when we speak of the seduction of the analyst, the genitive has a double meaning: seduction *of* or *by* the analyst in relation to the patient. We have seen that a seductive quality is inherent in the very nature of the analytical relationship, in the way the analyst invests the patient. However, there exist other forms of seduction by the therapist, often operated unknowingly: more deceitful and in subtle form, which have their origin in unresolved problems related to power, or the insufficient elaboration of narcissistic problems having to do with grandiosity, exhibitionism, and aggressiveness. A fascination for the wound is natural, in the sense that lacks demand compensation, satisfaction, seduction. And it is because of this opening (that is, the need of the patient to find a response to his suffering) that the analyst can conspire with the patient's tacit request for seduction.

The analysand will inevitably tend to idealize the analyst and often—especially if there are narcissistic problems—will be induced to project *outside* the setting hostile and disparaging sentiments. Analysts with analogous problems respond by colluding with the patient, tending to encourage the idealization, power, and control, and consequently will assume a dominant position with respect to the patient who is essentially submissive and masochistic. Another form of seduction consists of colluding with the *affective* requests of the patient by adopting a method of treatment that offers an immediate pseudo-intimacy. Thus the narcissism of both will be satisfied, but the basic pathology will unfortunately remain intact. This form of mutual gratification on the part of patient and analyst creates an apparently well-matched sodality, advantageous for both and thus lasting. However, a constantly positive transference can conceal a hostile symbiosis with an strong tendency to dependence (Grinberg 1981).

Once more in reference to the term *seduction* as regards its etymological significance, as a movement through which one is conducted to a place "other" than one's own reassuring position, it is possible also that the therapist is swept "elsewhere" by the patient. Roy Schafer (1983) states that it is possible to speak of seduction in the analytical relationship when one of the participants succeeds in making the other abandon his (or her) role.

The influence of the patient on the unconscious sentiments of the analyst—countertransference—is at the same time the most powerful form of seduction to which any analyst can be exposed. The analyst is an individual who, for very particular reasons—for instance, a continual confrontation with his own phantasms, his own wounds—has chosen that particular occupation. If we admit the fact that the conflicts and the wound for which we took up the profession of psychoanalyst are the same that bring our patients into analysis, it will not be difficult to understand that it is precisely at the point of this shared, painful nucleus that both are most vulnerable, most exposed. On the other hand, analysis is interminable; that is, no analyst ever terminates *definitively* his own introspective efforts.

The analytical process, therefore, animates the phantasms of seduction. However, if these phantasms are to be psychically transformed, they must be—I don't say unmasked, but identified—and recognized as familiar figures, old acquaintances, direct ties to the earliest emotional experiences, when becoming subjects coincided with the first object loss. It is with mourning over the loss of the first love object that the first phantasm of seduction is created in us. Driven from Paradise, we have never ceased to desire it and are endlessly seduced by it. Subsequently, we have been driven to resolve this enigma that constitutes us as subjects. The passion inspiring any *opus,* from art to the religious experience and love, is the response to this longing to create something, the origins of which are the love object's "always being elsewhere."

Analysis, due to the characteristics we have described, is one of the most adapted to this undertaking. In analysis, the original seduction is reconstructed, but the therapist is called on to dissuade the patient from making a simplistic and in the end sterile reading of this problem. Recognizing the phantasms does not necessarily imply simply giving them the names and faces of our fathers and our mothers, forever imperfect, absent, traitors or insufficiently affective, and precisely because of this defection even more seductive, in that they are impossible love objects. If it were, we would remain tragically bound to a destiny of frustrations, in the expectation of impossible compensation—and neurosis is the true evidence of this insistent request for impossible satisfaction.

Instead, what is necessary, through a radical change in perspective, is to recognize not only the compulsory quality of transference love as a repetition of something else, a repression, an unattainable scene of desire, but also its highly symbolic value at the service of the highest creative functions of the psyche. The transference is not only the ally of the patient's transgressive and regressive desires but is also the most powerful instrument for growth and development. When the patient, ensnared by eros, finds himself confronted with an overpowering desire for the analyst, he expresses with his vulnerability and defenses also those deep strata of his personality, the existence of which he never suspected. Confronted with this alter ego that demands love, comprehension, and assistance, his only means of finding remedy is asking the therapist for help, which must be immediate and concrete. In these circumstances, the analytical contract, the rules of the setting and the commitment of the therapist, represent the necessary institution to direct and give "form" to a *transference love* which, because of the violence and radical nature of its requests, could trap patient and analyst in a dead end. "What must I do now with the love which you, by asking me to lower my defenses, have activated?" the patient at that point asks desperately.

Liquidating this request with a textbook interpretation, reading it as an Oedipal reactivation, an incestuous request and repetition of a "perverse and polymorphous" eroticism, does not do justice to the albeit unconscious will of the patient to accede to his authentic desire. For concealed behind this request for love addressed to the analyst is the deeper question relative to his own desire: "What do *I* want?"

Jung strongly asserted that the psyche tends toward totality, a tendency of the individual toward the realization of his own personality, to the development and expression of his own creativity. Neurosis, instead, keeps the individual loyally bound to an internal phantasm, to its powerful seduction that imprisons him in an "elsewhere," robbing his present of completeness and project. Transference love is for the patient in some ways similar to homeopathic remedies, the principle of which is, "poison cures poison": the phantasm of the analyst can be superimposed over the internal phantasm to the point of substituting it, and this seems to the patient the best treatment.

Recognizing desire as a tending of the soul toward that which transcends it and perceiving in the dimension of desire the unhealed trauma between Ego and Self, between the horizontal and vertical dimensions of existence—that which moves the psyche to represent itself and leads the individual to ally himself with his fellows, signifies overcoming the "rough, literal interpretations" that immobilize the Ego—that is, a facile Oedipal and regressive reading of the transference—making possible acceding to the symbolic dimension.

According to Hillman (1972b),

> until my daemon has caught fire, I remain stuck in my transference and have legitimate need for the spark of another's eros for my self-development. The less the other can reveal his eros, the more I will demand it; for how else will my process be kindled? My own individuation impulse, my desire for psyche, must be ignited. This love for psyche—and not the analysis of "transference reactions"—alone resolves the stuck transference.

Thus, it is not the other alone—whether in the role of analyst or patient—who will satisfy desire and eliminate phantasms, but two individuals *together,* through reciprocal feeling and suffering, through the imagining and narrating of themselves and the love for the psyche that will heal us.

Six

Three Voices

Edward could not but see in her the most delicate, feminine creature it had ever been his fortune to know. He would almost have wished that she tripped and fell, in order to be able to gather her up in his arms and hug her to his heart. And yet, he would never have dared to, and for more than one reason: he feared offending her or doing her harm.

—J. W. Goethe, *Elective Affinities*

Analysis is surely one of those situations in which sentiment has the most profound effect on the life of the individual—in this case, the patient—inflicting at times a pain difficult to overcome and transform. The searing intensity of the emotions involved revives experiences from very early childhood, at which time we sought a container in order to accept and differentiate our experiences in relationship with the world. During these phases the child has need of a figure capable of teaching him to experience his own emotions without either repressing or being overcome by them. Psychic discomfort, in its various forms, is nothing more than the crystallizing of inadequate reactions that block the individual's capacity to realize his own process of development. Psychological therapy is presented as a return to those phases of existence during which development was blocked and distorted. This return to infancy involves both the affective vulnerability of the patient and his entrusting himself into the hands of an analyst.

Since therapy is conducted in the sphere of the emotions, the relationship formed by the two partners constitutes the syntax of the language with which they communicate. Thus, there are times when the difficulty encountered by the analyst in entering into contact with his own interior reality can become transformed not into incomprehension but into the risk of a more or less conscious manipulation of the other. This is possible because of the suffering of which the analyst, like the patient, is the bearer: a painful, open wound the effects of which could engulf them both. Favored by that difficulty the analyst experiences in entering into contact with his own complexes, it can burst into the relationship, demanding expression, and the forms in which this wound can be disturbingly inserted into the analytical relationship are many.

Although the analyst may be brilliant in intuiting the patient's most secret states of mind and consequently in mirroring them in an empathetic resonance, it is possible that the analyst himself lacks a mirror. That lack creates in him his need of the patient. At times the partners in the analytical relationship become trapped in an invisible web of seduction, which has been woven by both, together—and not only by the patient, who in the transference repeats infantile patterns, in the attempt to win the inadequate affection received during infancy. In the web of this seduction, the analyst can find himself bereft of a key to decipher his own expectations. In this way, his ability to accept and contain the desire of the other, utilizing its energy for the transformation of the patient, can become compromised. In these cases, the therapist can respond to the request for affection and comprehension formulated by the patient with his own unconscious request for affection.

This situation is created in a more visible and destabilizing manner when the analytical couple is made up of both sexes—in particular, when the analyst is a man and the patient a woman. Unconsciously seducing the patient in order to obtain affection—directed not at the role he assumes, but at the suffering individual concealed behind that role—permits the analyst to enter into contact with his own wounded infancy, creating a bridge with unknown emotions that are not easily expressed, having long lacked a code for communicating. However, in this way, he ends up asking the patient to give him precisely that which the patient seeks in the therapy. In these circumstances,

the analyst's willingness to lend an ear to the other, to comprehend him, is no longer exclusively in the interests of creating
that atmosphere of total, unconditional trust essential to healing
the patient's wounded parts, his growth and emancipation, eventually also from the analytical relationship itself. It is "a giving"
unconsciously directed, in the secret hope of receiving, of *being
treated by the patient.*

In a brilliant passage from a letter to Sabina Spielrein, Jung
(Carotenuto 1980, 169) writes:

> Return to me, in this moment of my need, some of the love and
> guilt and altruism which I was able to give you at the time of
> your illness. Now it is I who am ill.

The secret of every unconscious analytical seduction is contained in this need, this expectation, this electing the patient as
savior, no less and no differently than the patient does as regards the analyst. However, instead of saving and being saved,
very often what occurs is a sliding into a condition of increasing
unconsciousness, in a blind process in which neither analyst nor
(even less so) patient is any longer in a condition to help the
other. Only by critically examining his own efforts will this become clear to the therapist. This new contact with his own
wound, reconnecting the consciousness with the thread of emotions, can provide both with a way out of the labyrinth and the
way to transformation. However, this is not always possible. And
when it is not, the results will be different; there will be a bursting in of the emotions, which destroys the analytical container.
The two partners are forced to separate, to retreat painfully to
nurse their own wounds and to search only within themselves,
and no longer in the other, for the healing potential. In bitter
solitude, they can elaborate the web of mutual needs to which
they have fallen prey, utilizing incomprehension, errors, and failures in a process of evolution. What is achieved through the analytical relationship with its lights and many shadows must thus
depend on both partners. At times, resentment and disappointment can create a wall between them, at which point it becomes
impossible to leave the past behind or utilize what has been experienced and learned. At others, patient and analyst assume the

weight of the experience that they have created and, despite the errors and suffering involved, accept it as an important component of their personal history, the humus of a difficult growth (Carotenuto 1987b; 1988, 196–203).

The story narrated here is suspended in time, situated in a desert of the tartars that divides and unites the space of the imaginary and the space of a possible reality. It is a story that merely sketches its two protagonists, leaving out their real connotations and presenting simply the image of the soul. It is not the record of a clinical case, a transcription of words and actions observed in the analytical setting, but a "fable" of sorts. It is a story beyond space and time, as anything created by the soul must inevitably be, one that could have occurred in any setting and involved any analyst and any patient. As a paradigm, it is thus universal. In the main lines of this story, the famous and the anonymous intersect, and eventually merge: Sabina, Carl, Toni, Otto, Anais, René, Elma, Sandor, August, Margaret, Victor, Hilda, Emmy, Frieda, Erich, Eloisa, Jasmine . . . And yet, beyond their diversities, these stories recount the same dream, follow essentially the same plot. The unique quality, the thread of each single experience is thus woven into a single tapestry. It is one story, a paradigm, to describe the emergence of powerful emotions that explode, burst in, unhinge, and at times even dissolve the analytic container by contaminating the symbolic space with the space of reality.

As all fables will, our story begins with a "once upon a time." Once upon a time there was—and perhaps still is—in a place beyond time and space, which only the soul can recognize . . . With a constantly changing cast, this event has left its mark on the history of psychoanalysis, and continues to, in the sanctuaries of analysis, despite the passing of one hundred years, despite the increasingly longer training period required for analysts, and despite more and more sophisticated and refined techniques. It is the story of an impossible dream nurtured by the child persisting in the adult: the dream of a love so total and absolute as to soothe pain, even canceling it forever. Expectations, needs, and violence merge, to create a mixture of suffering and desire, and the process necessary to growth becomes difficult and painful. Our story is told by three characters: the Patient, the Analyst, and the Narrator. It is the Narrator who in the end will reveal the secret meanings of an encounter.

NARRATOR: Once upon a time, a girl and an analyst met for the first time on a rainy, spring afternoon.

However, their story actually began long before that afternoon meeting, which, like all meetings—although they occur at a particular instant in life—have been prepared for in the hidden corners of the soul. The passage of time—the time of consciousness and external reality—can only translate into a real event—something that has always existed in the soul.

Weighed down by her pain, which was apparently what kept her anchored to existence, the girl encountered her destiny on that ordinary, rainy afternoon. It was a meeting that would change her life, but of this she was not yet aware. As she walks down a tree-lined avenue, immersed in her own thoughts, dreams, and emotions, she nurtures a fragile hope that her confusion might lessen, her pain cease, and her being in the world finally find meaning.

From the moment she decided to consult an analyst, time became strangely contracted. The usual rhythm, the flowing along of the days and hours, has mysteriously changed. And only the encounter exists: a date, an hour written down in her agenda. Numbers seem to her to make up a magic formula: the first signs of the enchantment that will envelope her. It is difficult for her to unravel the skein of the emotions she experiences. However, one sensation prevails: the certainty that the darkness will somehow be dispersed once and for all. From the black and formless chaos of her past, a new woman would emerge. That look of indescribable sadness in her eyes when the burden of life becomes too unbearable would disappear. The drudgery of life without a purpose would cease, and the mask of false gaiety would no longer be necessary.

In the midst of distracted passersby, the girl muses over her dream of rebirth, thinks of the man of her analysis. What will he say to her? Her heart begins to beat rapidly. She is afraid. In order to overcome this anxiety, which grips her and ties her stomach into knots, she imagines a conversation with him in which the tone she uses is familiar. And in what other way should she address him, after all? He is her friend, the voice of her soul. But how should she formulate her request for help, for care, in order to persuade him to respond?

As she approaches the entrance, one desire, one request overrides what has been, what had occurred in a distant past and is still painfully evident in her glance, in her gestures. To find once more the happy child who in some small space of time she was, or perhaps would like to be now, for the first time. This is the desire, the ingenuous wish that is also a guilty one, because it negates the tragic aspect of existence, the impossibility of a liberation that would magically cancel out experienced pain. When her eyes meet those of the other, the man of the encounter, this will be the silent request: "Heal my wound, drive out the illness and pain in me, restore my smile, instill in me the hope of a different life."

GIRL: I feel so much pain and loneliness; I have burned all my bridges behind me. What is left is only a swath of burnt earth. And I am left with my void, my anxiety, my sensations of death.

The countenance of the illness within me eludes me. Images, suspended in dreams, recount my suffering, but they are undecipherable. Lacerated animals, murderers, violence and theft express my secret pain, buried in lost memory. I ask you to help me find a key to understanding. For only thus will I find a sense to the suffering that poisons my existence and renders me a stranger to myself.

You do not know this yet, but I know you and feel I can trust you. Others have spoken of you to me. Hidden in a crowd, from afar, I have studied your eyes, your face. I have seen your hands move in a way that is strangely familiar to me. One day perhaps I will understand for what mysterious reason I feel that familiarity. For the moment, this feeling that reassures and troubles me at the same time is enough.

I dreamt that *my mother and my father prevented me from coming to you; I dreamt that you and I were taken prisoners by a band of murderers, but that you succeeded in freeing yourself.* Will you succeed also in freeing me from the Enemy hidden in my soul who every night tries to kill me? Will you succeed in preventing him from secretly sabotaging my existence?

NARRATOR: Questions crowd her mind as she awaits the hour of the appointment. In recent months she has begun retracing the different stages of her life, searching for answers to the many questions that insistently arise.

GIRL: Since I was a child I have done nothing but look for the reasons for the waves of pain that inundated me. The world around me was incomprehensible, the reactions of adults unpredictable.

For years I have analyzed every memory, every emotion, without succeeding in undoing the knot of pain that prevents me from living. I pretend to live, while an invisible wall separates me from existence. Often, in the endless night, I have wished I were dead. And yet, I have not given up; I have gone on struggling.

But now, I am tired. A distant past, which I mistakenly believed to have pushed away from me, continues secretly to poison me.

NARRATOR: She approaches him in the hope that he will come to her aid. Even before their relationship begins, she has elected him as her savior.

Breathlessly, she climbs the stairs—perhaps before she reaches the door she will flee. But she feels it is her last chance, and she rings the bell.

ANALYST: I am tired; rain depresses me. I am waiting for a new patient—I know only her voice. There was a brief telephone conversation, a few minutes, but that sufficed to arouse my curiosity. I am anxious to see the face belonging to that voice. She had a cracked voice that reveals a false gaiety, a pretended security, obviously an attempt to conceal a desperate need for help. In listening to that voice, I was strangely disturbed. It is not the first time this has happened. What am I searching for in that voice, in the face of a woman I do not yet know? Perhaps a response to my own unresolved pain. Or perhaps that pain that reappears with each patient. Protected by the silence, I introspect once more. I am perfectly aware that some patients more than others represent a challenge to me, which becomes obvious from the first encounter. But I, too, almost without wanting to, challenge them. I challenge them to discover who I am; I challenge them to perceive in my face the features of the child I once was who still inhabits me. I promise protection, I sell them the *passepartout* to wisdom, and yet I secretly hope to be *myself* accepted, *myself* nourished, *myself* loved. I have spent years learning to suspend my own desires, to hide my own emotions, because only those of the patient before me count. And yet, paradoxically, I have never entirely succeeded in eradicating this infantile need for love.

NARRATOR: A web of invisible projections is woven around the protagonists of our story. What occurs in the years following this first encounter will also be the unraveling of that web, a web that will have compromised lucidity and awareness. Although in different ways, for both analyst and patient, this encounter will be a journey back to the mysterious and unexplored areas of infancy. Peeping out from behind their adult faces, the children inhabiting both will recognize each other and converse together in a long process, in an alternating of comprehension and pain.

PATIENT: Here I am; the words that I utter with great effort tell a story and all the while I scrutinize your face in order to understand your feelings, to decide whether or not you are sincere, whether you will really help me. I pretend to know my suffering well, and I speak of it with detachment, lucidly, rationally. I do not want my voice to shake, or for you to see at once all my pain. I both trust and do not trust, for too often have I been dis-appointed and wounded. A long series of betrayals characterizes my relationship with the world. When I look at you, however, a new hope takes form. The tone of your voice and your reassuring glance enchant me. I let myself be caressed by the promise hidden in that tone, in the way you look at me and address me. I want to believe you. I need to believe you.

ANALYST: Here she is; now she will ask me to begin to live a life unknown to me. I smile at her; she is intelligent, perhaps she will not misinterpret . . . Now I will tell her that, together, we will discover the cause of her suffering and lift the dark veil shrouding her pain. At this promise she lifts her head and smiles. Suddenly, in spite of myself, I feel immersed in that smile, in that look allusive of a tender, infantile torment . . .

NARRATOR: He already knows that the task at hand will not be an easy one. However, he is also confident that he will succeed in maintaining, even in the inevitable involvement that has already begun, a detachment operated thousands of times that will make it possible for him to truly help her. She goes on with her story, all the while watching him as if to fathom the extent to which she can count on him.

ANALYST: In me she seeks the response to her suffering that continues to darken her smile.

She has the air of knowing how things are; her kind of awareness troubles me. Perhaps she intuits that I also seek in her a response, a hope.

NARRATOR: The girl and the analyst mirror each other. Both have wounds, carefully concealed from the world, for years explored but never healed. They are united by the same pain. The girl recounts a story, but her dreams recount old sensations and new emotions. She reveals herself, partly aware that she is revealing herself, partly vulnerable in an infantile and unwitting way. She is well aware that this exposed condition consigns her into the hands of the other, plunging her inevitably into an asymmetrical situation. She is troubled and frightened, intermittently withdrawing into herself, hiding what she feels—all the while, studying the analyst intently.

The previous night she dreamt of him in feminine semblance: the feminine quality of his gestures the first time she saw him. She has always found that mixture of strength and gentleness attractive.

PATIENT: Can I be falling in love with him? In the dream *once more someone attacked and threatened me; once more I called for help. You came to my rescue, bringing me a medicine that cured me, a heart tonic. Then it was you who felt ill and I healed you with the same medicine. You put too many drops in the glass, but I, by decreasing the dose, healed you.*

What is the meaning of that dream? Perhaps that the process just begun will consist of reciprocal care. I will read to you what I wrote in my diary:

> It would have been unbearable that someone forced me to be healed. In the dream, instead, I also was in a position to tell you something, to exercise some "power" over you, to "heal" you.

This is the first dream I had after our encounter. And is it true that the first dream in analysis contains the germ of the entire therapeutic process? Could it be that our destiny is revealed by this dream? I perceive a lost child in your glance. Is it this child I wish to heal, to make smile? What I feel is strange: I entrust myself to you, to your knowledge and your experience; I scrutinize your face for the reassuring features of a good father, a tender mother, and yet my soul intuits in you a secret fragility. I have come to be helped by you, and yet after our first meeting I have already dreamed of healing you. I wonder how I could heal you, I who am so confused in life. But there is no deceiving the heart. It is a strange mixture of fragility and decision that has made me curious, which has seduced me.

ANALYST: She has entered my dreams like the image of someone I have loved greatly. The troubling emotion I experienced upon awakening was a familiar one. She had always been within me, with her penetrating, innocently cruel gaze, in her revealing me to myself. There was a void within me ready to receive her, an absence, a lack, a lack of love. That's it: love. I hesitate to use the word, but it would be useless to lie to myself. And yet, I cannot be so powerless before her. I cannot permit this child to compensate for my lacks, that her intense emotions gratify my painful craving for love, so similar to her own. I know that I cannot abandon myself to a desire that would prevent me from helping her. I know that I must not violate the pact. My task is contained in this renunciation. Only thus can I use *also my* desire for love to cure *her.*

NARRATOR: Time silently weaves its web of seduction. Hope and desperation alternate. A man and a girl meet with established regularity, a ritual. Seated face-to-face, they converse. But the encounter is not one of peers. She is urged to lay herself bare; he must assist at that unveiling. His role is one of accepting and comprehending but, although this occurs in conditions of considerable intimacy, his presence must remain discrete, withdrawn. He must offer his presence, his capacity acquired over years of placing himself in question and laying himself bare, in order to

94

penetrate and be immersed in the sphere of the soul. It must be a spare and warm place, a uterus in which she can once more form herself in order to be reborn into the world. Any other intention must be set aside, any other desire forgotten. For herein lies the analyst's difficult task.

PATIENT: Once more I undertake this way. The seasons pass while I perform my ritual, unchanged. You are the priest of this strange rite that will liberate me from my malaise. I contemplate my past, retrace it together with you. I speak, I question myself, in the attempt to explain a destiny that has left so painful a mark. I find no responses, and neither do you. However, you are beside me, and this alone counts.

I describe my suffering, mitigating the tension with a smile, with a look that reveals the trust placed in you. Perhaps you too were a wounded child; perhaps you too were betrayed and misunderstood. Ours is therefore an alliance, a complicity based on a shared feeling.

Last night you were once more in my dreams. *In my dreams, our faces were close together. Desire and fear mingled. Fear of this contact was so profound, so intimate, this fusion in which I am without defenses. While we kissed, the sensation was one of sweetness, and the impression was that I loved and was loved for the first time. I felt my soul open and enter completely in you. It was beautiful and terrible at the same time.*

I am troubled. My dreams reassure and at the same time frighten me. Upon awakening I have the wonderful sensation of well-being, protection, and tenderness. However, this sensation is soon overcome by frustration and apprehension. The anxiety is so intense that I feel I will go mad. I do not dare call you. I need your reassurance; I want you to tell me what to do. My dreams beckon you; they involve you telling me something that I do not yet understand.

ANALYST: I am troubled. You look deep into my eyes, penetrating me as you speak. I realize that you are able to read my thoughts: you are daily learning to interpret my gestures, my expressions, the tone of my voice. I feel vulnerable. I look away, examine my agenda. But it is impossible to flee; I cannot avoid this confrontation. A ringing telephone comes to my rescue.

PATIENT: My life is slowly beginning to flow. I want you to be proud of me and how I have learned to face existence. I have stopped hiding myself, stopped using a screen to protect myself. You are my model; I observe you and learn. If you have succeeded in facing the pain that is in you, that pain that I have come so well to intuit, then I can do the same. I want to do what you do, be like you. Although you are silent, I know that you approve. At times I have the impression that you are putting me to the test, but you are never disappointed. In the intervals between our encounters I have imaginary conversations with you, in which I describe to you what I am doing and what I am feeling. I imagine your reactions, your comments. Who knows, perhaps your soul hears my voice, hears my constant calling you to me. Inexorably, my life has begun to revolve around yours. You are the hub of my budding existence. Without you I am lost. At times I wander the streets near your house, so as to prolong a contact that is never enough, limited as it is to our ritual that becomes progressively more frustrating. I am not yet able to pronounce your name. Something stops me. The intimacy that I sometimes imagine between us frightens me.

Embarrassed, I hesitate to describe my dreams in which we make love. Then I decide. I know that I must tell you everything if you are to help me. But I am afraid of this desire that delivers me, naked, into your hands. You call it "transference," and I could possibly hide behind that definition. But if it is only a game of simulation, a virtual reality, why am I so afraid to detect in your expression, if only for an instant, the least indication of disinterest? The rules of our pact are no longer enough for me. I do not want you to pretend that you care for me; what I want from you is not professional interest. I want your affection, your tenderness. Do not betray me; do not leave me alone! Yesterday you were tired, and in the heat of the summer afternoon you were half dozing; you listened to me with difficulty. I pretended not to notice, but without your glance, without your smile, I suddenly felt alone, and everything around me lost all meaning. In your eyes, which did not look at me, I had ceased to exist.

Last night I dreamed of *a woman who nursed a child. You were there also, holding a baby's bottle. I watched you, fearing that you did not want to nourish me.* It is an infantile love of which I dream, as though all at once I had returned to the earliest phases of my life. Does the secret of my malaise of living, my incessant pain, lie in that distant time? Meeting after meeting, you take me back to those days, buried in memory without words. I let myself be guided on that voyage in time, as the present slowly dissolves. It is only we two who exist and visit those places unknown to the soul, among its images beyond time, its unchanged emotions. Only this counts. But now that you are the center of my life, now that I have given you absolute power over me, could I be in danger of being destroyed? Could the god be transformed into a demon? Is it possible that love becomes torment, and the promise of birth conceals a mortal trap? Could that desire of yours deep in your eyes to help me conceal a subtle desire to test your power to destroy me? Once more, I am afraid. Once more, dangerous murderers populate my dreams, and sometimes they have your face.

Today you told me not to be worry, that you would help me. I trust you.

When the hour was over, you accompanied me down the stairs, smiling sweetly at me. There was admiration in your eyes. Are you by chance falling in love with me? I let myself drift in this dream, your glance, your words, that smile with which you receive me. Whatever name we give to the sentiment that unites us, I now know that together we will succeed in overcoming the pain, that we share an understanding and affection. And ours is a tender affection, hand in hand, together in search of courage to continue down the path taken. Ours is a tiny oasis of sweetness in the midst of the desert we inhabit. With you I feel secure. You appear in my dreams as one who defends me from all violence, even from my own past. And I would defend you and protect you from evil also, that evil that is in you, or the evil of the world. Is mine an impossible dream?

ANALYST: Once more, she crosses the threshold of my studio to open her soul to me. Her step now has a different rhythm. She holds her head high now. A new hope is evident in her determined step. In her dreamy eyes, I perceive an offer of love. For an instant, I let myself be contaminated by her illusion; I experience its sweetness, but also its sharp pain. I cannot bear this torment, which wounds me with its impossible promise. Nothing remains but to return to reality. I could tell her what I feel, but she is so fragile, and she might misunderstand. So, I remain silent, and smile tenderly at her. At such moments, her eyes capture me and her smile disarms and very nearly disorients me. And yet, I know that, upon awakening, what she is happily dreaming will seem only a cruel betrayal. Banished by the dream, we will find ourselves alone. No one at that point can guide us; no one can protect us from each other; no one can defend us from our suffering. Thus, we accept the sentiment that unites us, to experience it only in the heart's depths.

NARRATOR: Slowly, the circle tightens around the protagonists of our story. It is seduction—an invisible, impalpable seduction. A tender trap, subtle and all-embracing. Each one believes himself capable of controlling the game, of being able to withdraw the moment it becomes too dangerous. The risk would appear to be a calculated one, just as the concessions, the giving, the receiving—a self-deception that could result in the perdition of both, causing them to slide impotently into a dream that would inevitably lead to a bitter awakening.

PATIENT: I try to resist the power you exercise over me. I fill my life with music, images, emotions. I lose myself in the crowd

97

and avoid you by traveling. I let myself be courted by other men, tender and distant. But the men I meet cannot take your place, and a strange sadness, a subtle melancholy pervades me when I realize that I want no one but you. Thus, I stop struggling and surrender to a love I can no longer control. It is an impossible, sweet, and desperate love, which nourishes my dreams and gradually consumes my will to live.

ANALYST: A strange apprehension inhabits my nights. A woman's face dominates my dreams: an image both unchanging and mutating. Memories of a distant past blend with the present, secret traces of a voyage to the ancient Orient of memory. *I see her: she has a cruel expression. Boldly gazing at me, she says to me slowly: "Enough! I am taking back my life. I will no longer follow you. I am tired of you and your arrogant analytical lucubrations."* I wake up, disturbed. Is it you who threatens to leave? Is it you who re-evokes an early abandonment? Why do I think of her, so far away, so different than you, why is her face confused with yours? I close my eyes and I encounter you again in the depths of the soul, where finally I can say to you what during the day I am forced to keep to myself.

"Listen to me: I am certain that I really love you; there is nothing false in my affection for you. The interior landscapes we discover together are real. Therefore, do not become weary if I flee from impossible illusions in order to construct with you only empires of truth. I am not the man of dreams come true."

NARRATOR: The man and the girl continue to meet. With the passing of time, the stakes in the game have become their very lives. He has risked compromising his career, his professional status, his very stability. An exaggerated faith in himself aids his fall, just enough, into the spirals of a dream that he would like just once to see realized. For her—who, understanding the enormous power she holds over him—what is at stake is the opportunity of truly becoming a woman. Ingenuously, she believes that she has nothing to lose. In her youthfulness, she believes that she can and must meet this challenge if she is to realize a dream of love, at times tender and innocent, at others secretly disturbing. The confines of the analytical relationship have become confused and totter at the threshold dividing dream and reality. And the game becomes daily more dangerous.

PATIENT: You are not happy, I know. I see anxiety in your eyes. You go on looking for a love you lack. I am that love. But I cannot imagine my life forever tied to you, or perhaps I am afraid of it. I would like only to dream this love, without expectations. I am afraid to confess to you what I feel. I fear your severe look, your frown, signs of a concealed irritation, or embarrassment for me. And yet, I know that I must let myself go completely, that I must confide all my emotions. They are intense, overwhelming. But you will not stop caring for me, will you?

In my dreams, we make love, and it is a sweet and troubling image. *Your body seems to conceal a secret, like the Trojan Horse of Ulysses. My mother hates what is happening. This makes no difference to me; I continue to seek your sweetness, the pleasure you are capable of giving me.* In another dream, *in the castle of Paolo and Francesca, a man and a woman murder the governor who opposes their love. An enormous, poisonous serpent encircles them, killing them. Their bodies are dragged away by a mysterious and invisible force. I feel compassion for the two lovers.*

There is something darkly obscure behind this love of mine, something obscure and terrible, which bears the echo of my past, the malaise that afflicts me. Loving you is like being born and dying, alternatively and infinitely.

ANALYST: She is late today. While I wait for her to arrive, images that speak to the body and not only the mind arise, swirling dizzyingly in my mind. I remain silent, watching and listening. *I begin reading a book, but she is late and the book burns in my hands. Surely I have a fever, and only she is capable of healing me. We are alone. She often describes how she was happy when her father was still alive, and her eyes light up with a joy that is beyond my reach. My mother no longer has time for me, but I have become her confidant. Then she goes out, and I feel betrayed, abandoned, angry—but at the same time proud to be so grown-up, to share her anxieties and aspirations. I love her, of course, but it is also possible that I hate her and do not have the courage to tell her . . .*

The sound of the doorbell and the sight of your face bring me back to the present.

PATIENT: I didn't have the courage to tell you what I felt. Perhaps we will succeed the next time. I need a sign, some small gesture. I am afraid of making a false step, of failing to give you what you expect from me. I imagine what I will tell you. I mentally repeat a thousand times what I will say; I offer you my love a thousand times over. Listen to me for once: we have talked about everything. There has been enough talking! We have had enough of this game of hide-and-seek. I am here, and I want you for myself, for myself alone. I am here, and no one else. And you know this! We have had enough of rules, of time divided into short encounters. I don't want any more rules in my life, and I love you. I have had enough of analyzing this desire; I want to live, and I cannot do this without you. I want to make you feel the infinite tenderness I feel. I want to read on your skin the secret of my soul. I want this desire for love to be satisfied, this sweet and cruel desire. Don't console me: don't tell me what it means or what it represents. If one day I sought you and if in the end I found you, it means that we were destined to share everything. You cannot deny this abandonment; it would be a lie for which I could never forgive you . . .

ANALYST: She moves with such suppleness and quick elegance. She has become even more beautiful. But I cannot be her prey. I will not give in to her sweet, cruel temptation, her divine provocation. I will resist her charm. I will close my eyes and listen.

PATIENT: I observe you as I listen to your words, your silences. I wonder what you think of me, what you feel for me. I do not understand what your game is, your being present and being absent, your flight. Your sudden withdrawals destroy me. I sink silently into the void; my image disappears, swallowed up by refusal, by your impenetrable look, your expressionless tone. I imagine that I have disappointed you, tired you out. I take my revenge with silence. I remain motionless before you; I try to look at you with indifference, while my soul shatters and dissolves. A dark anger rises in me, together with tears I keep back. I pretend to be distracted; I leave without a word. I go out knowing that I have condemned myself to a long, tortuous death, until our next meeting.

ANALYST: There are silences, once more unspoken sentiments that fail to find expression. I feel anger, and I think I can no longer trust you. I deny myself your look, your smile, your affection. I fool myself that you will have understood. The dream disappears, along with your silent offer of a reciprocal and unconditional comprehension. I turn away from you. I bury myself in work. I have other things to think about. Or, perhaps, I am only rejecting this cruel pain that lacerates me. I don't know what to do. Words, heavy as rocks, prevent us from communicating. I am tired of searching for phrases that you cannot hear, lost in yourself, in your impossible dream. And yet, I want to tell you that from the dream a different occasion can arise, overcoming the limits of that reality separating us. But you must listen once more to my voice; you must once more trust me. I will tell you, if you want me to, what I imagine. I would like you to come and work with me and thus satisfy your desire to heal souls. I would like to nourish that talent of yours of reading the heart's secrets. But you must be patient; you must transform your desire for love, take it beyond the limits of real life. And this is the tie that can unite us; this is the dream that can come true; this is the way to be together.

NARRATOR: Both realize that they are caught in the same net. But neither seems to know how to escape. Overcome by a desire that knows no limit or horizon of the symbol, both must admit partial defeat. They continue together to search for a place where treatment and love innocently coincide, but their search becomes progressively more difficult and exhausting. The comprehension that up to that point they had provided each other begins to be undermined and permeated with bitterness and anger, while the temptation to flee that unbearable onslaught of emotions becomes ever stronger.

PATIENT: Now more than ever I feel your fragility becoming an obstacle between us, forcing you to flee. I miss your comprehension, your strength. I put myself in your hands and experienced an infinite fall. You are unable to hold me in your arms, unable to contain my anxiety. You are afraid of my love. I look at you, not understanding. I do not feel that I am not asking you for anything, or perhaps, lying in wait behind in this absence of requests is in itself a total, absolute request. Your fear disorients me. You are no longer able to console me. That which until now attracted you now seems to represent a mortal danger for you. I fear your look in which I can read your fear of my offer of love. But I don't want to wound you. I dream that together we will succeed in overcoming the pain we share. I dream that together we will face life. But you can no longer trust me. At times, you caress me with your eyes, then the sight of me seems to burn your soul. You retreat, frightened; a veil comes over your eyes, and you become silent, inaccessible, impenetrable. You leave me alone to deal with the ingenuousness of my giving myself, with the impulse of my desire. I am once more lost. I have lost my friend. The man of the analysis is dead, and rising from his ashes is another whom I do not know and who frightens me, but who I cannot stop loving.

ANALYST: I look at you in silence, and my heart leaps. I can confess neither my fear nor my desire to you. I should like to use this love of mine to help you to grow, to guide you, but what I feel is stronger than my desire to help you. The sight of you inflicts a torment that I can no longer bear. Your eyes implore love and I do not know how to love you; I no longer know how to be with you without wounding you, without violating our pact. My soul is devoured by this impossible dream. I am prisoner of it. I have lost my strength. My knowledge is inadequate. "Countertransference." But this is by now no more than an empty word. I am losing the battle. I feel confused and alone. You dominate my dreams. I remain awake to avoid them. I want to flee from you, but I cannot do without your affection. I am jealous of your life, of what I know of it exclusively through your descriptions. At times my comprehension dissolves into a desire for revenge for what you force me to feel. I remain silent, in order not to reveal to you what is going on inside me, but for how long will I succeed in doing so?

PATIENT: I feel confused and lost. I cry because I am overwhelmed by anxiety. You are distant, inaccessible. I do not know how to speak to you, how to reach you. Every gesture of mine, my every word, causes you to draw into yourself even more. My desperate gestures are senseless, impulsive, and caused by my obsession. The dream is becoming dissipated; there exists only this endless torment, interrupted only by the rare instants of happiness when you become once more the person you were, and smile at me. Then I smile once more, and hope, and am happy. Once I more feel alive, until the next inevitable plunge into the abyss, the void. My life by now consists of this impossible, infinite alternating between closeness and distance. I feel exhausted, but I am unable to relinquish my dream of love.

ANALYST: You did not come today, and I missed you. I feel abandoned, betrayed. I want to see you, to listen once more to your tales. I want to dream with you, to accompany you on this voyage into existence. You phone your excuses. Something unexpected, you say. I am not completely convinced. I realize that you are trying to punish me with your flight, because I prevent your dream from permeating reality. And yet, like you, I desire nearness. I wish I could tell you what I feel when it seems that you are indifferent to my suffering. You have left me, betrayed me. You have turned against me, as though I had nourished you with poison, while I felt I owed you everything, because I obtained everything from you, nourishing myself and never being satiated. You rejected that which I could offer you, as though my nourishment were unacceptable, disgusting.

PATIENT: While I waited for your arrival, I tried to put down on paper the tumult of my emotions:

> I would like to stop a moment to reflect, in order to dispel the chaos of my emotions. What I feel is strange: the trap has been set, the prey has been captured. And I am perplexed. There is no joy in my "triumph." No, on the contrary, I feel bewildered. Now that I am certain of having succeeded in my intent, the game has proven to be a mortal trap. I am the prey. What do I want from this relationship? An impossible love? An infinite tenderness with the lost taste of childhood? An exhilarating and dangerous venturing into the labyrinth of Eros? The body overwhelms the psyche. I have no idea what will happen.

Rereading what I wrote, I realize how complex and dangerous our game really is. We continually alternate in the roles of hunter and hunted. In this game of seduction, each one is both seducer and seduced. I feel a dark and troubling anger. I discover that I possess a savage side, which until now was concealed behind a mask of rationality and moderation. My roots belong to a timeless universe, where emotions burn and devastate like the lava of a volcano. Fragility and violence are alternating and constant in this passion in which I am both woman and child. At times, my anger excites you, but it is a game that is too dangerous, and I am frightened. I frighten myself and you frighten me. How can you defend me from my emotions; how can you defend me from yourself?

ANALYST: I abandon myself to the intense cold of this winter's night. This relationship with you becomes progressively more difficult for me as it is to respect the rules of our pact. I admit that I need you. My role has been compromised; my capacity to interpret a sentiment that is now part of me wavers. I can only dream that one day we will finally be outside the tempest. At that point, you will also know how wonderful it was to take this mortal risk together, remaining united, and finally triumphing. It will not have been easy, but it will be wonderful precisely for that reason. No important achievement is without effort, without difficulty. The suffering and dismay of the present will seem to us lighter, will have a sense. From this pain and confusion, I am certain, something new will emerge for both of us. Making our way through our sharp and lacerating emotions, our project will finally be realized. Then you will have grown, you will have learned to walk on your own, and the words you hear will describe distant pain. But tonight, the dawn is still far off. I listen to the voice of silence and let myself slide into dreamless darkness.

PATIENT: I howl in anger and desperation. I have the impression that I have been nothing more than a game for you, a game in which I feel I was the weaker. Perhaps you were only playing with my life, with my sentiments, feeling yourself strong before my vulnerability, my dependence, my trust in you. I would like to kill you, slowly and painfully. I feel betrayed, used; a broken toy. I feel that I have meant nothing to you, that you only needed a prey. You love an image of something that does not exist, which you continue to search for in the eyes of every woman. Perhaps neither of us is capable of loving; perhaps we are both only searching for an image capable of satisfying an old need. But now that reality has taken the upper hand, I am disoriented. I do not know the man before me; I do not understand his attitude. Where is the person who offered to help, protect, and understand me? My requests frightened you, but I remind you only of your promise, of the reason for which I came to you in the first place. Have you forgotten how much pain there was in my soul? Have you forgotten how much fear and anxiety permeate my life? Why are you no longer capable of listening to me, understanding me?

But I no longer know how to speak to you. Everything has become confused; my mind splinters. My suffering now re-echoes the old pain. All that which I believed I had left behind now reappears before me. You can no longer save me or help me because it is you who daily inflicts this death.

I continue to write letters to you, which I keep. I need to understand, to speak to my soul, and you are my soul.

I am afraid; I feel I am going mad. Why do I feel so awful? The world is dark and threatening tonight, and once more my phantasms squat in the darkness threatening to assail me. I want to disappear. I am incapable of feeling love for anyone, and life has no meaning. I seem to have been mistaken about everything. You are the only person I truly love, but anything beautiful I feel remains imprisoned inside me. There are only tears of anger, of pain. I understand nothing.

I wander through the streets like a wraith. I have lost track of myself and am unable to find myself. My soul is the prisoner of a man who I must live without, incomplete, unrealized. I wrote in my diary:

The void has returned—quickly swallowing up my will to live. I have lost the will to struggle. I no longer believe in anything or anyone. Perhaps nothing, no one, is capable of warming my heart. Reality melts, while I remain, contaminated by unreality.

The nights are inhabited by nightmares. My dreams have become threatening. You are no longer there to understand them, to reassure me with your affection, your presence. Loathsome beings, zombies, and vampires express the anxiety of my existence. I am murdered a thousand times over by monsters who arise out of the earth, gelid creatures who suck the blood of their victims in order to steal their strength and life. I struggle against them in an endless battle, at times victorious and at others defeated. I would like someone to help me, but I have no idea who that might be. I am unable to trust anyone. And then, who else but we could really understand what occurs, without rendering it banal with empty words, or interpretations incomprehensible to the soul? Who else could comprehend the subtle dynamics of this obscure relationship between love and death?

It is not easy to accept the death of something, the end of a relationship. The years of our encounter were nothing less than life, rebirth, and a euphoric expansion in the world. Now there is only darkness, pain, void, absence, and death. Perhaps I unconsciously sought all this, brought it on by consigning to you every bond, every interest. The external world has disappeared, absorbed by this relationship. The result is a frightening asymmetry in which I experience your power, your strength, as opposed to my dependence and my need. I attempt to free myself from this yoke, but cannot. It is like sliding slowly into madness. My madness mirrors yours; my violence speaks to your cruelty; my need and my fragility encounter your vulnerability. This mortal embrace suffocates me: I am as though caught in the grip of a giant serpent. I must break free once and for all, but every opening closes and once more the game begins, in the same way, endless. I need sun, air, life, and love. And instead, I deliver myself daily to darkness, death, and solitude. What can I do?

ANALYST: I watched you today as you walked away. The sun was setting on the horizon, perhaps a presage of a by now imminent end. In an instant all our meetings passed through my mind, in the ever-changing rhythm of our emotions. I now know that I was interested in you because you offered me a place in which I could feel secure, a tranquil port in which to anchor, protected from life's anxieties. Often, when it seemed particularly difficult to resist the dream, we would tell each other that it was only an illusion. But what a strange and persistent illusion it was, if during all those years we were unable or unwilling to do without one another.

I remain, staring into the night, then slowly abandon myself to its darkness. I slide once more toward dreams of you. *An abandoned house and enormous suitcases—the baggage of our past. We separate without a word to go to distant places in flight from our roots and old phantasms. Years pass and life seems good to us. The echo of each of our successes reaches the other and unites us. The distance is not colored by forgetfulness. Distant and close, in a union that time has not destroyed. A design repeated, unchanged, revealing a comprehension that goes beyond immediate exigency, as though our tie had thus acquired an absolute and transcendent substance. Together, as though it were possible to be united to overcome the limitations of existence, which inevitably leads to the death of the body and its passions.*

NARRATOR: With time, the space in which these phantasms are contained and comprehended has become more and more limited. Reality violently attempts to enter the imaginary.

PATIENT: I take my leave of you in silence. I trust neither words nor gestures. I need to be alone, to face this pain that is destroying me. We do nothing but harm each other. Now I am the one who, in order to survive, takes refuge in the inaccessibility of distance. I write you letters you will not read. I write them myself, in order to give a meaning to what I am about to do:

> It is over! I have struggled uselessly for too long to avoid this break, this definitive separation. I am left only with emptiness and pain. All I

have achieved over the past years has disappeared. I feel I have lost the only important thing in my life: the love I felt for you and that made me feel alive. What remain are shadows, scraps of existence, and this is no longer enough to warm my soul. At the beginning, I searched for a god, then I loved your childlike fragility. However, two lost and bewildered children can be of little use to each other. The moments of pain outweigh the moments of happiness. I grew in your gestures of affection, in your looks permeated with desire, in your words that comprehended the mystery of my soul. I cannot describe that experience. It was heaven, the entire world, warm milk, the love of someone who loved and desired my uniqueness, my diversity. It was life. You made it possible for me to embody myself, to become truly real. You guided me through the unknown areas of my soul. Then all illusion was miserably shattered, torn by incomprehension and fear and thoughtless gestures, anger, revenge, jealousy.

The desire to live and fight is vanishing together with this autumn light. I would like to slide into the darkness of oblivion. Everything seems to me empty and useless. But I no longer care. Words have become too burdensome. I am no longer able to communicate. Only gestures, the body, still have a voice. But I silence them, incapable of seeking contact with another human being. I no longer feel the need to rebel. One resists only if there is hope, and I have stopped hoping. The dream has gone. I withdraw into myself, into my shell of impotence. I would like to seek a contact that would give me back life's warmth, but it would be pointless. I look at you, immobilized by my tenderness made barren. I feel death inside me. My body has become a heavy shell that I struggle to drag along and that I would like to forget. My womb is swollen with death, a death that operates in secret and in silence from within. It is as though all the ills of my life were centered at that point of my being, that place of love and life.

The days pass and I push them aside, repetitive and relentless in their anxiety. I am tired. Love is the only thing that can counter death. I slide more and more into the arms of darkness. I do not know what will happen to me. But this suffering, permeated with the sensation of emptiness, is less searing than the explosive pain I experience in seeing you.

ANALYST: I feel once more an agonizing nostalgia, the same overwhelming sensation one feels upon hearing an old, never-forgotten song. I cannot see you now, but if you have faith you will also discover a marvelous dimension in which you and I and all love stories still experience the same burning desire and the same hopes. If you seek me, I will always be there for you because of the importance of the symbolic love you gave me. But even if you do not, be certain that I am with you and remember you always. I love you, my grown-up little girl, beloved woman, fulfilled presage of a future only dreamed.

NARRATOR: Begun amid a thousand hopes and promises, the story concludes painfully, leaving the girl and the man of the analysis ultimately alone to face their phantasms. In the months to come, both will often think of what occurred and ask themselves what went wrong, analyzing words and gestures, in the attempt to find a satisfying response. However, it is difficult to explain passion. At best, it can be narrated, recounted, or sung, as by poets and artists. Only they are capable of finding the means to express what is inexpressible. Of all the "prohibited" loves, that which explodes in the analytical relationship is one of the most dramatic. The pain it causes is not the result only of the violating of a pact, as is the case in adultery, but also of the impossibility of considering the violation of this pact a free choice of the patient: a patient overwhelmed by the phantasms of the past. The face of transgression is confused with the troubling possibility of abuse, because anyone asking for help moves in the world with an infantile soul. The phantasm of incest casts its shadow on this relationship, obliging patient and analyst alike to admit unspeakable desires, experienced in the dangerous twilight zones separating the imaginary from reality. Never more than in love do we learn to know the dark depths of the soul—depths that become even more somber and troubling when they emerge in a relationship that confuses the space of the imaginary with that of reality. It is there that confines disappear, that everything becomes confused, making it more difficult to find the key to deciphering what occurs. This is an exhausting task for both partners, and even more difficult for the patient, who is left alone to elaborate a suffering in which past and present mingle.

WOMAN: Today, after so long, I saw you again, and we talked once more. Many years had passed since our last meeting, and the pain of those distant days had been placated. There was a strange lightness between us. The time of requests was over. I have forgiven you, and you have forgiven me. And only we could do this; only we could absolve or condemn each other. The road to forgiveness was long and difficult. We traveled it separately, divided by a pain it was no longer possible to share.

I had fled, putting an ocean between us, letting the sounds of another language make me forget your voice. I lived in exile; I exiled my soul. Once more, I exiled my emotions; once more I left a swath of burnt earth behind me; once more I burned the past—the past shared with you. I crossed the desert, in order that its silence might distill my pain, in order that in its vast, empty spaces I might find myself once more. Desolate expanses, to contain my images, my emotions. I wrote my story, *my mandala,* on

107

the sands, and I understood. Among those signs, at first incomprehensible, I captured the *Sense,* the sense of my story, the sense of our encounter. I glimpsed for the first time the reason for which I was born. Then I left the desert and returned to the world of people. Now I also can listen to the voices of suffering. My listening is light, my face smiling. I have learned to dance with pain, to play with life.

I took a plane home, and suspended up there among the clouds, I impatiently anticipated the appearance of a certain face. There was a man at the arrivals gate. He smiled at me. I once more tried to share my story, my emotions with him. And with him I learned a different kind of love, tender and playful. The old pain had finally been incorporated into a design that gave it meaning. Now I know that every event I experienced, every encounter, was necessary.

In the silence of the night, I write the story that I think you would have asked for: our story. In the silence of your studio, overcome by emotions, memories, I was not able to describe to you what had happened to me during the years that had passed since we had last seen each other. The happy expression on my face and the child I am expecting, however, told you something more than my inadequate words could. I realized that you had learned to trust me.

One more time, one last time, I returned to that past. Emotions and questions alternated as they once did, but they no longer have the bitter taste of anxiety. I have accepted the lack of response; I have accepted the existence of many truths, many explanations that overlap, all equally true, all equally uncertain and incomplete. The expression on your face, your gestures, your words, can no longer wound me. In the place of past pain, I retain only a small container overflowing with tenderness. I look back and smile. I smile at my unawareness, my need for love, my impossible requests; I smile at the frightened child in you, at your eternal need to be loved, at your flights, and your lies. The anger consumed and the pain decanted, I regard that also with tender detachment. I search in your eyes for the image of my femininity. You search in mine for the confirmation of your desire to be loved. You taught me the language of love, of seduction, of betrayal, of violence, permitting my emotions to be experienced, permitting me to comprehend my dismal past. I gave you my tenderness, a love in which to feel strong, I gave you a mirror in which to look at the child in you. You mirrored yourself in my vulnerability, in my total and absolute need to be loved. From our errors something was created. As we walked at the confines of death, destruction, and madness, our lives were fecundated. I cannot conceive of anything happening other than what actually did.

Last night I dreamed something that dissolved the apprehension produced by your telephone call, your strange seeking me after so long. When I heard your voice, the entire past once more suddenly assailed me, bearing with it emotions that I had been convinced no longer existed. But life inexorably changes us, and we are no longer what we were, except in rare instances, in fragments of memory, of dreams buried in the darkness of the night, in the secret parts of the soul. My dream was of an initiation. I now know that your task was that of initiating me to life. You had to accept and guide the existence entrusted to you. You had to help me to discover who I was, transforming my little girl's countenance into that of a woman. But you and I dared to risk confusing the dominions of the symbol with those of reality, and for this we paid dearly. At that time, so long ago, I believed that after so much pain, opening myself to life would be a light-hearted skipping through the grass. I was totally unaware of the suffering that awaited me. Your task was to initiate me to life and death. You taught me to be born and to die. Perhaps all this can occur in another manner, perhaps the road can be less painful, perhaps . . . I will never know. But, now, I can wish that your anxiety is placated. I can wish that you love and are loved, that you encounter that love that you are in search of and that is different than my love of once upon a time and my present affection. Now I can take my leave of you without pain, without regret, handing over to you my timeless affection.

NARRATOR: Played against emotions that can only be approximated with words, this story stands out for its exemplarity. The two protagonists, embraced in a spiral of emotions, were forced to look into their souls. Progress and suffering marked the road they took together. And in the end what prevailed was a transformation—achieved amid an infinity of torment, hesitations, failures, and successes—which changed both their existences. The desire to emerge from suffering, to grow, in order to represent one's own interior universe completely, is part of the hope of the patient who undertakes the "analytical voyage." The same hope and desire permeate the life of the analyst. The desire to aid a suffering humanity through the effort to resolve the enigma of his own being in the world constitutes the background of many stories. The analytical voyage is one way of self-confrontation, for both patient and analyst. In this confrontation lies the secret of a human multitude that suffers, and that errs, but that never ceases hoping to succeed in understanding the mysterious essence of the even greater voyage, which is our earthly existence.

Seven

The Language of Desire

All passions pass and are spent, all except the most an-
cient ones, those belonging to infancy.
— Cesare Pavese, *Il mestiere di vivere*

When we speak of seduction in childhood, we intend the emotional interaction that is established between the adult and the child, from the very first instants of life. Some seductive characteristics inherent in the physical conformation itself of the child and that could be defined as functional to his survival are easily identified. Among these characteristics, the physical conformation (the combination of some key stimuli such as a large, round head, large eyes, etc.) and malleability are essential to adaptation and survival, as they activate in the adult parental caring. This perceptive process in fact constitutes a mechanism that neutralizes aggressiveness and creates responses of cooperation and caring. It is in relation to those characteristics and what is called "submission behavior" that we can speak of "innate unleashing mechanisms" (Eibl-Ebesfeldt 1970) and inhibition of aggressiveness toward the young during the course of the evolution of the human species.

The newborn infant, with his naturally seductive behavior, activates responses that are in turn seductive and accepting. The adult approaches the child with tenderness, smiling and using an infantile tone of voice, his words accompanied by caresses, affectionate facial expressions, and gestures. The child is rocked, lulled, held tightly against the breast. The effectiveness of these soothing and calming gestures of submission is therefore such as to create in the adult an identification with the child who, in communicating, assumes the same attitudes. In this sense, we can say that a characteristic of seductive behavior is the adopting of infantile ways. A similar strategy has been observed in the behavior of animals. For example, the method of courtship of some bird species consists of approaching the potential companion miming the attitudes of small birds still in the nest (Montagu 1981). In fact, in many bird species, beginning with the dove, the "kiss" that seals the love preliminaries is identical to the "mouth-to-mouth" position by means of which the adult bird, male or female, feeds its young, with the sole exception that no food is involved.

It would seem that physical conformation and the type of signal emitted by the newborn creature constitute the means to guarantee its survival, a weapon—if you will—meant to compensate for the impotency and manifest vulnerability that, whatever their guise, activate in man contrasting, destructive impulses, a kind of incitement to annihilation created by the sight of helpless creatures. This should, however, not surprise us, as it is a primary, archaic, and very powerful drive that was subsequently sublimated, inhibited, or otherwise channeled by the various cultures. It is by virtue of our quality as cultural beings that we can be horrified by violence perpetrated on children or the weak in general. Only a few thousand years ago it was considered more than justifiable to abandon unwanted infants or expose or murder them when they were abnormal—one memorable example of this being the Spartan practice in ancient Greece of throwing deformed infants off the mountain cliffs.

Eibl-Ebesfeldt states in *Love and Hate* (1970) that anyone in need of help or desiring to create an affectionate response (for example, during courtship) relapses inevitably into the role of the small child. Adults as well, when menaced by superior forces or soliciting an affectionate response, can unconsciously use seduction, in the attempt to be accepting, obliging, or empathic.

Freud, in his *Compendium of Psychoanalysis* (1938b, 615), raises the maternal figure to the status of a model for all the love experiences of the subject:

111

> By her care of the child's body, (the mother) becomes its first se-
> ducer, as the prototype of all later love relationships—for both
> sexes.

As always, in Freud the need is constant to anchor a present process to roots in the past, through events and persons the seductiveness of which emerges in the symptom. It is the seductiveness of the phantasm rendered visible in passion, through the mysterious impulses of desire—those multiple, unconscious mechanisms that govern the attraction of looks or confer to certain imperceptive signs apparent in the facial expressions of another the inexplicable fascination of an enormous power over our imaginary, the subjugating power of certain gestures or a certain tone of voice.

Holding—the capacity of the "good" mother to hold the infant in her arms, to contain, cuddle, and sustain him—is essentially a primary form of seduction, if by this term we intend the imprinting that will subsequently be determinant in the very quality of the child's life, his subsequent way of being into the world—whether he allows himself to be seduced by his curiosity, or respond to the seductions of the world around him with anxiety, panic, and fear. As a defensive response to invasive, mortifying, or uncontrollable adult seduction, manipulating attempts and narcissistic maneuvers, the child cannot but adapt, abandoning his own authenticity. In order to survive psychologically, he needs his parents, needs to love them and defend them from his own aggressive drives and anger, even when these are more than justifiable. He must by necessity present himself in a seductive way, constructing for himself that defensive armor that D. Winnicott (1971) defines as the *false self*.

The act of primary seduction makes no sexual distinctions; male and female receive the same care. Have you ever asked yourself why it is that a male couple in an affectionate pose disturbs more than a female couple does? It is possible that the more indulgent attitude toward female homosexuality is due to the fact that in the initial phases of female development, a strong identification with the mother is normal.

Between 1895 and 1897, Freud theorized that at the basis of hysterical disturbances and neuroses was sexual trauma: the adult seduction of a child, which becomes trauma because at that point the child is still incapable of integrating that experience. It is through the analysis of dreams, symptoms, and above all the various forms of resistance in the patient that Freud arrived at the formulation of his theory of repression as censorship, as a defense against anxiety. When, by means of a determined associative process, a memory is related to a "seductive scene," the subject defends himself from that memory and the strong emotion it arouses by repression.

From these mechanisms of dissociation derives the formation of a pathogenic unconscious nucleus, as repressed affects remain in the unconscious, all their energy intact, and consequently compromise the conscious development of the individual. The precocious quality of the traumatic event and the physiological and psychological immaturity of the child do not permit an immediate onset of the trauma, which is thus postponed, "set aside" until, as an adult and in concomitance with an increased libidinal (that is, sexual) investment on objects, that event is once more evoked, and is able to release its explosive charge.

For Freud, it is a question of legitimately establishing the tie discovered by him between sexuality, trauma, and defense—demonstrating that it is the very nature itself of sexuality that has a traumatic effect and that, inversely, it is possible to speak of trauma and discover the origin of the neurosis only when sexual seduction has intervened (Laplanche and Pontalis 1985, 45).

According to this early etiological model, the *time* of the trauma actually goes well beyond the circumscribed duration of the traumatic event. The "seduction scene," during which the child is submitted to an attempt at seduction by an adult, is sexual and traumatic only in its subsequent re-evocation in the memory of the subject, at the time of a possible erotizing of the memory; the child possesses neither the physiological conditions of excitement nor the capacity for representation with which to integrate the event. Only subsequently, when by association a "second scene" recalls the earlier one, will this acquire a pathogenic character that in retrospect is attributed to it and that it originally did not possess.

With the theory of seduction, we might say that *all* trauma comes, at the same time, from the exterior and the interior. It comes from the exterior because sexuality comes to the subject *from the other,* and from the interior because it is unleashed by this interiorized exterior, this "reminiscence" from which hysterics are said to suffer, and in which we can already recognize the phantasm (ibid., 48).

However, by the end of 1897, Freud had already made the first major modification of the traumatic model and, in a letter to Wilhelm Fliess of September 21, he claims to have given up the theory of seduction in the form previously formulated: "I no longer believe in my *neurotica."* He perceived that the motive of seduction could be functional to the Oedipus fantasies of the patient, just as he perceived how "there are no indications in the unconscious, so one cannot distinguish between truth and fiction that has been invested by affect" (Freud 1985, 298).

We know that the abandonment of the trauma theory marked the passage from a "concretist" concept of the origins of neurosis—which took into consideration only concrete facts materially experienced by the patient—to a less rough and schematic, more subtle and evolved concept, according to which also that which occurred in the imagination has weight and substance and leaves its mark. The traumatic events referred to in the reconstruction of the infancy of Freud's hysterical patients could not be verified in reality, but this did not annul their real pathogenic charge or their intrinsic truth. As psychic elaboration, and as fantasized, imagined events invested with a strong affective charge, the episodes experienced only in the imagination generate "visible" effects on the analytic scene, where they become those phantasms of infantile desire with which the therapist must deal. Gradually, Freud (1915–17, 227) accepted the hypothesis of the aetiological importance of infantile fantasies, recognizing the elements of proposition present in seduction:

> I thus learned to comprehend that the hysterical symptoms derive from fantasies and not from real events; only later would I recognize in this fantasy of seduction on the part of the father the expression of the typical female Oedipus complex.

In a letter of January 3, 1899, Freud cites a fragment of self-analysis, on the basis of which he is able to confirm that "fantasies are the product of later epochs which, beginning in the present, are projected backwards to early infancy." And he continues: "To the question 'What happens in early infancy?', the answer is: nothing. . . ."

A few years later (in 1906), the official retraction of the theory of seduction would be concurrent with the publication of "My views on the part played by sexuality: the aetiology of the neurosis" (Freud 1905). Seduction, according to Freud, has the same role in the sexual history of the infancy of those who have "remained normal" as it does in the sexual history of the infancy of neurotics. In other words, according to Freud (1905, 222), the event is less important than its *repression:*

> Thus, it was no longer a question of what sexual experiences a particular individual had had in his childhood, but rather of his reaction to those experiences—of whether he had reacted to them by repression or not.

Forty years later, Sandor Ferenczi would also take up the theory of seduction. On the occasion of the XII International Congress of Psychoanalysis (held in Wiesbaden in 1932), he made an important presentation, "Confusion of tongues between adults and the child" (1933). In it, he once more affirmed the importance of sexual trauma as a pathogenic agent and confuted the objection that it was a question of the sexual fantasies of the child ("hysterical lies"), stressing that that idea was contradicted by the numerous confessions of patients in analysis who claimed to have used violence on children. Ferenczi (1985) confirmed this position in his *Clinical Diary,* in which his analysis of the aetiological factors of neurosis referred once more to seductions that were proved to have actually occurred during infancy and were not fantasies, thus returning to the earlier concept of Freud (who requested urgently that Ferenczi not read its contents in public). Ferenczi refused, and that decision to be autonomous earned him criticism and accusations from Freud and his group. Freud accused him of having allied himself with the children, thus demonstrating an unmanly comportment. In addition, both

115

Freud and Jones agreed that Ferenczi was paranoid, since precisely in "Confusion of tongues between adults and the child," he asserted that anything patients remembered of their trauma was real. Ferenczi thus colluded with the disturbances of his patients.

Clearly, certain criticisms are *always* suspect, if they come from the custodians of orthodoxy, those who confuse theory with *credo,* Templar Knights of a secular Holy Sepulchre, at one and the same time warrior and priest, ready for the "cause" to "believe, obey, and do battle"—and, above all, to excommunicate. However, *in this particular case,* the clashing shields and excommunications would appear to have been particularly unreasonable. The elaboration of the infidel Ferenczi happens to be rich in interesting discoveries and intuitions, above all for the modernity with which it approaches the infantile experience and the dynamics of the child's identification with parental phantasms, at a time when a true infantile psychoanalysis as yet did not exist.

According to Ferenczi, the child considered himself obliged to respond to the desires of the parents, under pain of death: the emotional conviction of the child being, "If I don't love them and don't identify with their desires, or if I do not let them seduce me, they will kill me." Letting himself be seduced is equivalent to a scheme for survival. In order to survive conflict, a defense mechanism known as the "identification with the aggressor" is activated in the child. The implication of that defense is the assuming of the guilt of the other; that is, the guilt that the other, the adult seducer, does not feel. The act is perceived as being wrong; however, no one—except the child, obviously—assumes the responsibility. The parent who refuses to do so is obviously also a parent who projects his own Shadow onto the child. The adult introduces into the child's language (or tongue) "of tenderness" his own language "of passion," (thus explaining the title of Ferenczi's presentation):

> On the other hand, the language of passion is that of desire, by necessity marked by prohibition, guilt and hate. . . . The phantasm of the primary scene, with its violent aspect, is the evidence

of a true introjection of adult eroticism by the child. (Laplanche and Pontalis 1985, 50)

Seduction is thus also accompanied by other types of violence, suggesting to the child the association between sexuality and violence. In this sense, according to Ferenczi, seduction is not a form of love, but of hate.

Another form of seduction is that adopted by parents who bind the child to them by means of what Ferenczi calls the "terrorism of suffering." We are familiar with the child's desperate need to smooth over all disorder and conflict within the family. In so doing, he takes onto himself the burden rejected by the adults, and does so, according to Ferenczi (1933, passim; 1985, 288 foll.), not altruistically but in order to restore the lost peace.

Clearly, then, when we speak of seduction in the bosom of the family, we are attempting to circumscribe a very complex series of phenomena. *Seduction,* in fact, is not only the direct, violent, and explicit sexual seduction of children, but also any form of manipulation to which they are subjected through the use of the deceitful methods of emotional blackmail and the abuse of power to satisfy or frustrate the other, by exploiting his dependence.

About 15 years ago, J. M. Masson published *The Assault on Truth,* in which he criticizes Freud for having abandoned his theory of seduction. According to Masson, Freud retracted his theory in order to avoid social censorship and isolation by the academic world. That retraction, in his opinion, was a betrayal of the very *truth* psychoanalysis claims to seek. Citing a copious literature containing case histories, observations, and documentation, Masson concludes that seductive experiences referred to by patients are authentic and not to be attributed to fantasy. There has been a rehabilitation of Ferenczi's position as regards credence given to patients' descriptions of traumatizing events in early infancy. Ferenczi supported Freud's original thought—the trauma theory—and opposed Freud's subsequent abjuration, reaffirming that the origin of neurosis is definitely sexual trauma. In this context, the phenomenology itself of the trauma should be considered from a different angle. In the adult-child relationship, in the love relationship, it is possible—and this is the thesis of Ferenczi—to encounter a "confusion of language." This would

117

occur when the child imagines that he plays a "maternal" role with the adult, a game of tenderness, while the adult responds with the language of passion, which is the language of sexuality. This primary misunderstanding in the communication between adult and child has consequences in the formation of character and neurosis: the response of the child, faced with what is, at the very least, strange behavior on the part of the adult, is the development of anxiety and fear. Given his extreme vulnerability, the disproportion or inequality produces in him feelings of inadequacy and impotency. Instead of defending himself, the child ends up identifying with his aggressor. The dynamic is then transferred, and the aggressor serves as an internal object, and as such falls under the influence of the primary processes and can thus be transformed in a hallucinatory way. Thus, in the child the primitive situation of tenderness is allowed to survive, but at the cost of a splitting of the ego. A further internal process is created with the introjection of the feeling of guilt. Identifying with the adult-aggressor, the child assumes the responsibility of the adult, and the ingenuous game of tenderness is transformed into something turbid and reprehensible. It is in this context of self-guilt that the child perceives the parent's incongruous and contradictory attitude toward him, his withdrawal from the perverse game once the seductive act has been concluded.

The reaction in psychoanalytical circles to Ferenczi's thesis is only too familiar, and Masson investigates the negated truths, in the intent to unmask the "betrayal" of a certain psychoanalysis that has ceased being concerned with the painful reality of the psychic events. It is irremediably bound up with real events, in order to focus its attention, in both therapeutic research and practice, on the more ephemeral and unstable aspects of the psychic life: a comfortable and reassuring (if sterile) choice, a disengagement (if not an out-and-out desertion). Masson (1984, 144) writes:

> But by shifting the emphasis from an actual world of sadness, misery, and cruelty to an internal stage on which actors performed invented dramas for an invisible audience of their own creation, Freud began a trend away from the real world that, it

seems to me, is at the root of the present-day sterility of psycho-analysis and psychiatry throughout the world.

It is not my intention here to go into a controversy that has re-sulted in a taking of position and diatribes within the psychoan-alytical associations. However, I will say that expressions have come from other authoritative quarters in support of a clear-cut rejection of the tendency to prefer the fantastic aspects of infan-tile experiences and their narration to the effective significance of real events and the real traumas to which infancy is submit-ted. Alice Miller, a sensitive expert on the problems of abused children, and John Bowlby are two notable examples of those taking this position. Certainly, when approaching the question of the seductive maneuvers by the adult world as regards children, we inevitably encounter the most powerful taboos and the most assiduous attempts at concealment. There is an incredible amount of injury and oppression inflicted on children daily, and this is something that not only must be admitted but also shouted to the four corners of the globe. And if, as we have said, that negative seduction is perpetrated not only through sex but also using far subtler, more devious—and consequently more perverse—means, it is clear that the concept of "mistreat-ment" should be extended considerably.

According to Ferenczi, seduction of the child by the adult is also a metaphoric rape, as it violates his psychological and senti-mental equilibrium, through the intrusion of passion where there is place only for tenderness. The seductive act then consists of "deviating" the child to the point of forcing him to assume a role that is not his. Therefore, infantile seduction also involves being conducted "elsewhere," being diverted (seduced) away from one's own truth (for example, the truth of one's own biological and emotional maturity).

In his *Clinical Diary* (1985, 289), Ferenczi deals extensively with the problem of the seduction of the child by the adult and how that early experience of seduction influences the develop-ment of the Ego:

> An early imposition of forms of untimely satisfaction disturbs the normal development of the Ego.

By "early imposition," Ferenczi intends both the practice, in vogue with nurses of the time, of putting the child to sleep "making recourse to masturbating his genitals," and the "frequent and brutal masturbation aggression perpetrated by adults," and naturally also cases of real sexual relationships. Ferenczi explains how this would alter the development of the ego: the genitalia of the child have not yet gone beyond the "stage of innocent touching, without passion." The child does not have "sufficient capacity of judgement to condemn the conduct of such authoritative persons" (in fact, should he attempt to do so, he would in all probability be accused of lying). He feels threatened and intimidated, and above all he risks being "deprived of love." In the attempt to avert that menace, the child can also begin to doubt his own perceptions, or else withdraw from the conflict, "taking refuge in day dreams" and performing like a robot the tasks of the vigil, finally embracing the most drastic solution, that is, escape by means of a total identification with his aggressor.

We could ask why the child resorts to so "uneconomic" a solution. Well, as Anna Freud put it so aptly, identification in itself constitutes one of the most powerful weapons available to the ego against those external objects capable of causing anxiety (1936, 119):

> The child introjects some characteristics of an anxiety-inducing object and so assimilates an anxiety experience that he has just undergone. . . . By impersonating the aggressor, assuming his attributes or imitating his aggression, the child transforms himself from the person threatened into the person who makes the threat (ibid., 123).

An interesting aspect of the concept elaborated by Anna Freud on this defense mechanism of the ego is the conviction that it contributes powerfully to the formation of the Super-Ego. She even went so far as to suggest that the Super-Ego could coincide with the identification with the aggressor: "What else is the Super-ego then if not the identification with the aggressor?" (Sandler and Freud 1985, 404).

Ferenczi speaks, in this context, of "identification love." Identification love leaves the ego unsatisfied, also because immediately following an early seduction is the sensation of guilt felt by the one seduced: according to Ferenczi, even the feeling of guilt would be derivative of the identification mechanism. In other words, the child perceives of a feeling of guilt in the aggressor, and shares it.

It is perhaps this perception alone of the feeling of guilt in the aggressor that confers the character of guilt to the discomfort of the ego; in other words, it is due to the disturbance caused. The comportment of the person invested with authority after the completion of the act (silence, negation, anxious conduct), in addition to threats made to the child, is such as to insinuate in the child the consciousness of his guilt and his complicity (Ferenczi 1985, 290).

In this context, H. F. Searles, the author of *Collected Papers on Schizophrenia and Related Subjects,* affirms that the ambivalent situation to which the seduced child is exposed is strongly "schizophrenogenic": the pathogenic aspect is due to a situation in which on the one hand a sexual excitation is provoked, and on the other that provocation takes place in a context in which it would be extremely dangerous for the ego to satisfy it. In other words, that situation constitutes a situation capable of driving the other mad (Searles 1965, 245–246). This is a problem related to the alienation of the body. Alienation signifies "giving to another"; the body is given to another without that giving being motivated by love or affection. The body is given to another, ceasing to belong to he who gives it. The alienation of the body, of one's own sexuality, occurs through a passive experience, conceived solely to please the partner, to be ensured of his love. The body is forced to submit to a true "estrangement." An estrangement conceals and at the same time reveals a deep fracture between affect and sexuality—"deep" also meaning the hold on the present of a remote past.

According to Ferenczi, the origin of the estrangement of the body, the primary cause—or at least one of the causes—of its alienation lies in the seductive behavior assumed by the parent toward the child. As we have seen, this behavior arouses sexual excitement in the child, but at the same time produces an intense conflict between the need to satisfy the excitation and the prohibition to which the ego is submitted due to the incest taboo. We have briefly given Searles' ideas on this matter. We might add that the childhood of many schizophrenic and border-line patients was passed with seductive parents. Those patients had thus experienced the conflict produced by their parents' behavior. Relational psychologists speak in these cases of a "double bind," or "paradoxical prescription," in the sense that on the one hand there is an excitation to be satisfied, and on the other the prohibition to act accordingly. The satisfaction is prescribed and at the same time prohibited. That situation of "double bind" is then aggravated by the child's basically imma-ture genitalia. This we might call a "corporeal double bind," in the sense that satisfaction is demanded *from an immature body*. In other words, a body is prescribed to *already be* what it is not yet. The request is made, with authority (the authority of the parents), of a body still immature to be a body already mature and to act as such.

For that redefinition of the context of seduction, Ferenczi had excogitated the expression "confusion of languages." That confu-sion not only is present in the adult-child relationship but also exists in the adult himself and is projected onto the child. We can then—as regards the parent—legitimately speak of a confu-sion of languages in both the extra- and intro-psychic relation-ship, depending on the extent to which he is unaware of the se-ductive, sexual significance of his action, of his *advances* made to his child. And here we have the confusion of languages: the unconscious says "sex" where the consciousness says "affection, loving care." The parents tend to defend themselves from the value of the "sexual language," converting it through rationaliza-tion (after all, they are the parents and the children are theirs, and it is only natural that they behave as they do), to the context of affects. That confusion present in the parent is reflected cata-strophically in the psyche of the child, who, despite his imma-ture genitalia, perceives in some way the sexual implications characterizing the adult's *advances*. He nevertheless encounters the unconsciousness of the parent, because he experiences those approaches as behavior perfectly congruous with his role. The confusion of the child and the collusion with the adult, in the attempt to preserve the love object and avoid hate and anger and be accepted and loved, is manifested as a compromising of his capacity to distinguish between what is good and what is evil, between just and unjust, and above all between what is desirable and what is not. From there the passage to madness is brief. But why should so much confusion of language be generated in the parent? In most cases, the answer lies in another confusion, that which reigns in the relationship with the partner. The more the partner withdraws from the intimate relationship, abstaining from speaking their language of love and sex, the more he will utilize—with the purpose of extracting from it an unconscious excitement—the child's need for intimacy and affectionate warmth.

Behind the confusion of languages and seduction there is the pressure of a double frustration. If *versagen* is composed of *sagen* (which means "say") and *ver* (which negates it), in some way this word contains both concepts, the "say yes" and the "say no": at the same time, a promise and the negation of that promise. It is interesting that the term is constructed in the same way as *verfuhren,* which means "seduce," to indicate a relationship that in fact can be found somewhere between frustration and seduction. Remaining in the realm of Freudian terminology, when is it that I actually "frustrate"? Only there where I promised, where I made the other understand that I said yes to him. Therefore, I frustrate when I negate that promise. The frustrated parent in turn frustrates the child. Between adult partners, frustration lies in having negated a promise of love and sex. Between parent and child, the frustration lies in having negated the promise of affection.

The intimate relationship between *Verfuhrung* (seduction) and *Versagung* (frustration) becomes even more evident if we consider that a seductive parent identifies with a parent who in fact refuses. We have established with our etymological examination of the term *seduce* its meaning of bringing someone to a place that does not belong to him. Therefore, seducing the child means taking him to the place of sexuality after having promised him to take him to that of affection. To this, we must add the frustration referred to above: the frustration of the parent is a shadow that the child cannot avoid taking onto himself, with devastating effects on his psychic equilibrium. The parent uses the body of the child to obtain excitement; he therefore violates that body, invades its privacy, frustrates it, in the sense that following the promise once given is the *negation* of the body, the refusal to acknowledge the person possessing it as autonomous. However, at this point something incongruous can occur. The child, abandoned to the solitude of his anxiety, can react—and more often than not this reaction is in the form of an excessive, *overcompensating* attachment to the seductive parent. In his solitude, which mirrors that of the parent frustrated by the partner (and in all probability the child is aware of the parent's solitude), he in fact feels as though forced to ensure his love. A. Lowen, a student of Wilhelm Reich, wrote in *Betrayal of the Body* (1967, 94–95), which was published on the eve of the student and worker protest movement of 1967, that attachment in its turn reinforces the initial fact, which was the alienation of the body.

Giving the body to another, in a situation of unbearable psychic stress, the child definitely frustrates himself, negating himself the possession of what most rightly belongs to him. We have seen how the immaturity of his genitalia prevents the child submitted to the seduction from understanding completely what is happening to him. It is then a question of providing a response to a sensation that he in any case perceives as prohibited. The response will consist then in his alienating the body. That alienation can be defined as a sort of "freezing," an anesthesia more than an amputation. The child does not *feel* it because feeling renews the guilt (derived from the identification with the aggressor, or with the assumption upon himself of the parent's guilt). The life of this child, whose experiences we have described, continues in silence, which is also the silence of the body. The fear of losing the affection, albeit incongruous, of the parent prevents him from speaking or revealing his own incestuous secret. And there is also the fear of not being believed, of being considered mad or even responsible for what has happened. Life continues therefore in silence, a silence tormented in some cases by the memory of that experience, a memory that is isolated from the emotions experienced on that occasion. That isolation reinforces in a vicious circle the alienation of the body with which the seduced child attempted to attenuate the effects of the aggression to which he was submitted. What appears evident from the experience of many women who go into analysis is their experiencing their own sexuality passively or in order to please the partner, never for themselves.

There is, however, another area of research on the theme of child seduction: a psychoanalytical reflection of the most attentive sort on the *imaginary* of the child, his personal, albeit fanciful vision of what occurs, a situation of which Jean Laplanche is one of the most stimulating interpreters. This perspective offers us the possibility of a *double* reading of the theory of seduction. In a limited sense, we have that literal form of seduction dealt with in this chapter—the *sexual attack* of an adult on a child who, due to his immaturity, is not able to elaborate the situation. (This is the first way of understanding seduction by Freud.)

In a wider and deeper sense of Laplanche, seduction refers to the maternal care that—regardless of intent—is the "vehicle" at the same time of sexual messages.

In this context, the immature child, with his as yet unstructured unconscious, finds himself faced with an adult whose unconscious is already formed who transmits a multitude of verbal and nonverbal messages. (These are precisely those "enigmatic meanings" that create unconscious nuclei that the child is still incapable of elaborating and that are partially unconscious for the adult himself.) The child is therefore called upon to attempt to *resolve the enigma of the maternal seduction* (Masciangelo 1988, 449).

During the course of analysis, there is a pressure to resolve the enigma of seduction, the origin of which is in early infancy—at times literal and violent in cases of real sexual seduction, but more often that which has been operated in us from the moment of our birth, the seduction the mythical roots of which Laplanche and Pontalis (1985, 51) have identified, that "myth of the origin of sexuality by introjection of desire, of the phantasm, of adult 'language.'"

Thus, each of us nurtures a phantasm of seduction, the roots of which are in the dawn of existence. The mother who appears, gratifying the child's desires, and the mother who disappears, withdrawing from the "fusional circle" to live *elsewhere* her capacity to "give," can converge—in unison with the intimate experiences of the oscillation of the maternal presence—in the unconscious representations of the child. Although not necessarily representations bound to sexuality, they in any case belong to the area of desire. The primary identification with the loved object, and consequently, that immediate gratification and omnipotence the fusion provides, must work loose and leave the way clear to the perception of reality. However, no one abandons immediate gratification if it is not substituted by another, because desire—like aversion—has desperate need of investing a precise object.

Imagining and fantasizing constitute the first means with which the individual substitutes the absent object of desire with an image. The force of the image on which the child projects his entire experience—hate, fear, and love—is such that first Freud and later Jung would use "phantasm" and "unconscious phantasm," respectively, to stress the capacity of the phantasm to interact with reality—actually molding it and perverting it (for example, into fetishism, which according to Freud concealed a phantasm of *perverse* seduction). Thus are created seduction fantasies, fantasies of desire, Oedipal fantasies, and those bound to the "saga of the family" (Rank 1909); wherever there is desire and the expectation of gratification, a corresponding fantasy of satisfaction emerges, to compensate for the lack, for the loved object's *always being elsewhere.* We believe that the fantasy does not only serve a "vicarious" function—that is, that of providing the child with a "hallucinatory" surrogate for the absent love object, thus providing substitutive gratification. On a much deeper level, through the imaginative activity, it permits the child to enter into contact with the tension that the absence of the loved object generates, to pause in that empty space, inhabiting it with his own fantasy productions that are translations of his early emotional experiences and the first attempts to elaborate them. Fantasy crystallizes in an image the deeply ambivalent feelings that the child nurtures toward those persons with whom he lives. Anger, expectation and disappointment, hope and fear, combined with the images of the parents onto whom the child projects those contents, are the chaotic material that fantasy visualizes and orders. And fantasy is also colored by affects, becoming that precipitate of images of an emotional tone that Jung calls a *complex.* For this reason, the appearance of desire and its development are inextricably bound to "dealing" with phantasms.

The psychological development of man is closely related to his capacity to tolerate the detachment from forms of immediate gratification which, if protracted too long, rebound, castrating him. The child must leave the maternal womb at a preestablished time, pain of death. He must tolerate the separation from the mother; first at his physical birth and later at the moment of his "true birth" (the birth of consciousness), that form of fusion and primary identification that made his psychological survival possible, but which when protracted beyond the time of maturation can become a mortal embrace.

Each passage from one phase of development to another implies a phase of disintegration, a crisis in the acquired equilibrium. All of this, however, is essential to growth, and it is reasonable to assume that the individual, who must continually generate himself, will possess the psychological means to tolerate frustration and overcome difficulties. Totality and wholeness are not of this world, and it is part of the human condition to be lacerated, divided, always in search of a refuge, a port, a goal as an ultimate destination for peregrinations, to move desire.

Our love objects are always elsewhere, and when by chance or by circumstance our desire recognizes in a face, in a place or in a work (of art) the traces of its phantasm, there is seduction. Nostalgia is reactivated, and with it that hope that had never really died, that that face, that place, that beauty might heal our splitting. And, instead, as though the result of an obscure spell, nostalgia is sharpened, wounds are reopened, and the stage is invaded by phantasms. The other "wound," "strikes," appears and disappears, and we are once more the child of yore, vulnerable and at the same time hopeful, once more astonished at our own fragility and the overwhelming power of the other.

Eight

Providing a Face for the Phantasm

The amorous discourse is usually a smooth shell
Enclosing an image, an extremely soft glove around
the loved one.
        —R. Barthes, *A Lover's Discourse: Fragments*

The moment we are captured by the seductive action of the other, we become *victims.* Psychic energy is catalyzed by this new pole of attraction, and in these circumstances we can even reach the point of believing that our very lives are in the balance. And although there are obviously far more serious trials in life, there is—at least in the psychological context—something profoundly true in the idea that the force of seduction threatens our very existence. No other experience succeeds in mobilizing and channeling our psychic energies in one direction as does the contact with our *phantasm,* which is precisely what occurs in passionate love. By *phantasm,* we intend that constellation of affects and unconscious images through which our pleasure and anxiety pass. And it is precisely for this reason that a good deal of the patient's unconscious dynamics becomes perceptible with the emergence of the transference. It is through the experience of emotions, in all their manifestations (love, anger, fear), that the map of the patient's deepest feelings emerges, in terms of an absolutely personal language. And it is that map, subsequently deciphered together with the patient, which will lead to consciousness where there was only a compulsive desire for acceptance conditioned by the "impossible" requests of the patient.

The game of seduction is, like any game, ephemeral. And yet, as long as we are captured by it, we live in a total and absolute dimension in which we are brought face-to-face with our most threatening and, at the same time, most stimulating fantasies: "Oh love, oh mad illumination and crimson menace," exclaims P. Neruda in a love sonnet (1960, XXXVII). One can die of love or fantasize total union. In any event, the beatitude of acceptance, like the pain of abandonment, is intense.

As we have seen, one possible interpretation that might shed light on the nature of this intense sentimental experience is that which traces its roots to an early experience: that of being at the mercy of the other. We are born absolutely helpless, as the initial supremacy of our parents represents all good, all light; in other words, power. The condition of the child is one of total vulnerability. The child must be provided everything if he is to survive, and that "everything" is provided exclusively by the other—someone to nourish and protect him, anticipate his needs by giving them form and a response. That "someone" need simply withdraw to decree the end of the child's existence. The hidden roots of seduction are in the fertile ground of dependence in which is created that constellation of power, imagined or real, of the other. As insecurity is structural to that love, dependence must be structural to the condition of the one who loves when faced with the *power* of the loved one. This condition could be described as a state of psychic necessity; as essential as the need for air or food, it can become an instrument of torture. We have delegated to the other—with his power to appear and disappear—the significance of our existence; it is he who will decide our worth, he who will judge whether we are necessary or superfluous.

The fascination that the powerful one exerts lies precisely in his apparently being arbiter of the destiny of the other as well as his own. But after having observed the effects on the one submitted to the power of the loved one, we might ask what occurs as regards the one *exercising* that power—for example, how much of it is obligatory, dictated by unresolved compulsions or unhealed narcissistic wounds? As our intention is not to place seduction in the sphere of neurotic illusion, a distinction should be made between the various types of seductive behavior: between healthy illusions of love and the compulsive need to use personal attractiveness to win admiration and esteem and inspire positive reactions. Power causes the emergence of the darkest aspects of our desire, and in the relationship it appears not as power over things, but actually possession of the other's soul. In the love situation, that psychic aspect Jung called the Shadow emerges with renewed strength. Never so overwhelmingly as in the amorous state do the more controversial aspects of the personality emerge, in that there we can observe an absolutely unscrupulous use of power, influencing the behavior of one who loves. What would one not be capable of, what would one not repudiate or trample underfoot in order to conquer the love object? We would never succeed in deciphering the most secret dimension of the other were it not for these critical situations. Thus Jung stated that love, in the sense of *concupiscentia,* is that dimension of the soul that causes the unconscious to emerge. Therefore, latent in the need to seduce is the need to exercise power, albeit a bewitchingly masked sort. Common sense is helpful in revealing this aspect of seduction that is conducive to evil and perdition.

The experience of being seduced is above all one of privation. We are deprived of tranquility, of the levity of life—but above all, of that charitable blindness that prevents us from examining, and therefore being conscious, of those internal aspects we call complexes. The love experience awakens precisely those affective nuclei related to our most primitive drives, the most extreme requests for love and the most archaic forms of ambivalence. The other, who violently invades the space of our everyday life and our imaginary, can exercise an overwhelming power, if only because he exists "beyond" and "despite" our need. He has the power to disappear from the scene, abandoning the love territory created by our desire. He can do this, and it is this freedom that confers the power experienced by the other as threatening. The other is free to not be there, and his absence can only reflect and create a constellation of that basic lack existing in each of us. Saying "I miss you" is tantamount to admitting an extreme fragility and vulnerability, a dependence on someone who eludes our desire. Thus, we feel divided; it is as though the potential of our corporeal experience and that of our soul is awakened and can be realized only in the presence of the loved one. We succumb to the other, suspended in a Limbo somewhere between life and death.

130

When we succeed at seduction, when we enter the heart of the other and realize that we have become necessary to him, we are reliving another condition the roots of which are in very early experience: the omnipotence and deification of ourselves, the election of the self as the center of the universe.

"You shall have no other god before me": it becomes imperative for us to convert the other to our religion, make him our devotee; in other words, seduce him. In a famous verse of Sappho, she describes the one before her 'appearing as blessed and like a god.'

The seduced is in adoration of the loved one. This unconditional surrender, as lightning swift as the conversion of St. Paul, is a fundamental characteristic of the love experience: being captured with an immediacy impossible in any other circumstance. One speaks of seduction as a hypnotic state. Plato would call it "divine delirium." It is ecstasy, being beside oneself.

For the duration of this love, this being before an object charged with mystery and divine fascination, there is the urge to wrench him from his extraneousness, forcing him to emerge from the obscure setting with which he is still confused, in order to render him intelligible. Is this a desire for power? At the root of seduction, of both seducing and being seduced, there is therefore a dual dimension: the exercise of power and self-deification. Is it the old fear of parents projected onto the other that renders him divine? Or is it also the fear of the power of the other, which can be exorcised only by a countering/preventive power, by legitimizing oneself as divinity? In other words: from legitimate self-defense, we pass to excessive defensiveness, "attack is the best defense," or *si vis pacem, para bellum*. And if it is the relationship with the other that is feared, it would be well to remember that it is usually fear that causes the first shot to be fired.

Perceptible in the seductive act is the attempt to neutralize the presumed aggressiveness of the other, capturing him with our love. The behavior of Don Juan is one example of the powerful emergence of this subtle fear. The seductive strategy of that legendary personage leads us to suspect the existence of an unconscious fear of the other and his power, which can be exorcised and controlled only through the ritual of repeated conquest of *mille fanciulle più una* (a thousand-and-one maidens). In fact, cynicism, irony, and insolence usually mask a deep fear of relationship, which is neutralized by means of adroitly maneuvering the other into an impasse.

The heady sense of this power over the other is one of the prizes in the type of seduction we will call instrumental. Think of the child when he realizes the power he wields over the adult he has succeeded in seducing.

There is another type of seduction—more ephemeral and banal, but not for that reason less effective, common, or penetrating—that reveals these aspects. It is the manipulative seduction to which we are all exposed in a consumer society. The signs and images of the seduction of publicity are everywhere, aimed at capturing our desire, at creating in us the need of the object being publicized. We are seduced to buy, but commercial seduction is perverse in that its true objective is *not* allowing the "pleasure" of possessing what has been purchased to last too long. In order to perpetuate a condition of need, an uneasiness must be induced, an eternal state of dissatisfaction, of insatiability. In other words, the consumer is rendered perpetually vulnerable to conquest by another, latest product.

We might ask whether the relationship we have indicated between seduction and power in the end does not impoverish it, eliminating the value and fascination of what we have defined as not just an experience but actually a constant in our lives. Is it possible that a theme that for centuries—even millennia—has inspired creative masterpieces in both art and literature is at bottom nothing more than one more variant of the eternal game of the abuse of power? The truth is that that relationship is just the smallest part of those particular aspects of seduction. For seduction is a considerably more complex contest, as it is a movement from Me to the Other, by means of which the deepest nature of our desire is revealed. There are various forms of seduction, each one representing a way, more or less unconscious, of experiencing our own subjectivity and entering into contact with the subjectivity of the other. The methods of seduction reveal to us what image of ourselves we wish to provide the other, and in an even deeper sense, what image of ourselves we keep most concealed. The other can function as a mirror to confirm our imaginary constructions: in other words, as nothing more than a transitory means to reflect our preferred image of ourselves. Or else, more painfully, he can represent with his inflexible otherness the challenge of a difficult confrontation with our own internal images—for example, Narcissus captivated by the seductive aspects of his own image, Echo seduced by the unending flight of her love object, or Psyche discovering through a dark love story and at great cost the way to being an adult woman, or lover.

What we will consider here is this substantial difference between the two forms of seduction—one that could be defined as being an "end in itself," and the other "instrumental." These two forms of seduction correspond to two different, if complementary, ways of approaching the love object.

The first consists of recognizing diversity, accepting the other in his *otherness,* while the second consists of manipulating the other, reducing him to a mirror, or even in searching outside ourselves, in the other, for something familiar in that it is *ours,* in projecting onto the other our phantasm, an aspect of our interior theatre.

We have seen that these aspects are complementary; there exists no relationship that is not based on a reciprocal game of projection. However, it is possible to separate the two aspects, at least in the sense of distinguishing those relationships in which the projective mechanisms operate powerfully and massively by suggesting very unconscious subjects from those based on an elevated awareness in which the other is recognized and accepted with all his differences. In the latter, the other appears to us as an already differentiated subject, with a fairly stable identify and a "basic trust" that permits maintaining a distance.

The difference between the two forms of seduction is the same as that between an infantile—we might even say pregenital—form of relationship with the love object and the tension and attention typical of a more mature stage of development.

The process of the psychological maturing of the individual could be defined essentially as one in which the infantile dependence on the object, based on *identification,* is gradually modified to become a form of mature dependence, based on a *differentiation* from the object. Characteristic of the phase of infantile dependence is that form of love that Balint calls "primary love": the object is loved as responding to our needs, but is permitted absolutely no autonomy. For the child, the mother exists exclusively as responding to needs and confirming omnipotence. The scope of the libidinal straining in the direction of this love object is of a predatory type: when we speak of oral or "capturing" means, we refer to a very primitive form of "love," which often as adults is expressed by the phrase "I could eat you up."

One example is the seductive aspect of the instrumental type of seduction operated by some narcissistic pathologies, in which there is the desire for a mirroring and confirmation of one's self and one's own needs in the other. These individuals are usually described as "loving themselves only." Obviously, it would be unwise to make hasty generalizations, in that there also exists a "healthy" narcissism, or "natural" narcissism, such as the narcissism attributed by Freud to the feminine universe.

Freud was interested in the different forms of object choices (1914b), making a distinction between choices for support or protection (the search for love objects that reproduce the maternal model, therefore the nursing woman for the man or the protective man for the woman) and narcissistic choices, in which the individual, through the object, loves what he himself is or would like to be. Freud explained that it was not a question of making a clear distinction between individuals belonging to one or the other type, as each individual is capable of making an object choice in either direction. As regards the seductiveness put into action by the narcissistic type, Freud would include most women as "naturally" narcissistic personalities, especially women with pronounced aesthetic qualities, in whom "a kind of self-sufficiency would intervene, compensating them for the sacrifices society imposes as regards the freedom to choose their own objects" (ibid., 459). These women above all love themselves and in their choice of partner look for dedication and adoration. They are extremely fascinating to men, precisely because of their particular psychological constellation, which renders them narcissistically inaccessible and exercises "a strong attraction for all those who, having renounced any totality in their own narcissism, are in search of object love" (ibid.). That the narcissistic factor has particular importance for women would seem reasonably evident. They invest their love life in a narcissistic way, exploiting, for example, their corporeal ego, both through care of their bodies and their clothing, as well as in a broader sense the care of those narcissistic extensions of the ego, such as their houses, companions, and children.

In their search for confirmation of their own value, narcissistic individuals inevitably arouse the envy of those who mistake their apparent inaccessibility for smug self-sufficiency. However, that envy is totally unjustified; the desperate need seducers have for those confirming "mirrors" is an anything but enviable condition. In fact, the level of psychological immaturity of this type of seducer renders impossible establishing a true object relationship, that is, one between autonomous and differentiated individuals, each possessing sufficient power of their own and consequently having no need to subject the other. Consequently, it is not in the other or the adoration of the other that they expect to have their existence confirmed or find the necessary basis for their self-esteem. The exercise of power, in whatever form it may assume, is always a collusion, an abuse operated to the detriment of the other, who is thus deprived of his own authentic personality. In this context, we might cite Theodor Adorno (1951, 177):

> Only the recognition of the distance in which those closest to us mitigates extraneousness, assuming it in the consciousness. While the expectation of a total proximity each time already achieved, which is precisely the negation of extraneousness, exerts on the other the ultimate injustice, negating him virtually in his particular essence, thus negating what is human in him, "assigning" him, incorporating him to the inventory of possession.

This is the most sterile form of seduction, since it is only a preliminary to an operation in which the other, for the seducer, is not a human being to whom to relate but an instrument, whose sole function is to assume the role conferred on him in a "game of simulation." In instrumental seduction, the vocation for power finds fertile ground, as apparently its ultimate and sole aim is keeping the other in the palm of his hand. As Jean Baudrillard stated, it is always a question of arousing the other's desire. And it is for this reason that in ritual contexts or in certain forms of animal behavior, the sexual act is the official sanction of conquest, the ritual act of submission par excellence.

We discussed earlier how seduction is the taking over or invasion of the other's imaginary: if the seducer is to take possession of the lover, it is necessary that he permanently occupy the center of the other's desires. How often have we heard the question, "But do you want me?" Here, desire means not only the recognition of the other's role as absolute protagonist and therefore a constant presence in our imagination but also that this presence is not "pacific" and guaranteed once and for all, but is precarious, uncertain, ours but not entirely, something that could at any moment slip through our fingers.

Instead, the type of seduction we have described as being an end in itself involves a game, a confronting the unknown concealed in the encounter with the other, which could be described as a venturing into the reality of the other. Thus, the recognition of difference and diversity is also the acceptance of the intrinsic limit to the movement toward the other—who could refuse, reciprocate, or withdraw altogether from the game, thus exposing us to frustration. This type of seducer is well aware of this. He is not afraid to express his own desire; however, he takes into consideration the unknown factor of the other's desire, since included in his notion of the seduction game is the basic freedom of the other. In love situations, there exists still— at the threshold of the third millennium—a certain type of psychological request, a way of interaction between partners that subtends a well-known relationship model characteristic of the primary relationship. In the partner, we seek support, care, altruistic love, a capacity for warmth and accepting, all of which would be perfectly comprehensible were it not for the fact that, in order to obtain it, we advance requests to which only an *ideal* partner could respond. Or better still, to which only our mothers—if we were fortunate enough—could respond. The pathology of the couple, of whatever type, and specific unconscious collusion is based on an insistence on impossible requests for satisfaction. Thus, we have the *couple neurosis*.

We have said that the main characteristic of the end-in-itself type of seduction is that the one playing the game, as it were, within the reality of the other exposes himself, takes risks, while in instrumental seduction the other must—or is expected to—assume the role assigned him; in other words, he must essentially cast off his characteristic of being "other."

Of the two types of seducer, only the former can be considered psychologically adult and in search of a true object relationship, moving totally toward the other; that is, toward that which he perceives as diversity. The instrumental seducer, on the other hand, does not see beyond himself, as he is basically unable to recognize the diversity of the other without experiencing a subtle fear. Otherness is paradoxically that which must be neutralized—and, consequently, not recognized. This seduction serves to accomplish precisely this.

In the instrumental type of seduction, very often the unconscious attitude of the subject intending to conquer is, more or less: "I will be as you desire me." Essentially, this means abdicating one's own individuality, as the only way of conserving it—as though making oneself an illusive mirror for the needs and desires of the other were the best way to succeed in finally being someone, in finally having an identity: the paradoxical identity of one who has none, of one forced to change form like a chameleon. However, this illusion is destined to be destroyed: often it is the subject himself who flees, who upsets the game, in the hope of avoiding the destruction of the illusion in the further illusion that he is "in control" of things, that he is perfectly capable of deciding when he has had enough. What characterizes this type of seducer is that his love objects express a total adhesion, which could be summed up by the phrase "I am hopelessly in love with you because in you I see myself." The love objects seem to exist because they have been invested by the other with meaning: it is the other who ensures their substance and meaning. They become the shadow, the reflection. The other is their ideal ego, incarnating all perfection to which they have no right, and they dedicate their existence to this ideal; should it disappear it would mean the end of everything.

This is a very common form of collusion, which usually dramatically dissolves with the withdrawal of the "stronger" of the two who, once he has obtained the other's unconditional surrender and had his own uncertain self-esteem bolstered, can then redirect his energies toward another love object.

The art of seduction is instead really the art of devotion, as described in the great lyric poetry of the Middle Ages. It is through the submission of love that we acquire the comprehension that it is only through another that we can accede to a new galaxy of meaning, and it is thanks to this obligatory passage through the tight web woven of desire and absence that we can be transformed.

But to what does the seducer submit the seduced? Put briefly: his own truth. Once more we might cite Baudrillard (1979, 112): "Being seduced means being deviated from one's own truth. Seducing is deviating the other from his truth." We proceed, comfortable in our certainties, until that moment when an encounter averts us, upsetting our equilibrium. The other captures us, and we rush happily toward our own ruin, as all our certainties shatter around us. And yet, we continue on, through a dangerous and unexplored territory. Love causes an alteration in our relationship with reality. But what exactly does "altered" mean in psychological terms? It means that our usual psychic order has become extraneous to us, defective, fragmentary, unsatisfactory; we would not have been capable of embracing the unknown dimension of the adventure if some laceration had not already occurred, if a renewed sensation of "lack" had not set us unconsciously to seeking a response.

At that point where all certitude has been destroyed, the deification of the other becomes our new creed. *Our* truth has been lost. We are all familiar with that particular form of identification in which we unconsciously begin to imitate the gestures of the loved one, speaking as he does, assimilating his opinions, even to the point of seeing the world through his eyes. We say of the loved one, "He (she) has become my very life." In certain cases, dignity itself is lost: "I would do anything for him (her)." And in that state we probably would. The other has averted us from our own truth. On the other hand, even the truth seduces, inasmuch as its attraction is irresistible. And, like every "obscure object of desire," it is always elsewhere, somewhere "other," than where we are.

Nine

I Have Vision, Therefore I Exist

. . . you walked along the riverside, a
flowing jar of water on your hip. Why did
you suddenly glance at me through the flowing
veil, which lit the darkness and grazed me like
a breeze gently urging the waters to the shaded glen?
                                    —R. Tagore, *The Gardener*

Seduction is easily perceptible in certain characteristics, attitudes, and qualities: those particular aspects of which the other is the unwitting repository and that exert an attraction and a subtle, irresistible fascination.

Although admitting that our desire is activated by unconscious and extremely subjective factors, we cannot deny that certain elements are particularly effective and pressing and create an irresistible emotional response. A certain tone of voice or a particular glance can be the source of a powerful, mysterious fascination. A sinuousness or delicateness, a way of moving, can become the essential elements of a seduction—forms registered by the unconscious to subsequently be translated into the opportune conditioning: instantaneous conditioning, expressed as *coup de foudre* and love at first sight. Thus, while observing the other, listening to his voice, or admiring his physical appearance, we are ensnared, lured. The reference here is obviously to the above-cited etymology that unites the Greek *thélgo* (I seduce) with the Germanic *dolg* ("strike, wound"). Everything falls into place exactly, as if we were programmed to react to that particular stimulus, and no other.

Some aspects of the language of seduction are universal: for example, the troubling quality of a voice (song or words) or a glance. There is a popular saying that "the eye attracts love," and there is a French proverb, even more to the point: "Le mouvement des yeux est le langage des amants" ("The eyes express the language of lovers").

There is no cultural or artistic tradition that has not recognized and celebrated this intimate relationship between the glance and amorous fascination, between vision and love. This relationship was already noted by Plato, who in his *Phaedrus* (255 c–d) compares love to an "illness of the eyes." This comparison led Plotinus in the *Enneads* (III 5, 3) to consider a strange etymology of Eros, a name that could have derived "from the fact that he obtained his existence from vision." The first object of contemplation for the soul is the *beautiful,* the sight of which provides the individual all enjoyment and realization. It thus follows that every object in the perceptible world that is apparently the depositary of this archetypal beauty arouses desire, awakens Eros.

Medieval poetic tradition takes up once more the Platonic concept of love: love is awakened always by the contemplation of the loved one, and the eyes are the principle means of seduction. "O, Deo, che sembra quando li occhi gira!!" is the ecstatic, fear-charged confession of Guido Cavalcanti (1986, *Rime,* IV, v. 5), a poet extraordinarily true to this concept of love attraction expressed by a glance, and the wounds of love inflicted by the eyes of the loved one:

> Voi che per li occhi mi passaste 'l core
> e destaste la mente che dormìa,
> guardate a l'angosciosa vita mia,
> che sospirando la distrugge Amore.
>
> . . . .
>
> Questa vertù d'amor che m'ha disfatto
> Da' vostr'occhi gentil' presta si mosse:
> Un dardo mi gittò dentro dal fianco.
> *(Rime,* XIII)

The metaphor for the love wound inflicted by a glance of the loved one is also described by Petrarch (1953), in its total fulfillment and its highest expression:

Io temo sì de' begli occhi l'assalto,
ne' quali Amore e la mia morte alberga,
ch'io fuggo lor come fanciul la verga;
e gran tempo è ch'i' presi il primier salto.
                    (*Rime*, XXXIX, 1–4)

The acceptance that love "vien da veduta forma che s'in-tende"—once more citing Cavalcanti—or that it is stimulated by the contemplation of a form capable of penetrating the senses, is accompanied by another distinctive characteristic of sight: the eye is a mirror upon which the image of the loved one remains impressed, and through this the heart is reached and the soul touched. However, the visual perception of the loved one is not sufficient to transform aesthetic attraction into erotic attraction. For this, an internal, interiorized vision of the woman is neces-sary, which is possible only through the real image being al-lowed to decant in her absence, in her being distant in time and in space. The soul can retain the image of the loved one and with it converse, rue, despair. Physical distance does not pre-vent, and sometimes even intensifies, the anticipation of love, which is transformed by distance and obstacles into an ex-tremely refined psychological awareness and introspection. The image of the loved one thus loses its real connotations and be-comes transfigured, a psychic image contemplated not with the external senses but with an inner eye, the eye of the poet. What this internal vision deciphers and reveals are the most subtle, most secret, and most complex psychological processes of the love seduction that, when successfully put into words, have given us some of the highest forms of Western romantic literature.

Medieval psychology conceived love as an essentially imagi-native adventure, and the seduction of the love object as the ability to occupy permanently the imaginary of the one seduced:

> The medieval discovery of love upon which . . . there has been so much discussion, is the discovery of the unreality of love; that is, its fantastic aspect . . . It is only in the culture of the Middle Ages that the phantasm emerges as the origin and object of love, and the condition of Eros moves from vision to fantasy. (Agam-ben 1977, 96–97).

In fact, in this process of interiorization, the woman becomes the image of the Anima, the heterosexual component of the male psyche.

The communication of the glance, therefore, marked the beginning of the erotic transport; it is the necessary initiatory rite, the threshold leading to the realm of the seduced, of lovers. Endymion, when speaking of Artemis to a passing stranger, confesses:

> I awakened under the moon . . . and saw her . . . saw her as she watched me, with those slightly oblique eyes, fixed, transparent . . . I didn't know then, nor the day following, but I was already hers, imprisoned in the circle of her eyes. (Pavese 1947, 69)

But from whence this fascination of a glance?

If we consider the earliest experiences of life, we see the enormous importance of the eyes and the voice of the mother in the learning process of the newborn infant as regards himself and the environment. According to R. Stevens (1975), children are attracted by eyes from the very first. Looking can be gratifying for the child if what he sees is always a smiling face, which in its turn will be related to other kinds of gratification, such as food or bodily contact.

The infant, a few weeks after birth, already follows the movements of his mother with his eyes. His first experience is intimately permeated by the mother's gaze as she watches over him, as she studies him in order to anticipate his needs and respond to them; it is a look that placates, that communicates love or anguish, that can pardon or wound. The proof of the mother's presence is the nearness of her loving glance. The infant can begin to explore his world only because it is still a space included in the maternal vision, which contains it and gives it meaning. At that point, exploring the world is still— according to M. Klein (1937)—exploring the body of the mother. The basis for his feeling of identity is therefore provided by the mother. The child discovers the "mother" object, and through the object discovers himself. We know that the child studies the facial expressions of the mother, perceiving even the slightest change of mood, in order to prevent undesired effects of mater-

142

nal malaise, which would produce deep anxiety in him. Each child—and in particular the children of depressed, anxious, insecure mothers—thus structures a particular receptivity that is extremely sensitive to every maternal sign, and in particular to her look. These apprehensions are registered and utilized to foresee if what appears will be a mother who is a source of anxiety or not. The mother's glance can thus function as a mirror, furnishing the child with the reflection of his gestures and his still-premature experiences, presenting to him the world in a more comprehensible form. D. Winnicott would illustrate the specular mother-child condition as follows: "When I look, I am seen; therefore I exist" (Winnicott 1971, 134).

The theme of the look, of the power it emanates and the anxiety it can produce—central in phenomenological thought in the 1950s, from Merleau-Ponty to Sartre—was investigated also by psychoanalysis, in particular by Jacques Lacan (1975), who initially followed the direction taken by Freud. While Freud associates the "scopic drive" with psychopathological problems such as fetishism, voyeurism, or exhibitionism, Lacan recedes in his analysis to the point of identifying looking as the primary function (principally in the form of being *looked at*) in the constitution of the subject and in the structuring of desire. And it is in relationship to desire that the look is connected to the feeling of deep anxiety: the appearance of a look produces a troubling sensation, previously intuited by Freud. Lacan continues, eventually developing the theme that Freud left unfinished, stating that being observed by the other renders the individual an object, but a particular object as he is aware of being seen. I see that the other looks at me and the other, to whose look I am subject, in turn knows that I see him. Therefore, the look of the other specifies a particular way of my being here: My *being* depends on a desire, an expectation, a judgment. What is more, the look delimits a field and a distance. It is through this distance that the subject perceives himself as being separate from the object, and therefore the value of the desire emerges, to which full satisfaction is denied. We can desire only beginning with the distance from the object, or once more only in that we are subjects lacking something, and for this reason "inclined to alienation," to being captured by the desire of the other, on whose look depends the structuring of the image of the subject. The Lacanian formulation taken up once more by A. Green in *Narcissisme de vie, narcissisme de morte* should consequently be comprehensible. According to it, desire is:

> The movement by means of which the subject is decentralized— that is, the search for the object of satisfaction, the object of the lack, activates in the subject the sensation that his own center is no longer within himself, but outside in an object from which he is separated, with which he attempts to reunite in order to reconstitute by means of the recovered unity-identity, in the well-being that follows the experience of gratification—his center. (Green 1980, 26)

The power of the look in the seductive game becomes even more radical. The look that subjugates me and that, paradoxically, at the very point at which it renders me object, confirms my existence as a subject, can occur or not occur, independent of my will. Love is an event that cannot be controlled. It is incredible that so important a phenomenon, upon which the very existence of man is based, is apparently so fortuitous, so left to chance, the imponderable. Freed of the bonds of the consciousness, the magic moment of the appearance of the other who seduces me is and is not, at pleasure.

As adults, the love object changes, but not the way in which it seduces. There are crossed glances, the happiness caused because one has been looked at, the wound that the absence of the glance of the loved one inflicts. "Ceasing to be loved," wrote Marguerite Yourcenar, "means becoming invisible" (1957, 93). Thus we are enlightened as to the essential value of the amorous attention and glance of the other, the absence of which threatens our very identity. As adults, we look to orient ourselves in relation to those around us, to decipher them. But there is a more obscure, more troubling dimension to the fascination of the glance, on which some light must be shed if we are to reveal the essential ambivalence of every erotic movement, every opening toward the other. In the seductive game, not only can the look confer or deny the substance of the other, but it can also deceive, cheat, kill.

The look of the seducer can in fact be a predator's look. If we consider the close relationship between seduction and envy, it is extremely probable that in the seducer there is, albeit unconscious, the desire to annex, appropriate, or "phagocytize" the qualities of the other, along with an equally unconscious destructive intent, identical to that aroused by envy.

If we analyze the various semantic aspects of the Greek word *baskàino* (I seduce), we find a considerable amount of negative meaning, because besides meaning "I fascinate," "I enchant," and so on, it also has connections with envy and casting spells. It might be useful, in this sense, to make a comparison with Neapolitan writers concerned with the powers implicit in the look and spells—in other words, the evil eye. The most prominent among these was Nicola Valletta, author of a text published in 1787, *Ciclata sul frascino volgarmente detto jettatura*. The book opens with a citation from the *Georgics* of Virgil (I.2.490): *felix qui potuit rerum cognoscere causas,* a citation that returns in the title of the first section of the book: "The fact that a man fails to comprehend the evil-eye does not necessarily mean that it is not true" (Valletta 1787, 46). It is interesting to note how in the second section of the book, Valletta removes fascination and the evil eye from the realm of the devil, defining it as a "natural, bad influence." In the fourth section, the author approaches the etymological aspect. His first statement relates directly to our discourse on seduction (and in particular on the seduction of the eyes). Valletta states that the word *jettatura* (evil-eye) "derives from *gettare* (to cast) attentive, and immobile, eyes on someone" (ibid., 51). In Tuscany, for example, there is the use of the terms *affascinamento* (enchantment), *mal d'occhio* (ailment of the eyes), and *gettare incantamenti* (cast spells). Valletta also provides the interesting derivation of the Latin term *fascinum* from *fando* (that is, the verb *dire,* to say), as proof of the sensory, perceptible pervasiveness of seduction, which is not limited to sight but avails itself also of speech and, as we will see, other sensory means. As to vision, Valletta brings the etymological discourse around to envy, beginning with the Greek verb *baskàino,* which, he observes, "is pronounced almost *phàesi kàino,* that is *oculis, aspectu occido.* Thus, *baskàino* means to envy (ibid., 53). Virtually, it means a look to kill, as well as drawing the other inside oneself with the eyes, as though there were some subtle, in-

145

visible connection between envy and seduction. We could say that envying—or, better still, the existential condition of he who envies—corresponds to one who is inexorably seduced. It is at this point that Valletta ties the discourse of fascination or charm to fantasy, stating that "the spell of fantasy acquired great force" (ibid., 101), thus establishing the strong relationship between seduction and fantasy. Fantasies unite seducer and seduced, as for each of them the loved object is the possessor of qualities he previously did not possess. One may think, "If I could just touch her face," or "If I could just exist near her," thus intimating that the simple concession of physical proximity was enough to improve the quality of existence or confer well-being. How could we forget the Biblical "woman having an issue of blood," certain that simply touching the mantle of Christ would mean being healed? What does all this imply? It implies the activating power of a form that we see and that sees us, the initially visual constellation of seduction. Before being able to speak, we see and are seen: before being able to speak, we are carried by other eyes to a place that is not ours, or not yet ours. It is precisely this—our being forever "elsewhere" in relation to the look of the other, to our object of desire—that makes of the captive glance the most powerful form of seduction. And its force lies in the fact that it operates in silence, initially with imperceptible signals, energizing and activating unconscious contents. The look enlivens the drive, and is the first threshold that, once crossed, renders seduction almost certain. Of course, the theme of the seductive capacity of the eyes brings us closer to Romanticism and its dream-need of a mirroring that is also a promise of fusion, a sliding toward an undifferentiated union, being swept toward the irrational. The passion of love also includes this. In fact, it has always been considered a form of possession, the response to which is control by reason, the virtue of wisdom:

> We should recognize that the terror experienced when faced with the absurd, the fear of the Dionysian powers of the love passion, are understandable. Is there anyone so cold-blooded as to claim never to have experienced these feelings? Love, to which we owe our very lives, can also lead us to certain death . . . that very impulse which determines life and creation can also tend towards

destruction. Thus, the languid gratification of sentimentalism, the insipid sweetness of romance, often mask a latent violence. (David 1971, 180–181)

The appearance of the other who captures our desire inspires fear, as we rightly intuit that the difficult road of the love circumscribing the limits of our illusory freedom will give us the exact measure of the suffering that that love itself generates, in order to provide a space for the soul and initiate us to psychic reality. The experience of seduction and the reality of the encounter, eroticism, solitude and separation, are phases in a process involving a loss of subjectivity and the rediscovery of renewed identity. The lover completes all the initiatory steps to psychological transformation, and for this reason many find it difficult, if not impossible, to surrender to the seductive game of the other. In the erotic experience

> . . . the aim is not the pleasure of the ego, but its dissolution, in order to create that opening through which the other part of ourselves can make its troubling entrance with the strong tones of life and death for that which we were and which, after every act of love, we are no longer. Either one experiences this vertigo or the game remains superficial, without substance or depth . . . There has been no knowledge . . . because the first nexus, that which links death with rebirth, has never been created for the sake of caution, in order to avoid losing the abodes of the ego. (Galimberti 1989, 208)

Paradoxically, protecting oneself from the pangs of love is translated into a more serious suffering, because it leads to nonsense, negating us access to our most profound reality, which, although troubling, is also potentially transforming. Every transformation originates in the spheres of loss. Examples are the separation from images that have become obsolete, the transformation of libidinal ties with our internal objects, and connections that change and impose on us a different elaboration of our affects and our way of relating to the world. Inscribed in this radical passage is the possibility of an interior renewal that, in the wake of a continuous peregrination of desire, provides us with an intimate knowledge that is more profound and transparent, as well as the awareness that we are basically ambivalent.

Let us return to those aspects related to the senses to which our desire remains bound. For example, consider the allure of hair; the charm of "golden locks" or "beautiful raven tresses." The strength or virtue of a person has often been symbolized by the hair: one very familiar example of this is the Biblical tale of Samson. Lovers in a certain genre of romantic literature will often present a lock of their own hair as a gift to their beloved, and in many fables, the hero frees the fair prisoner by scaling her tower-prison with the aid of her long braid. The practice of cutting one's hair and giving it away has always been seen as the token of a deep bond and, as we know, in many ancient cultures the hair represents one of the magic symbols of appropriation and identification. Often, cutting the hair of kings and priests is taboo. It is in the hair that vital force lies, and vital force implies the notion of soul and destiny. Thus, the cutting of one's hair and giving it away signifies communicating to the other that, for the sake of our love for him, we willingly deprive ourselves of a part of our vital energy, abandoning ourselves trustingly where there is the danger of losing our souls. Also, being allowed to comb someone's hair is often considered a sign of love and trust. It is a gesture of intimate contact, which assumes the significance of rocking, falling asleep, and caressing, and we know that caressing the hair has a hypnotic effect, pleasantly erotic and relaxing. This would explain the presence of magic combs in many fables; for example, the golden comb of the lady of the flowers in Hans Christian Andersen's tale of the *Snow Queen*. The erotic and sensual importance attributed to hair resulted in the obligation of tonsure for Christian penitents, hermits, or anyone else wishing to practice temperance. In a similar way, women were forbidden to tint their hair and were later instructed to cover it in a dignified way. Anyone transgressing these rules could be denied access to religious functions, even refused burial "in consecrated ground."

Along with hair, other details and parts of the body of the other thus became evocative symbols, a powerfully subtle and mysterious, subliminal communication: coded messages, the meaning of which can be immediately understood, even without possessing the "key." Take, for example, the irresistible charm of hands, which Gustave Flaubert describes so masterfully in a memorable passage in *Madame Bovary* (1857). The scene is the meeting between Emma Bovary and her seducer, Rudolph, at a country fair. He approaches her and, taking her trembling hand in his:

> This gentle capture is only the first scene in Rudolph's well prac-
> ticed seduction scenario . . . His long experience allows him to
> calculate the extent and tolerance of Emma's impatience for his
> touch, and he decides that six weeks will be exactly the right
> emotional distance. (Kaplan 1991, 327)

The satisfaction that we experience in contemplating certain parts of the body or some insignificant detail of the desired object is linked to the erotic quality with which we confer them or, better still, to the fact that they become *symbols* of something other than what they "naturally" represent. Beyond fetishism, a far more subtle and pervasive symbolism is given to certain characteristics of our love objects, causing the hand, the foot, a certain glance, to become, during the period of fascination and falling in love, very powerfully erotic. We have specified "during the period of falling in love" because it is at that point where an attraction exists for the particular extirpated from the consideration of the subject possessing it and from the affective investment, or the tendency to isolate and concentrate all attention on that aspect exclusively to the detriment of an attention to the entire individual, that we enter the sphere of "perversion." That which is of interest to us here is the fact that in seduction the affective condition is the primary one for the symbol; one emotion provokes another in a chain reaction of subtle, unconscious associations of similarity or contiguity. We then say that where there is eros, a different style of perception follows, a different qualification of the object, admired not so much for what it really is but for a certain excessive significance, for a particular value it assumes in the eyes of the lover. And yet, this consideration subtracts nothing from the objectivity of the love experience, or its transforming potential. For the person who arouses desire is *that* person and no other. Eros causes a man to desire

149

not a woman, but *that* particular woman. It is only she, with her mysterious charm, with her special way of smiling, of withdrawing, of speaking or moving, who arouses a desire that is primarily a desire that elevates the other, that places her on a pedestal, idealizing her. Freud considered this aspect of love as one of the most disconcerting. He also considered that it is due to idealization—and according to Freud—to the fact that "the object is treated by the same standard as the Ego, thus causing a considerable quantity of narcissistic libido to flow onto the object. . . . The object is loved because of the perfection we observe for our Ego and which we then, indirectly, wish to procure to satisfy our own narcissism." (Freud 1914b, 445)

Through the process of idealization, the image of the other becomes the seductive image par excellence, possessing all beauty and perfection, and for this reason there would be, from the psychological point of view, no point in attempting to establish an objective concept of beauty:

> What seduces man is never natural beauty, but ritual beauty. Because this is esoteric and initiatory, while the other is merely expressive. Because seduction lies in the secret created by the levity of the signs of artifice, and not in a natural economy of sense, beauty or desire (Baudrillard 1979, 126).

What is beautiful is what seduces; we are seduced exclusively by what appears beautiful to our subjective perception, in our personal view. Erotic symbolism in fact can assume very particular forms; for example, idealizing certain imperfections in the loved one, which can become the essential attraction and principle erotic quality. Ellis Havelock, in *The Psychology of Sex* (1933), cites the attraction of a limp, strabismus, and certain particularities of the skin. The Persian poets offer a vast variety of images and metaphors glorifying the mole of a woman beloved. It is, however, absolutely normal that erotic symbolism be manifested as the need to idealize also the "ugliness" of the desired one. Stendhal calls *crystallization* this process in which certain qualities of the loved one present a roughness upon which the emotions of the lover can be deposited like crystals.

The special quality of the encounter leading to seduction is the fact that the other who appears on our horizon, with his particularities and his imperfections, corresponds exactly to our most secret desires. It is as though we were internally programmed to react to certain messages exclusively. The seduction encounter functions as does an imprinting, because it permits some potentiality to become expressed only in the presence of that particular aspect of the sensible experience that the person seducing us would appear to incarnate and possess in its most exact form. We have mentioned, in referring to the seduction of the bodily aspect or in a broader sense the entire person, that in normal love experiences that particular sign does not prevent the affect from investing the entire person. What is more, it actually becomes the most evident sign of the interest that that person as such arouses in us. The attractive aspects of the man or the woman desired form a complex, a harmonic whole, which creates the desire for complete possession. However, what occurs in the sphere of perversion is something quite different; for example, in fetishism attention for a particular becomes exclusive and the object is isolated from its context. In this case, the normal ways to sexual pleasure become inhibited, necessitating finding other more complex, sometimes morbid forms of the erotic symbols to substitute normal excitation. At this point, we are dealing with a "partial" object—a specific object, that and no other, which can be a part of the body, clothing, or an object belonging to the person desired. This object is seductive; that is, it is capable of exciting erotically and possesses an erotic symbolism. Obviously, these objects do not in the least possess an "objective" beauty. Nonetheless, they fascinate, in the etymological sense of the term; that is, they "bind with a magic operation," enchant—veritably exercise a form of witchcraft. According to Havelock (1906, 61), "all fetishism is by necessity morbid obsession . . . an obsession is a kind of fascination aroused by an object or by an idea which provokes a shock of sorts in the subject in contrast to his habitual ways of acting or his ideas."

Seducer and seduced are therefore united by an intense imaginative activity as regards the desired object. The other, who appears before us, triggers off a deep imaginative process, a contact with the troubling images of desire. It is through this present/absent interlocutor that one's own phantasms emerge, that invisible web of unconscious affects by means of which are defined enjoyment, anxiety, illness. We are all constantly subjects and objects of seduction: we conquer and are conquered. In the game of seduction, the responsibility is reciprocal; it is a circular situation in which there exists neither "guilt" nor "innocence." Consider the game of seduction as an evil form of sorcery to which we fall victim—unquestionably a way of avoiding responsibility, but equally tendentious.

As we have said, seducing means above all *permanently invading/colonizing the imagination of the other.* An illustration of this is the frequent use of the verb "to conquer." Seduction is one of the forms of manifestation of that which Nietzsche (1888, XXIII) defined "the war and mortal hatred between the sexes." The other must be conquered. Having made himself the instrument for evoking our internal images, he becomes precious and absolutely necessary to us; losing him would be equivalent to losing ourselves. Therefore, it is necessary to subjugate him, conquer him, prevent him from escaping. He is the bearer of an unexpressed image, of that other person who we also are but can never attain to completely (Jung 1940–50, 128). And the force of "possession" in love resides in the fact that the other is invested with a numinous quality that transcends reality, because it is the numinous quality of the encounter with representations of our own complexes. In the search for a union that would make possible realizing that mythical androgyny, synonymous with completeness, that harmonic re-conjunction of the separate parts—which remains the ideal aspiration of the consciousness— the power of seduction lies in the promise that the other by his mere appearance would appear to incarnate, but that continually frustrates, because the other is forever unyielding, forever "elsewhere." And herein lies the mystery of otherness:

> The way of feminine existence consists of hiding, and this quality is in fact modesty, discretion . . . a way of being which is a withdrawing from the light. The transcendent quality of femininity consists in finding oneself elsewhere, a movement in a direction opposite to consciousness. But it is not for this reason unconscious or subconscious, and I see no other possibility than that of defining it mystery. (Levinas 1949, 56–57).

Ten

Proposals from the Misty North

In love, torture or during an operation, one of the two involved must inevitably be the torturer or the surgeon.
—F. Nietzsche, *Frammenti postumi 1887–1888*

What exactly are the characteristics of the seducer? Before setting out in search of a possible definition for this personality, it might be wise to make the following premise: there is a marked homology, a consonance if you will, between seduction and being swept away, seized as it were by the seductive image of the other. Making a distinction between seducer and seduced implies isolating and separating aspects that are essentially inseparable, given that we are seducers to the extent that we have been marked, disturbed, or disoriented by an object that seduces—and therefore seduced from the outset. Being seduced, on the other hand, also implies an active role, that of reconstructing an image of the other on the basis of a personal elaboration and an interpretation of characteristics the other apparently possesses.

The troubling force of the desired object depends to a large extent on the desiring subject and the personal contribution of that subject to the construction of the figure of the seducer. Consider, for example, that a person can exert a fascination in spite of one's self—that is, unaware of or without realizing the entity of emotions he arouses. In fact, a certain type of seducer can, unknowingly, appeal to a sensitivity and a propensity the result of which is that he incarnates the Animus projections of certain women. Thus, Jung spoke of women-Anima, referring to a certain type of psychic attraction exerted by female figures who are effective bearers of the projections of the Anima of men who prefer to comply with the desire of the other. They gradually incarnate the image of the eternal female deposited in the male unconscious, rather than discover and gamble on their true identity.

In consideration of the possible responses to our initial query—that is, whether in fact there exists a typology of the seducer—we have decided to proceed from the reflections of Kierkegaard on the theme of seduction, its nature, and the players involved. The interest demonstrated by Kierkegaard—who, incidentally, provided one of the first unconventional interpretations of the figure of Don Juan—in the phenomenon of seduction most certainly derived from personal experience, which he then described in *Diary of a Seducer* (Cantoni 1990). The date of that work, included in the first part of *Enten-Eller,* was 1843, which was approximately two years after he broke his engagement with Regine Olsen. The beauty and intensity of that love experience appeared to him so overwhelming that he chose to end it, thus freeing himself to follow another road, dedicating himself to a philosophical and spiritual quest.

The love story of Kierkegaard and Regine lasted from September 1840 to October 11, 1841, when he broke the engagement apparently without any particular reason, sending back to Regine a ring accompanied by a note in which he asks her to forgive him for not being capable of making her happy. He had realized that his love for Regine was too intense, and as such—by his own admission—would have involved him totally. Thus, it was that intensity which decreed its end. He had inevitably to move away from an experience so committing as to constitute an unbearable weight. And he would subsequently submit that experience to a different elaboration through his writing and philosophical contemplation, consigning to meditation and ethical reflection the torments of his soul. However, a general aversion for a "bourgeois" institution or the fear of being suffocated in the not exactly stimulating role of husband are not sufficient to explain his flight. This is all the more so because, in the desperate attempt to free himself of this bond, he went so far as humiliating himself by making himself despicable and petty in the eyes of Regine. In fact, it was after Regine's violent reaction to his philosophical attempt to destroy the relationship that he decided, as a last resort, to play the part of an abject being, in order to exasperate her and convince her to abandon him. His efforts would succeed, and the inevitable result caused scandal in the middle-class milieu of Copenhagen. Kierkegaard consequently fell into a state of absolute prostration.

Kierkegaard's depression, which would keep him in a perpetual state of sadness, lasted up until his death. He was constantly tormented by the fear of going mad, obsessed by the idea of suicide, and prone to atrocious attacks of anxiety. A vein of black humor led him to compare his life to a "long night." He was convinced that he was utterly incapable of maintaining harmoniously a couple relationship. That malaise could be related to a certain episode in Kierkegaard's life: his father, paralyzed by a constant fear of divine retribution, one day confessed to his son his sin of sacrilege. In a moment of madness, he had cursed God, blaspheming against the Holy Ghost. He had imprecated against God in rebellion and anger in the face of a difficult, even hopeless situation. This sin was aggravated by his sense of guilt at having lived together with his female servant after the death of his wife, and he was thus tormented by thought of divine punishment. His confession convinced the philosopher that his father's life had been cursed. And the resulting trauma caused him, in the autumn of 1835, to fall into a very serious state of depression.

He explains the reasons for having broken his engagement with Regine in *Colpevole O non Colpevole? Un Martirologio, Esperienza Psicologica di Frater Taciturnus*. This text is considered by the author as the best of his works, albeit of difficult comprehension. In it, Kierkegaard poses certain questions: for example, whether or not a soldier of God should marry; he should not if he must measure himself constantly against the attacks of an innate melancholy (dating from the time his father revealed to him his revolt against God and his blasphemy). He had been determined that the family curse, which weighed so heavily on him, would not touch or involve Regine. Therefore, there was no other choice but to sacrifice himself—he felt he was a leper and as such could not marry. In this work, there also emerges the profound difference between the joyful and sensual, concrete and ordinary involvement of Regine and Kierkegaard's attitude toward existence. He had believed that associating with so charming and joyous a young woman would heal him, but he soon enough realized his own extraneousness to the girl's infantile joy. Thus, his proximity to her could only result in her unhappiness.

At the root of these reflections there is a very deep sense of guilt, which he represents as an uninterrupted dialogue and a continuous confrontation with the phantasms of melancholy. As we know, *melancholy* is one of the aspects of depression; it is a form of continuous brooding over the fate of one's "lost objects" and one's own guilt in connection with their disappearance. In this work, Kierkegaard ultimately absolves himself of any guilt: the gesture of marrying Regine would have been beyond his forces and would also have ruined her life. Thus came the decision to break off the relationship with the person he loved in order to protect her, to prevent her from being contaminated by his "curse." He could then dedicate himself to spiritual matters, sacrifice his "human, too human" love, in the attempt to expiate the guilt of his father and the *karma* of the circular curse. But like any sacrifice that in reality conceals a castration, a self-inflicted punishment, the solution was not liberating.

Jung stated in reference to this love experience and its particular development that Kierkegaard in reality was incapable of accepting that which the encounter with Regine implied: the encounter with the divine, the numinous. Certainly, this love itinerary *sui generis,* which results in an inhibition of the love drive itself and in renunciation, has something in common with a certain ethic of medieval heroism, the impossible love of the troubadours for the beautiful *dame blanche,* as well as the melancholic, saturnine love of many poets, philosophers, and artists. It is difficult to separate the morbid aspects, related to the negation of desire, from a positive form of sacrifice of certain functions of the ego at the service of a higher level of development—we might say at the service of the self. In fact, certain forms of aestheticism—renunciation of material wealth and sensual enjoyment, sacrifice in the interests of superior ends—often conceal complexes or loyalty to an archaic internal object which in a way imposes absolute love through a symbiotic and totalitarian form of existence. Jung, apropos of the alchemist Opus—that initiatory itinerary which, beyond the complex symbolism of the search for the philosopher's stone, represents the road to individuation—affirms that the process of development of the personality in its totality presupposes a practically complete realization of all the psychic functions:

> Incomplete realization explains much that is puzzling both in the individual and in the contemporary scene. It is a crucial matter for the psychotherapist, particularly for those who still believe that intellectual insight and routine understanding, or even mere recollection, are enough to affect a cure. The alchemists thought that the Opus demanded not only laboratory work, but reading of books, meditation and patience, but also love. (Jung 1946, 283)

According to Jung, it is a question of a self-realization achieved through sentimental vicissitudes, and he stresses the transforming and cognitive possibilities offered by the authentic love experience—virtually a "discovery of a new world." It is impossible to conceive of personal realization in terms of a hypertrophic development of a single function, given that wholeness consists of the harmonious unfolding of all the potential of human nature. The unilateral is unnatural:

> The story of Faust shows how unnatural our condition is: it required the intervention of the devil . . . to transform the aging alchemist into a young gallant and make him forget himself for the sake of the all-too-youthful feelings he had just discovered! (ibid., 280–281).

Consequently, Eros is so demoniacal and overwhelming, and given the compensatory dynamics of psychic activity, that the subject ends up identifying with his own rational part. "That which is lacking in one area, determines an excess in the other" (ibid., 164). All unconscious psychic content becomes dangerous in proportion to the degree to which it is repressed. It therefore acquires a coercive, compulsive character that carries off, seizes, and submerges. Thus is the love rapture that creates the constellation of repressed psychic contents and becomes the principle means for entering into contact with internal images, the images of desire.

In his *Diary of a Seducer,* "which tells the tale of a diabolically cunning seducer . . . who, availing himself of every artifice, causes confusion and excess in an innocent eighteen-year old girl" (Cantoni 1990, V), Kierkegaard dissertates on the nature of seduction, postulating the existence of three phases of personal development: aesthetic, ethical, and spiritual. The seducer stops at the first stage, being incapable of passing to the ethical phase, in which man reveals himself. The aesthete, in fact, is an individual who absolutely refuses to reveal himself and who, in his remaining constantly concealed, neither confers nor desires to confer value to reality. The price of this game of hide-and-seek with the world is, according to Kierkegaard, that of becoming an enigma to oneself.

Although the ultimate scope of aesthetic love is always pleasure, the methods of seduction and its actors differ. Kierkegaard makes a distinction between two types of seducer: the sensual seducer and the intellectual seducer. The first type, to which Don Juan obviously belongs, moves within the "innocent" sphere of the world of nature, with the simple force of instinct and the vitality and spontaneity of a primitive, naive sensuality. He seeks pleasure in a direct, immediate manner, and the peak of his pleasure consists in his possessing the desired object—at which point the object loses significance and the seducer abandons the game to direct his passionate attentions elsewhere. Dominant in this attitude is a desire that, as it transcends the object, is insatiable. Certainly, one characteristic of the game of this type of seducer is inconstancy and fickleness—despite this, however, it is an extremely exciting and challenging one. The sensual seducer's method of fleeing from the relationship, together with the admirable *mise-en-scène* with which he seduces and succeeds in being forgiven his continual absences, flights and promises never kept, and his never being entirely present in the relationship, would appear to constitute an irresistible attraction for a certain type of woman (or man, if the situation involves a seductress). Kierkegaard in a very subtle way points out that for this type of lover *a* woman does not exist, only *women.* He in fact does not relate to the other as a particular being loved for herself, for her unique nature and history, but appears rather to pursue femininity itself, the *idea* of woman.

Obviously, this is an emotional field diametrically opposed to the experience of falling in love, in which desire is directed with absolute determination to a unique, irreplaceable individual. In the seductive experience described by Kierkegaard, any woman can be substituted for another, every loved one being merely an occasion for mirroring—and this is one of the more painful aspects with which the prey of a similar suitor must contend. While the reflective seducer is of a contemplative nature, one to whom "possessing a woman is less important than enjoying her aesthetically" (Cantoni 1976, 16), for the sensual seducer, the immediate quality of desire requires an immediate discharge of a drive, and his search for an amorous correspondence is connected not to the particular quality of the object but to her exploitation. Don Juan is not seduced by the qualities of the loved one, but only because they arouse his desire. He is seduced by the fact itself of desire.

The sensual seducer therefore enjoys the moment, the pleasure of the moment. But what is it that seduces in a similar attitude? What is the attraction, what does it give to the individual who is subjugated? Girls and women seduced by Don Juan are regularly abandoned, and it is easy to imagine how the already acute suffering is increased by the sensation of uselessness and devaluation created by the realization of never having really been loved. The passion of love that elevates lovers to the level of mythical creatures and which, paradoxically—while it annuls them in the ecstasy of fusion—renders them unique and irreplaceable for each other, is here replaced by another type of passion, which we could call "orgiastic." Our seducer does not seek the absolute in sentimental uniqueness, but in the plurality of the occasion and the forms that are offered him. He does not attempt to "nominate" the other as much as sweep him into uncertainty, into Dionysian exaltation.

Profound erotic experience, however, also implies a real encounter, a secret alchemy of desires, a reciprocity that can also be bound exclusively to the sphere of unconscious communication, but in any case presupposes the appearance, on the love scene, of one's own unconscious phantasms. Defining an encounter as a "love" encounter usually implies a particular experience that goes beyond mere satisfaction of a drive. Knowing how to love, being capable of abandoning oneself to the experience of love, is the result of a long and complex transformation of infantile impulses and the most elementary drive requests. The attachment to a libidinal object with a direct and immediate satisfaction in view is no more than desire reduced to its most elementary nature. Freud is very clear on this point: there can be no sentiment or any form of what we call love without the manifestation of our drives, of our instinct for satisfaction.

However, if we remain on the level of pure drives, if the drive were not even partially restrained and diverted from its primary ends, that cultural form of reciprocity we call love could not exist. In "Contributions to the psychology of love," Freud points out the importance of the frustration of the drive (a frustration that from the structural point of view is associated with the original phantasms and the Oedipus complex) for a mature organization of the sexual and love life: "The physical importance of an instinct rises in proportion to its frustration" (Freud 1910–17, 429). Thus did he associate the birth of desire (which is different from the simple need to discharge drives) with the progressive ability of the individual to tolerate frustration, the absence of the love object: we become capable of loving only at the point at which we sacrifice the overriding request to satisfy a need. Love therefore carries the sign of a first sacrifice, an inhibition of the drive as regards its aims. Repression would in this sense be, according to Freud, a mechanism adopted by the ego for the purpose of favoring the renunciation of perverse and autoerotic infantile satisfaction, and the passage to a mature object investment, under the genital primacy of the "procreative function." This necessary frustration makes possible a transformation of the request for love itself, which is enriched by a fantastic—in other words, truly psychic—component. Thus there is the passage from an elementary drive request to a far more complex elaboration of a desire that implies the recognition of the autonomy of the other and, consequently, the recognition of one's own individuality and autonomy.

This transformation occurs under the sign of suffering—given that every elaboration of a separation, like every sacrifice of requests that cannot fail to appear legitimate to us, implies a *mourning*. Not everyone succeeds in tolerating this passage—

and here we have the particular form of narcissistic pathology, for example, in which the seductive pattern of behavior, the compulsive search for the throw-away partner, the possibility of living the relationship only for that brief period of falling in love, of the state of fusion and mutual idealization that reveal a fragile ego that fears being faced with frustration. The behavior of one who "seduces and abandons" is a defense mechanism to prove to oneself that the love object is not indispensable since it is absolutely interchangeable. The point is to abandon the game first, in order to avoid being abandoned, and therefore avoid the experience of a separation and mourning considered unbearable. This type of fragile ego is often the ego of the instrumental seducer we described previously. We will see further on how many psychoanalytical interpretations have been followed in the wake of the invention of Don Juan, how many dissertations on the psychology, personality, pathology, and myth of this personage. But let us leave aside for the moment psychopathological interpretation and instead consider the Dionysian element—that simple, instinctive inebriation that the sensual seducer seeks and apparently creates in the woman seduced.

This impulse results in going beyond all limits, eliminating all confines, where figures become confused and indistinct and are lost and practically canceled, and the division between subject and object disappears as though a lost original unity had been restored. The Dionysian experience inserts man in the perennial dynamism of nature, in the multiform chaos of the natural elements, in their endless transmutation of form. Lovers are lost in a flow of sensations, in a game without rules: the opposite of Apollonian equilibrium and order. It is an experience that upsets that rational organization of existence in which everything has a precise productive and economic function, in which everything can be pondered, measured, calculated, and contained. "However, counting and measuring are equivalent to negating. And failing to provide the necessary space to the forces of pleasure results in exposure to the ferocious return of repression" (Maffesoli 1988, 53). An exorbitant price is exacted by the regime of civilization, and Eros can function as a compensatory and re-equilibrating element. When Dionysus appears, it is the logic of playing, of the free movement, of the expenditure of energy, which sets the rules. It is often a tragic game because, as Apollonian order does not recognize the necessity of disorder, there will inevitably be the emergence of the perverse and exacerbated violence of repression. Of this, modern man would appear to have lost memory, this once-familiar ancient wisdom that admitted the presence of the "shadow" forces, approaching and controlling them through ritual. This, in fact, was the function of the Dionysian feasts during which the Greeks were permitted to liberate instinct and passion. Dionysus played with bodies, as did Don Juan. Dionysus was an ineffable, inexpressible god: the child of changing forms—male and female, god and animal, man and plant, a god at whose passage nature explodes in its full exuberance; a divinity of metamorphosis, described by Euripides in his *Baccante* as a stranger to female form, at whose passage through the city women fall ill and disorder reigns in the nuptial chambers. The Dionysian eruption unveils other forms of existence and other rhythms of time than those dictated by the logic of productivity and profit: an erotic time, a contact of bodies for the pure pleasure of that contact, a pleasant "waste" of energy. Freud's term, "polymorph perversion," is an apt one to describe the concept of waste, of an aimless playacting. There is an investment in and exploration of the body in all its erotic potential; it is the search for and abandonment to pleasure for its own sake. This is not pleasure at the service of reproduction, but the practice of a free sexuality, tinged with transgression if only for the fact that it goes against the imperatives of institutionalized relationships of sex and love.

> We might recall here how in the preliminaries to the sexual act, all the parts of the body come into play. Daily practice and the various erotic writings are proof of this. The sexual act is made up of a variety of corporeal stimulation which not surprisingly brings to mind the game of polymorph perversion, which is neither productive nor genital. The art of seduction is, in this sense, similar, as it invests the object of desire from many aspects, without completing any of the assaults. (Maffesoli 1988, 56)

The sensual seducer transgresses against the logic of civilizing the body, against subjecting pleasure to the order of reproduction—and his art of seduction, in its accusatory and destabilizing aspect, ends up being included in the list of deviations.

Dionysian rapture restores to Eros a collective and transpersonal matrix. The orgy annuls subjectivity: the Dionysian feast reunifies in a single body the participants in passion, to remind us that pleasure and voluptuousness are essentially "divine" and collective. In the light of psychoanalytical research—and we will see further on the types and number of interpretations psychoanalysis has provided for the figure of Don Juan—the sensual seducer appears to us as a typical expression of instinctive action: a brother of Pan, an adept of Dionysus. We know that instinctive behavior at its extreme is compulsive and archaic behavior. Compulsion is its fundamental characteristic, that typically instinctive attitude of "all or nothing." James Hillman, in *An Essay on Pan* (1972a), analyzes the behavior attributed to this Greek mythical figure. Pan represents the exaltation of compulsion and the panic it generates, rape as a form of conjunction and satisfying need, and nightmare. The blind impulsiveness of the seducer toward the object of desire, together with the desperate flight of the being attempting to escape that seduction, are images that belong to the mythic scene of Pan: the satyr in pursuit of nymphs. Apparently characterizing the comportment of this type of seducer is the absence of reflective consciousness. Through the flight of the nymph (which is also "taking distance"), Pan seeks the possibility of reflection, which by means of continuous retreating he transforms into his own instrument (Hillman 1972a, 108). At the same time, it is also true that our seducer—from the sublime Don Juan of literary and theatrical tradition to his modern imitators—chooses with care, albeit at times unknowingly, his victims: young or "mature," it matters little; what is important is that any "maturity" is exclusively physical. Contrary to the common belief that the seducer is utterly without discrimination, his prey must in fact always possess one fundamental characteristic—that psychological vulnerability born of insecurity and low self-esteem or, in other words, someone who has not yet come to terms with her deepest femininity. He therefore seeks the encounter exclusively in the interests of conquest: his seduction is not a prelude to love and recognition of the other, but is aimed at his own satisfaction.

163

But, one might ask, is this seduction? Is the seducer really seductive? Jean Baudrillard, making a distinction between seduction and provocation, wrote:

> Think of provocation, which is the contrary and a caricature of seduction. It says: "I know that you want to be seduced, and I will seduce you . . ." There is nothing worse than betraying this secret rule. Nothing less seductive than a provocative smile or behavior, given that they imply that it is impossible to be seduced naturally, and that blackmail or a declaration of intent is necessary: "Let me seduce you . . ." (Baudrillard 1987, 39)

Eleven

By the Hand of a Statue

It is ridiculous to seek comfort in the company of our fellow creatures; as miserable and impotent as we are, they can give us no respite: each one of us must die alone.

—B. Pascal, *Pensèes*

What is the origin of the myth of Don Juan? It is impossible to say with precision: myths have nothing to do with documentation, chronology, or registries. Even the nationality of the personage is uncertain. Various countries have been proposed in this context: Portugal, Spain, Italy, Germany. And as to the period during which this mythical character first saw the light of day, it might be the Middle Ages, as Kierkegaard sustains; the theatrical representations of the Jesuits (more intimidating than edifying; the ungodly punished, the atheist struck down by lightning); or some sixteenth-century *canovaccio* of the *Commedia dell'Arte*, the *Grand Siècle*, or the *Siglo de Oro* of Calderon de la Barca and Tirso de Molina. However, what is certain is the longevity of this "masque," the continuing interest in the personage and his adventures, which is truly surprising. In fact, the bibliography of Arman E. Singer for the University of West Virginia includes 4,303 entries on the theme of Don Juan, covering a range including music, literary criticism, painting, theatre, and cinema. This endless proliferation of variations illustrates that Don Juan rapidly became independent of the original text; beyond the various plots and constructions of the personage, Don Juan would appear to have had an autonomous existence, as he "passed from one work to another, and from author to author, as though he belonged to everyone and no one" (Rousset 1978, 6).

This is one of the characteristics of the myth, an anonymity of sorts, which has permitted the continual transformation of its nucleus in the wake of the *esprit du temps* and the fantasies of the collective consciousness. What are the elements of attraction that would account for the survival of this personage over the centuries? Why, we might ask, are we seduced by the myth of the great seducer? A response to that question would necessitate a deep analysis of the variables and constants of the myth. It is obvious that we are here confronted with an *imago* that is disturbing to the point of investing the collective imaginary. The fantasy of artists and the popular imagination have appropriated the particular traits, in this masque, of a character and a destiny, and have made of it a figure charged with human truth far more representative than had he been a real person. Like other *personages* that, although assuming the semblance of a particular individual, have become symbols of a universal characteristic (Othello, Madame Bovary), Don Juan has become a part of the history of usage, of comportment. Not only does he incarnate an individuality, but a particular sensitivity as well: a particular "illness" or *forma mentis,* a possession, something that although formed by the tragic characteristics that have conferred the personage with the mythic quality of heroes, nevertheless touches and stimulates our desires. We could then speak of a Don Juan syndrome, a sexual promiscuity–fed form of *seduction compulsion* to collect conquests. But, if we are to understand the psychology of Don Juan, it might be well to first examine more closely the history of that character.

The opera of Tirso de Molina published in 1630, *El Burlador de Sevilla y Convidado de piedra,* could in a sense be considered the first, official manifestation of the legend of Don Juan. The plot of that work is briefly the following: in the opening scene, there is a daring seduction—Don Juan Tenorio furtively enters the royal palace of Naples and seduces the Duchess Isabella—who is betrothed to Duke Ottavio—disguised as her noble fiancé. Unmasked, Don Juan flees with the help of his ambassador uncle and embarks for Spain. The ship on which he travels is sunk in a storm and Don Juan, rescued by his faithful servant Catilinon, seduces the woman who offers them refuge, the beautiful Tisbea, deceiving her with a false promise of matrimony. Despite the admonitions of the devoted Catilinon, Don Juan flees to Seville, where he is to wed the beautiful Donna Anna, daughter of Don Gonzalo de Ulloa. However, the news of his scandalous behavior has reached the king, who orders the libertine to make reparation for the affront to the Duchess Isabella, by marrying the other woman. Donna Anna does not particularly mind, as she is secretly in love with the Marquis de la Mota, with whom she plans a rendezvous. However, it is Don Juan who predictably keeps the appointment and, substituting the other through a ruse, enters the woman's rooms. Donna Anna is not fooled. Hearing her screams, her father Don Gonzalo rushes to her aid and is killed by Don Juan, who once more flees. In the village in which Don Juan takes refuge, he meets and seduces a young married woman. With deceit and false promises, he succeeds in expropriating the goods of her poor husband, calling on heaven to witness his innocent intentions: "might I die by the hand of a dead man . . ." begins his scornful, ironic oath. Back in Seville, he sees the stone statue the king has had placed in honor of the defunct Don Gonzalo and recklessly proffers it an invitation to dinner. At this point the narrative tone changes: the realistic vein is replaced by an intense and troubling symbolism. The statue in fact arrives punctually for dinner and in turn invites Don Juan for the following evening in the chapel of the deceased Ulloa. Contemptuous of the risks and ever rash, Don Juan repeats his challenge to the dead man. The dinner scene is tragic and when Don Juan, after having proved his courage, is about to take his leave, the hand of the statue seizes him and flings him into hell.

The plot has undergone extensive revision and transformations over time. The individual sensitivity of each author and his vision of the world, obviously molded by the *esprit du temps,* have resulted in various readings of this myth, and Don Juan is alternatively presented as maniacal or depressed, hero or scoundrel. It is interesting to trace the psychological evolution of this personage that has attracted and stimulated the creative fantasy of so many, in the fields of literature, painting, music, and theatre (writers such as Molière, Goldoni, Hoffman, Byron, A.

Dumas, de Musset, Stendhal, the painter Delacroix, and composers, including Rimsky-Korsakov and, of course, Mozart).

Molière's *Don Juan ou Le festin de pierre* was presented in Paris in 1665. Molière drew his inspiration not from the original version but from a transposition of the *Commedia dell'Arte* (around the middle of the seventeenth century). Successively, Lorenzo da Ponte wrote a lighthearted drama in two acts, *Il dissoluto punito, ossia il Don Giovanni,* for the opera of Mozart, inspired by Pierre Corneille's verse adaption of Molière's play. And in 1655, there was Goldoni's *Don Giovanni o la punizione del dissoluto.* However, the myth's power of attraction was strongest above all for the Romantics, and it has extended in various versions and reinterpretations on up to the present.

In a reading of the Don Juan myth as it has been represented over the centuries, what strikes one immediately is the increasing complexity of the psychological structure of the personage. The characteristics that identify him, be they positive or negative, have changed over time, so that it would seem that it is a case not of *one* Don Juan but of many incarnations of the libertine. Thus might we trace this evolution.

The original character, in the *Burlador de Sevilla,* was therefore a "burlador," and what was emphasized above all was his burlesque, jovially adolescent qualities. The seduction of the first Don Juan is described as a taste for the jest, as an exhibitionist theatricality, an artful playfulness intended to amuse. The adventurous aspect, the taste for the exaggerated and the excessive, the love of daring, the passion for sensational disguises and the shock of the unexpected, are the key elements of the personality of this protagonist. Throughout that century, although with variations on the theme, Don Juan was depicted thus. The popular vein running through seventeenth-century *opere buffe* portrays him as a transgressor, an unrepentant hero, a libertine too weak to resist female charms, an easy prey to eros, comic in his impetuous, licentious passion. The actors of the *Commedia dell'Arte* presented him as a personage without scruples, but there—even at the most dramatically sanguinary moments—the public is provided with entertaining devices and jokes. The entertainment, jesting, the thousand tricks and disguises would be the dominating character of the seventeenth-century stage—*if* it

were not for the distinct impression that these histrionic qualities, combined with a certain artfulness, rapidity of action, and
above all the carnival atmosphere, were permeated by so tangi-
ble an uneasiness and so exasperated a vitality as to create the
suspicion that they served to attenuate some underlying contrast,
to disguise a fear, to distract attention. One is reminded of pagan
rituals, the feasts, dances, and hammering rhythms created to
neutralize negative forces. And if we think of the epoch during
which this characterization of Don Juan emerges, it is not difficult to conclude that it represents the vital and reactive response
to the *memento mori,* the admonition of annihilation and death
characteristic of that century—the idea of the vanity of appear-
ances and that the only truth was the final one, which contained
and canceled: death. As Rousset pointed out (1978, 17), at the
basis of the myth of Don Juan was deception (*Burlador*) and the
encounter with death (*el convidado de piedra*).

Don Juan is the incarnation of the protest against the cult of
death, a vital response, exalted and exalting, transgression
bordering on the ridiculous, fear, illness, ruin. His sensuality, his
obsession for Woman seen as a source of pleasure, would represent a response of sorts to the morality of the Counter-
Reformation. However, it is Death that triumphs in the end, in
the form of an animated statue that drags the irresolute protagonist down into Hell. This element—the relationship with death—
more than any other places Don Juan among the myths: in fact,
the story of Death that returns is taken from an ancient, popular
legend, familiar throughout the Christian Occident. Death that
returns, and what is more, assumes the truly alarming appearance of a statue come to life, is a theme belonging to the sphere
of the *inquietante étrangeté,* of the unsettling—or, if you will,
the return of the repressed. Therefore, there are two principle
themes presented by the original texts, around which rotates the
leitmotiv of the guilt of the protagonist: the reckless quest for
pleasure of an unscrupulous seducer, and the real, great sin: the
derision of death, the profanation of the sacred. It is not so
much that Don Juan arrogates himself the right to inflict death,
but that he challenges death in the form of the statue, which he
mocks with his invitation and by the hand of which he will be
definitively punished.

These are the two nuclei to be analyzed, if we are to understand in what way seduction can be a challenge to death. We have seen how seduction is paired with death, how love and death are companions, how letting ourselves be averted by the other also implies jeopardizing our own internal order, allowing a change of form and consequently permitting a part of us to die. We know also that the erotic movement, by calling up phantasms and evoking repressed images, reveals the basic ambivalence of sentiment—that painful interplay of impulse and renunciation, of oblation and sadism, of adoration and hatred, which characterizes the manifestations of eros. The object of desire, which can be idealized and idealizes, which transfigures us and can be observed as transfigured, is the bearer of a promise of infinite gratification and compensation—a promise that, because it cannot be maintained, leads to disappointment and suffering. The person we love most is always the one who has the power to wound us; the very fact of being the loved object confers that object with the power to deal us death. The paradox confronting the ego is the confrontation of psychic opposites that had always been kept separate by the consciousness and that passion reunifies. The other whom we love represents in fact both ecstasy and perdition and is the dispenser of all good and all evil. Since that person exists and we admit loving him, the fear of losing him, of seeing him disappear, is created. Loving would at times appear to be a kind of masochistic gratification in pain, at others a perverse confrontation of forces, a struggle to prove our own power to ourselves and the other. A part of us perceives itself to be so powerless and vulnerable as to be compelled to find refuge in an intentional, premeditated exercise of power. Thus, we discover ourselves to be at the same time blessed and damned, tender and cruel. And there is the confrontation with the Shadow, with the least known parts of ourselves—where anger, envy, fear, shame, and those desires that we ourselves find reprehensible and deserving of only condemnation are harbored.

The first Don Juan who emerges from seventeenth-century works is apparently a naive seducer, primitive and fairly rough. He lives with an impulsive, joyous, candid sensuality, which we might describe as infantile were it not for the fact that, unfortunately, infancy is not that magic and innocent realm adults love to imagine, nor is sexuality lacking its dose of ambivalence. In fact, in order to achieve his aims, that pleasure-seeking and shrewd sensuality leads Don Juan to perpetrate all sorts of iniquity and violence. In order to win the desired woman, Don Juan must furtively substitute for her man and must duel with and even kill the father of his betrothed. He commits these acts of licentiousness without the slightest hesitation, without the least consciousness of guilt, with an impudence and heedlessness in which the sense of guilt is so split that we are to led to think that it is precisely there, in a sense of guilt that is as annihilating as it is unconscious, that the secret *causa movens* of his actions lies. But we will take up this point further on.

No sphere of human existence is so dominated by ambivalence and contrasting forces of drives as the erotic sphere, because with the bodily expression of emotions and sentiments, it is impossible to cheat, falsify, mask, or resort to etiquette. The body speaks, in spite of us or our intentions. The body rejects convention, repudiates formalism, and above all cannot negate itself if it desires, just as it cannot offer itself if it hates. We can defraud with words, never with the body. We can *say* that we love the other, delude ourselves that it is true, make an enormous effort in order that love might resist the ravages of time. But our body will conspire against our intentions, given that its law is one rooted in the truth of instinct and the unconscious, which are realms impossible to dominate solely with the forces of the ego. Through our bodies, the silenced truth is expressed along with our intimate, generally concealed desire and our innermost fears. We could say, paraphrasing a famous expression, that "there is no commanding the body." It would be practically impossible to caress someone toward whom we feel hostile, impossible to concede the confidence of our bodies to a person toward whom we feel rancor.

Thus, despite ourselves, through our bodies, through our eroticism, we transmit emotions that do not emerge into the light of the consciousness—sensations, thoughts, impulses impossible to translate into words and that we would not confess even to ourselves, so wounding and fear-inspiring are they. The body, however, admits and expresses them, and we feel disoriented by that transparency, by that courageous assertion; we respond "no," "enough," or "I hate you" where habit and fear would have us say "yes," "I don't know," or "I still love you." Thus, the real meaning behind the expression "making love" could be "doing battle." The common observation that the causes of disturbances of a sexual nature are psychological expresses this simple and painful truth. Impotence and frigidity are the technical denominations used to express far more familiar terms: fear, shame, inhibition, sense of guilt. The compulsive, reckless search for physical contact and erotic encounters is indicative of a discomfort and an interior disharmony, since in order to enjoy the other, our body has a time and a rhythm that is fed not so much by experience as by our interior, deep responses, which not only are extremely individual and subjective but remain too often ignored by our consciousness. Our body does not *practice* sexuality, it *enjoys it;* and by enjoyment we do not mean performance, conquest, enumerating or challenge, but desire. This is a mysterious concept to us, given that we are never there where we would desire to be and we believe that we have achieved our gratification using others. Seduction itself has its limits, precisely because it does and does not provide for the full enjoyment of the loved object but always requires that the object "flickers" and not concede itself, in order to prevent its being transformed into something else—love perhaps, or indifference.

Don Juan is continually seduced by the beauty of women and continually seduces. He desires that which, immediately after, he wishes to be rid of. His loves are of the "throwaway" type, and it is not possession he seeks but consumption. Don Juan consumes energy, consumes sexual acts, consumes his women as though they were merchandise. He does not want to possess them; to the contrary, he counts on liberating himself of them as quickly as possible. To the disoriented Don Luigi, his rival in love intrigues and duels, who asks him how many days he dedicates to his new conquest, he responds with cynical superficiality: "One to fall in love with her, one to enjoy her, one to abandon her, one to replace her, and one hour to forget her" (Zorilla 1844, 36).

This is tragedy, but Don Juan is not aware of it. And this blindness in fact leads to his damnation. It is an arrogant blindness that rejects healing, despite the attempts in many versions of the myth of the women who love him—the faithful Donna Elvira, for example, or the very much enamored Donna Ines in the *Don Giovanni Tenorio* of Zorilla cited earlier.

Twelve

Encountering Psychic Reality

Renouncing the ownership of one's own body, confer-
ring it to another is an action which can be included
in the imagination of the perverse; this implies inhabit-
ing the body of another as though it were one's own
and in the same way conferring one's own to the other.
　　　　　　　　　—P. Klossowski, *La moneta vivente*

As the vast variety of versions of this legend proves, the nuclei around which the story of Don Juan revolve—and that, analyzed more closely, would represent the very structure of his
character—are many. Don Juan is a very particular type of van-
quisher: insatiable, he could be described as suffering from
erotic bulimia. More than gluttonous, he is voracious; what
matter to him are numbers. But even more, he needs to catalogue, list his victims. In the *Don Giovanni Tenorio* of Zorilla
(1844, 34–35), Don Juan and Don Luigi enumerate the woman
they have seduced and the men they have murdered:

> DON LUIGI: There is my sheet. Count them.
> DON GIOVANNI: Twenty-three.
> DON LUIGI: They are dead. Let's see now . . . By the cross of
> St. Andrew . . . thirty-two!
> DON GIOVANNI: They are dead.
> DON LUIGI: That's what I call killing!
> DON GIOVANNI: I beat you by nine.
> DON LUIGI: You win. Let's go on to the conquests.
> DON GIOVANNI: Here I have fifty-six.
> DON LUIGI: On your list I count seventy-two.
> DON GIOVANNI: You lose.
> DON LUIGI: Incredible!

DON GIOVANNI: From a royal princess to the daughter of a fisherman, my love has embraced the entire social scale.

In the libretto of Mozart's opera, once more this particular need to *enumerate* emerges, and the aria in which the cataloguing occurs is more than an inventory; it is an arid auditor's account.

In Italia seicento e quaranta,
In Lamagna duecento e trentuna,
Cento in Francia, in Turchia novantuna,
Ma in Ispagna son già mille e tre.
(In Italy six hundred and forty, in Germany
two hundred and thirty-one, one hundred in
France, in Turkey ninety-one. But in Spain,
They are already one thousand and three.)

What is the significance of this need to go on with these conquests and to enumerate them? What is revealed is the psychology of the libertine: an individual versed in the art of seduction, but incapable of abandoning himself to love. Apparently, enumerating above all compensates for being incapable of truly possessing. It is a surrogate, a consolation prize; it is deceiving oneself of having in some way realized certain fantasies of omnipotence: to have conquered one thousand and three! These apparent riches, according to Kierkegaard, are instead indicative of an extreme poverty; the enumeration reveals that it is a question of an anonymous crowd, passersby, faceless numbers without out a story. It is an enumeration that allows for no distinctions, "lumping everything together," and ultimately reveals the total incapacity of Don Juan to love the single, particular, individual aspect of the other; each new victim is seen solely as increasing the booty.

The inability to develop a love tie is common in the narcissistic personality. The dominant sentiments in these individuals are impatience and frustration whenever the objects of their desire are not immediately available. They become restless and discontent, quarrelsome and irritable, as though something of vital importance were slipping through their fingers. And in fact, in their eyes, succeeding in seducing—that is, conquering and

175

subjugating—the other represents a confirmation of their value, a proof that they exist. I seduce, therefore I am. Their self-esteem is so fragile that a rejection can even cause—as I have personally had occasion to observe—acute psychosomatic reactions. The other who does not yield kindles painful sensations of insignificance, worthlessness, and loss of identity, because he has the power to confirm or nullify identity. But fortunately for them, the deeply narcissistic personality of these individuals succeeds in reducing to the minimum the risk of such traumatic experiences, simply by refusing a priori to attribute to the other an individuality, a peculiarity, a "uniqueness" that could render their response—be it positive or negative—significant. "I don't need you" is the message of the narcissist's comportment. It would be more realistic, however, if he were to say, "I cannot afford the luxury of needing you: I am too vulnerable to face that risk, I couldn't bear the anxiety that would imply." This anxiety dates back to his earliest experiences connected to the first relationships with the parental figures, as well as the manner in which he *invested them with affect*. Infantile narcissism in fact is also a reflection of the "investment" made by the parents on the child, an investment that can assume various forms. In certain situations, in which the very birth of the child is "hyper-invested"—for example, when the child has been long desired, when it is hoped that his birth will function to salvage the existence of the couple, or when the child is the long-hoped-for male child—the mere fact of his existence results in his being experienced as an extraordinary being to whom superior qualities will be attributed (Saraval 1987). Every physiological activity of his, from eating to evacuation, will be praised, emphasized, while aspects relative to his impotency, or worse yet, his destructiveness, will remain in shadow, without the slightest hint of reproach. This form of idealizing love does not allow the child to develop in a balanced way; his Self will "swell with illusory omnipotence" (ibid., 51). A child whose capacities, beauty, obligingness is continually praised is thus forced to repress as shameful all the manifestations of vulnerability, discontent, and aggressiveness, which he must experience and which he *must* conceal in order to conserve the love of his parents. He will then develop a false self, a hypertrophic and narcissistic self, causing to remain split and re-

176

pressed those affective contents not tolerated by the consciousness: vulnerability, impotency, anger—all sentiments associated with shame and guilt.

On the other hand, the unwanted child, lacking empathetic attention and care—the product of a difficult pregnancy, or in a situation or circumstances that do not dispose the parents to acceptance—will demonstrate a disturbed narcissistic development, in the opposite sense of the hypertrophic narcissism of the "gifted" child. He receives signals that diminish his importance, which mortify his desire to be loved or to love: anguished experiences of persecution, fear of being abandoned, and feelings of shame and annihilation structure an impoverished and depressed impression of himself, continually necessitating external confirmation and reassurance as to his own value, demonstrations of acceptance to counter his own feelings of inadequacy and discomfort. In both cases—"hyperinvestment" of the infantile Self on the part of the parents or insufficient care—the development of the child's sense of identity will be profoundly marked. In the first case, the illusion of omnipotence will inflate the sentiment of the infantile Self, preventing the child from encountering his own aggressive components and therefore allowing him to develop the capacity to bear what is bad in himself and in the other, and above all to find protection through love. In other words, he will be incapable of perceiving the sense of his own limits. In the second hypothesis, what is structured is a representation of the devaluated and depressed self that may be transformed into a tendency to fail in forming valid relationships, causing the subject instead to re-create with the partner the same original parent-child relationship, in which he will be frustrated by his incapacity to relate to his own love objects. As M. Balint (1932) suggests, these dynamics are related not so much to conflict as to basic *failures* in the process of the development of the Self. That failure can be traced back to a fundamental lack, a profound void or early wound that irremediably marks development, and that could be resolved only by the receipt of the missing aspect. The adult utilizes once more these mechanisms for adjusting, and not only defensive, ends. In any relationship, even including the brief and superficial relationship that the narcissistic seducer establishes with the partner, the adult once more reproduces and reactivates the original situation of the relationship with the parents.

In order to avoid entering into contact with those sentiments of dependence and fear, the narcissist prefers seducing, magically attracting to himself the other, capturing him with his desire and being loved himself in turn. The idealization is always present—a reciprocal, mirroring idealization—in which the seduced lives the enchantment of being the chosen, elective, loved one. This is possible because this personality—usually well aware of his seductive powers—and a master of the art of appearing as the one who will finally realize the expectations of the other—give the impression of being gratifying, sure lovers. Don Juan is only apparently in search of the other; what he is actually in search of is narcissistic confirmation, that corroboration of himself that he inevitably perceives of as fleeting. It is the sense of his own personal value that is constantly threatened, never definitively established, and perpetually in need of being confirmed by the dedication and mirroring love of the other. It is essential that this be understood; Don Juan, the seducer Narcissus, does not aspire to an authentic encounter with the other, and even less so does he seek possession. Once more, what he seeks is exclusively a confirmation of his own value. "If the other—so precious, beautiful, intelligent—prefers me to so many others, it must mean that I am worth much more," says our seducer to himself. The logic subtending this collector/conqueror behavior is clearly bound to the quest for power. This constant need of the seducer for casual sexual relationships, his interest limited to the brief period of the seduction and not the difficult and longer period necessary to consolidate a union; the inevitable recounting to friends of conquests and the strategies used to achieve them, and above all the need to assign to numbers the quantity of conquests; and the weight of proof of his own "value" all reveal that his choice of lifestyle is more the result of the need for power than an erotic need—intended, once more, as a profound transforming experience. It is a pressing, febrile, indefatigable need, the vain struggle to close a breach. At that point, there remains nothing more to do but catalogue the efforts, each success, as proof of a "duty" performed, the mortal remains of the defeated "enemies" lined up like cadavers at the morgue. And, in fact, as we have seen, that enumeration was not only of victims of seduction, but also of murder! Thus Mozart's Don Giovanni sings in the famous champagne aria:

Ed io frattanto
Dall'altro canto
Con questa e quella
Vo' amoreggiar.
Ah! La mia lista
Doman mattina
D'una decina
Devi aumentar
(And I, in the meantime, with this one and that
go courting. Ah! My list, tomorrow morning,
by a dozen or so will you be increased.)

That need to catalogue is a fixation that Don Juan shares with another famous libertine—the French Marquis de Sade. The list of the *Divine Marquis* also includes a vast range of erotic eccentricities, given that his interest was for the most part in perversion. This enumeration of rapes, crimes, and a wide variety of obscenities, unfailingly accompanied by the detailed and vivid description of the single "entries," in the final analysis puts into focus the other side of the capricious, inconstant, infantile seducer. In the end, he is a pathetic figure. Thus, the Shadow of this character comes into the limelight; that is, the phantasm of the rapist. That analysis may be considered offensive, if not hasty, by the legions of "Latin lovers" who vaunt being identified with the valiant Don Juan; however, it should be reasonably clear to the reader that our intention here is obviously not to judge *every* libertine as psychopathic. What we would point out is the imaginary—we might even say archetypal—substratum. The hero possesses every quality or is guilty of every depravation. Thus Don Juan has been described by many authors as an abominable creature; that is, he has been judged as an absolutely negative personage. The following is a passage from Stendhal's *De l'Amour* (1822):

Don Juan forsakes all duties which would liken him to the rest of mankind. On the great marketplace of life it would be a bad merchant who took always without paying . . . Women gifted with a certain elevated spirit who, once the first bloom of youth has passed, know how to see love only where it actually exists, usually avoid the various Don Juans who would have quantity rather than quality in the conquest.

The psychological reality revealed by the craving to enumerate is one aspect—as the imaginary of de Sade also reveals—of a maniacal psychology. However, as López-Pedraza rightly points out, "defining the line dividing the aspects of the fantasy of rape . . . and the psychopathic aspect . . . is no easy task, in life or in psychotherapy" (1977, 49). Thus, any simplistic diagnosis of the *case* of Don Juan risks producing a leveling effect, distorting and falsifying the complexity of the characteristics, thus depriving us of information that can *also* be provided by the dark world of pathology. In fact, López-Pedraza maintains, there exists a certain type of "initiation to psychic reality" that is actually affected through violence and transgression, provided that these remain figures of the imaginary, emblematic and significant as metaphors, and not models to be taken literally. Obviously, rape constitutes a crime and as such must be condemned and punished. However, this does not belie the fact that within each one of us there is space for a "theatre of the imaginary"—at times no less cruel than the famous *Grand Guignol*—where violence and horror are on stage: the personages and plots belonging to our psyche, our desire for imagination and initiation to the reality of the soul. Assuming their roles in these intimate and secret, interior scenarios are executioners and victims, sadistic phantasms and masochistic angels, rapists and sacrificial victims. In the dark, this imaginary world in which we are more audience than author, and that is capable of disorienting us, performs a function that we will gradually learn to understand. Here, we will simply say that although the Shadow of the daring Don Juan is violence and rape, it does not necessarily follow that Don Juan is a rapist, but that—like any mythical image—the image of Don Juan *contains and expresses* the reality of psychic opposites. If for our daytime consciousness the truth of desire is unambiguous (love is simply love, and in love there is no space for hatred, as certainly as white negates black, and vice versa), our primitive, nocturnal reality of the Anima tells us that the truth of desire is actually ambivalent, contradictory and conflicting, that we hate more than we love, that is possible to experience dependence and love for a frustrating object, even to desire one capable of dealing us death. Dreams—those windows opened onto the unconscious world—indicate to us that the psyche is a complex and ambiguous reality, the language of which is unknown to our consciousness, as it inevitably differentiates—it weighs, judges, measures, punishes, sunders.

Thirteen

The Dream of the Chameleon

He desires sensually, and seducing with the demonic force of sensuality, he seduces them all.
— S. Kierkegaard, *The Music of Mozart and Eros*

In love, Don Juan is a simulator, a pretender, a *play-actor.* He feigns sentiments not his own, impersonating—just as an actor would—personages "he is not." Dressed in borrowed finery, he passes for servant or friend and, in the conspiring darkness, takes the place of lover or husband. Don Juan is a *Burlador:* a sham and a cheat. But then, is not deceit a recurring theme in the universe of sentiments? In love, we resort to deception to overcome prohibitions seen as obstacles. But deceit is a tactical choice, and as such differs from simple transgression; it assumes an unsuccessful elaboration of what is forbidden and the reason it is, the absence of a sense of guilt and consequently any need for redress.

Anyone habitually resorting to deceit in the love relationship clearly moves in the narcissistic area of illusions, in which he is omnipotent and dominates reality through a magic control of its elements. The liar inevitably ends up confusing his own deceptions with reality, eventually failing to distinguish between what is true and what is false—which is what ultimately traps him. There is a saying to the effect that the liar has a short memory; however, what happens is that he forgets the imaginary constructions supporting his lies and thus reveals the hidden truth through a variety of lapses.

This attempt to magically control reality is an illustration of Don Juan's incapacity to conceive of his own limits—and the failure to perceive of limitations provides the basis of his illusions of immortality and omnipotence. Thus he permits himself every sort of deceit, every caprice, anything that attracts him or flatters his narcissism. In his arrogance he is utterly incapable of postponing satisfaction or renouncing pleasure, and the stronger the prohibition, the stronger his need is to challenge it, to prove to himself his own omnipotence. In the event of defeat, his habitual strategy is inevitably to negate what is true, like the fabled fox and the unattainable, *bitter* grapes.

Don Juan does not dismiss the possibility of divine punishment, but he considers it so distant a possibility that he feels he can ignore it, preferring to put off repenting until a "tomorrow" that slides progressively further into the future. He consequently possesses an unshakable faith in his own ability to handle any situation, which he does generally through the usual subterfuge and deceit. His illusion of omnipotence is fed by his reckless temerity and contempt for danger. The themes of challenging death and morality and incarnating the demoniac potential of the flesh rebelling against divine prohibition are expressions of Don Juan's excessive self-confidence. He is the accused rejecting the accusation, refusing to accept guilt. Writers dealing with this theme, above all during the Romantic period, have been very taken by the vitality of Don Juan's desire and his exuberant behavior, often considering these to be admirable manifestations of a solar heroism and Dionysian exaltation. Don Juan's arrogance was for many Romantics a sign of heroism and courage; however, other versions of the myth present it for what it is—a blindness and maniacal self-importance that eventually lead to his definitive fall. Once more, from the point of view of the libertine, deceit serves to overcome a serious obstacle to conquest: prohibition—that is, the Ninth Commandment, which prohibits coveting another man's wife. Don Juan challenges it, as he in fact challenges any prohibition: he divides loving hearts, couples, insinuating himself as a third subversive element within the love dynamic. He seduces ingenuous fiancées, discrediting their fiancés, and if the one to refuse to capitulate is the desired woman—who has no intention of violating a marriage vow—deception, disguise, or substitution will eventually produce the desired result. The prohibition about "another man's wife" obviously echoes the Oedipus prohibition as regards the child's first love object, which is the mother. It is in relation to this early prohibition that the child develops the sense of guilt and the fear of vengeance and punishment by the parent, a fear that becomes even more overwhelming in proportion to the child's projections of affective ambivalence onto the mother. Feelings of jealousy directed toward the parental couple and their love effusions, the envy and anger that can be aroused from feeling excluded from this intimacy, only amplify the child's fear of violent reaction on the part of the parent.

Jungian psychology considers libertinism, along with homosexuality and impotence, to be one of the possible effects of the maternal complex. In the homosexual, the heterosexual component is, in unconscious form, fixated on the mother, while in the heterosexual libertine, the son unconsciously seeks the mother in every woman. According to Jung, the mother complex leads to an unnatural sexualizing of the male instinct.

Other psychoanalysts claim that the comportment of Don Juan could be explained in terms of an unresolved Oedipus complex. Don Juan seeks his mother in every woman, but never succeeds in finding her. The Oedipus complex of this seducer would be structured on a series of unresolved narcissistic needs, which include the need to incorporate the loved object. As we know, from the outset, the infant enters into a relationship with the mother (and successively with the world) through oral activity and the ingestion of food. Nourishing himself, the child not only satisfies the need for nourishment but also enters into deep contact with a new reality, which the mother in her role as "first environment" represents in a special way. Being nourished is significantly an act of incorporation and consciousness of reality. This would explain why the metaphor of nourishment is so often used to express the assumption of something vital: we "nourish" ourselves with good literature, we speak of "nourishment for the soul" and "the spirit." In ancient Greece, Zeus "nourished all living creatures," just as the Eucharist, as "nourishment," for today's Christians is clearly a metaphor of the love of God (remember the words of Jesus of Nazareth upon the first celebration of the rite). But let us return to profane love. Among the endless versions offered us by literature and the cinema of the "nourishing" aspect of sexuality, we might cite the excellent metaphor of Italo Calvino (1986), in *Sotto il sole giaguaro,* of a universal cannibalism molding every love relationship and eliminating the confines between bodies. Thus lovers, in sensual ecstasy, will often use the expression "I could just eat you up." Obviously, this is usually not an indication of real cannibalistic tendencies, but rather a throwback to ancient images, something recalling those primitive experiences we have completely forgotten. And so, the rite celebrated in the arms of the other produces echoes of lost memory. In fact, incorporation is the somatic model, precursor of the mechanisms of introjection and identification. The child incorporates, along with his food, the "good" or "bad" qualities of the mother. Think, for example, of the concept that the milk of a depressed woman is "bad" milk, and that many infants born of depressed mothers refuse their milk. The mechanism of sucking is essential to survival, as well as to pleasure and the need to enter into contact with the world, to assume and metabolize its qualities.

There are three aspects of incorporation: the pleasure of ingesting an object; assailing the loved object ("I could eat you up"); and assimilating the qualities of the object, making them our own. In the phase of "oral organization," loving is also equivalent to avidly incorporating, destroying, and metabolizing the loved object. And here we have that ambivalence that will govern the dynamics of our sentiment and affects for the rest of our lives. When incorporation is experienced by the child as an aggressive experience, as an attack on the mother, the fear of being in turn devoured causes paranoiac anxiety that can at times be devastating. There are many reasons for this; the projection of the child's aggressive impulses onto the mother may find the mother unable to receive and re-elaborate them, so as to restitute them digested. In fact, it is the mother who confers meaning to the emotional elements that the child experiences, she who translates them and responds empathetically: "Don't worry, your aggressiveness will not destroy me." When, due to more or less conscious psychological problems, the mother fails to identify empathetically with the moods of the child and tranquilize his anxieties, frustration increases the child's anger, and the need to incorporate the mother becomes progressively tinged with aggressiveness and guilt.

Naturally, for archaic psychology (which sees the child as primitive man, as any individual passing through a regressive phase, as for example the psychotic), devouring the other implies the possibility that the other might do the same. The wolf of Little Red Riding Hood fame is an incarnation of those fears, as is the image of the witch fattening up Hansel and Gretel before turning them into a tasty meal. Psychoanalytically speaking, when there has been an insufficient elaboration of the problems related to the oral phase, the model of successive relationships can remain fixed on a relationship model of the incorporation-identification type. Unconsciously, the fear of being "devoured and destroyed" determines a defense of the type "I will devour and destroy you before you devour and destroy me." Of course, one can be destroyed only when he has been unveiled as being impotent and vulnerable, and it is this unconscious experience of impotence and vulnerability that underlies the narcissistic malaise.

The sadistic tone of libertine comportment, seduction through deception and remorseless abandonment; the quality of "prey" of the girls seduced by Don Juan, their being "savored," consumed, and quickly substituted; and the insatiable hunger of the protagonist all are elements that lend themselves to an analytical interpretation based on models of sadistic incorporation and unresolved narcissism. The spur to erotic success is dictated by feelings of inferiority and inadequacy, which the seducer contests with proof of his erotic prodigality. In fact, his narcissistic need demands that proof and requires that others provide it, as he lacks a solid and stable sense of identity. We could then speak of a dependence on narcissistic aids and a fear of losing love. From the moment Don Juan knows that he has succeeded in exciting one woman, he is once more riddled by doubts as to other women with whom he has not yet measured himself. The strategy of deception and false promises is the instrument that conserves his illusion of being in control and manipulating the other without being in turn manipulated and controlled. These rituals make it possible for him to negate fear, exorcise the evil potential of the other, and above all withdraw from the relationship when it threatens to become too involving or compromising—that is, when it becomes a question of establishing a relationship and consequently revealing his real countenance. There is nothing in the world Don Juan wants less than to reveal his real identity. The anonymous theatrical piece *Il convitato di pietra* (erroneously attributed to Cicognini) opens with Don Juan's obstinate refusal to be recognized by Isabella:

> ISABELLA: I will not leave you, even at the cost of death!
> DON GIOVANNI: Let me go, treacherous woman!
> ISABELLA: Let me at least know who you are.
> DON GIOVANNI: Incognito I came, and incognito I would leave.

This situation is repeated in the libretto of Lorenzo da Ponte (1787) for the work of Mozart, *Il dissoluto punito ossia il Don Giovanni,* once more providing the opening scene of the opera. The name of the woman this time is Anna:

> DONNA ANNA: Don't leave or else I shall kill myself. That I would let you flee, never.
> DON GIOVANNI: Mad woman! Futile request. Who I am you will never know.

The insistence on concealing identity—it should now be clear—is another way to protect an excessive fragility. The chameleon defends itself against its predators thanks to an amazing mimetic ability, by means of which it conceals its real identity. Don Juan also possesses this ability, which is manifested not only in the endless game of disguise and substitution but above all in the unconscious art of incarnating the male projections of the woman he must seduce, of donning the finery of the ideal gentleman, the faithful lover whom the ingenuous woman longs for.

It is interesting that, in the ancient African legend of Kaidara, there is a symbolic representation of the chameleon that fits the psychology of our personage like a glove. That animal and its physical characteristics and habits, analyzed in an anthropomorphic manner as the psychological attributes of certain individuals, provide a surprising daytime/nighttime polarity. The characteristic of changing color is one example: the diurnal sense is sociability, the capacity to establish pleasant relationships, the capacity to adapt to any circumstance; while the nocturnal sense is hypocrisy, malleability, lack of convictions, squalid opportunism, and a weak personality. Also, the chameleon's long, viscous tongue, with which it can attack its prey from a distance without requiring the slightest movement of its body, could be symbolic of certain human attitudes: for example, a carefully dissimulated avidity, a powerfully persuasive loquacity with which to overcome the resistance of the interlocutor. The chameleon's tongue deceives and conceals. The chameleon's prehensile tail is the symbol of the coward—the individual who resembles the chameleon possesses a facile sociability and an extroversion that leads to success, but also has another side characterized by a tendency to appropriate that which belongs to others without giving the impression of seducing, a tendency to act "behind their backs," of laying traps. Those who are familiar with the literature on the love life of Don Juan may be surprised at these analogies as well as the psychological delicacy of cultures we are presumptuous enough to consider "primitive."

As we have said, avidity, lust, superficiality, inconstancy, a defiant attitude, a contempt for danger, and opportunism all are defensive strategies of Don Juan, which serve to shield him from contact with something extremely distressing and menacing. These defenses, in the opinion of many psychoanalysts, would be tied to a sense of guilt related to the Oedipus ménage: there is always a rival to eliminate, a husband to kill, a lover to neutralize.

The theme of the punishment/guilt of Don Juan was taken up by Otto Rank (1922) in *The Don Juan Legend,* a rare monograph on the personage by a leading figure in that field, published for the first time in the review *Imago*. The tragic theme of punishment and guilt, which is the true leitmotiv of the libertine experience, has its origins in the failure to separate from the maternal figure and consequently in the failure to identify with paternal law and assume adult masculinity. If Don Juan seeks the mother in every woman, then every man—that is, the father, the legitimate "proprietor"—must be the mortal enemy par excellence. In other words, the love for the mother must not violate or ignore the limits set by the taboo of incest; if it does, it will inevitably bear the sign of the obscenity of a terrible crime that calls for punishment.

Recognizable in the many versions of the myth are personages clearly representing Don Juan's father, or his more or less symbolic substitutes (a brother in some versions, or the statue of the knight, which Rank identifies as the reappearance of the paternal phantasm). Don Juan assumes a hostile attitude vis-à-vis these personages, to the point of parricide (in a version of Holtei referred to by Rank (1922, 42), and (significantly) very similar to the parricide committed by Oedipus (during a heated discussion, he kills his father without having recognized him, because his father appears dressed as a hermit).

Don Juan, however, does not seem to experience the slightest feeling of guilt, nor has he any second thoughts about perpetrating his misdeeds. He abandons, postpones, falsely promises, murders, oblivious of any cause for remorse. Even the admonitions of his devoted servant, Leporello (father substitutes, even fathers, are ineffectual), fall on deaf ears. His death, as it is represented in *Burlador,* is—as we have seen—the result of his habitual, impenitent arrogance. Don Juan's final challenge—to death (in the guise of an animated statue)—is unsuccessful.

Another discerning interpreter of the myth of Don Juan was Melanie Klein, who analyzed this theme in "Love, guilt and reparation" (1937). According to Klein, Don Juan suffers from an unconscious obsession: he is oppressed by the terrible fear of the death of those he loves. It is a fear that could have cast him into the depths of darkest depression had he not developed a mighty defense: unfaithfulness, which permits him to prove to himself that his only love object (originally his mother) is not indispensable, since he succeeds in investing his energies on other women, toward whom he can demonstrate sentiments apparently strong and sublime, but that are in reality utterly superficial. This unfaithfulness is produced by an unconscious compromise, manifested in a dual attitude: Don Juan abandons the woman who temporarily substitutes the object of primary love and immediately afterward turns to another, showering her with the same instant attention, the same sudden passion. What is the explanation of this unconscious dynamic? Don Juan, by abandoning the desired woman, withdraws from the mother, saving her from his love, which he perceives as dangerous as it is avid and destructive. By means of this defense, he above all attempts to free himself from his painful dependence on her. It is an ambivalent movement that attempts both to save the mother (from the fear of losing himself in her or being devoured by her originate) and to withdraw, in order to protect her from his own voracity. Turning to the future conquest and providing her—he believes—with pleasure and love, he protects the loved mother. However, the fear of a lethal dependence unleashes those destructive, avid, and angry tendencies that cause him to continually attempt to substitute the first object of desire. Implicit in this ambivalence is that, if on the one hand sexuality is experienced as the power to protect the mother and render her happy, on the other it represents a hidden threat, to himself and to the other.

Among the most frequent causes of the incapacity to love or to establish satisfying relationships with the opposite sex are mechanisms of splitting and repression of emotions perceived as threatening to the psychological equilibrium. From birth, the child attempts to defend himself from all states of physiological and psychic tension that place his survival in jeopardy; with the structuring of a stable consciousness of himself and an ego capable of relating to others, the child learns to protect himself from those emotions that threaten the love bond with his parents and other significant persons close to him. He protects himself not only from communicating those emotions, which would cause a punitive reaction on the part of adults, but above all from those unbearable emotional states concealed in the circuit of unconscious communication between child and adult, from the first moments of life. The depressed parent, for example, unconsciously communicates to the child a request for "salvation" and help that paradoxically reverses the roles in the relationship: the child-parent must defend and protect the mother (the "defenseless little girl") from her anxieties. The child develops a surprising sensitivity, by means of which he deciphers the needs of the mother and learns to communicate to her only that which does not threaten her equilibrium. He thus learns that certain emotions are "bad" (because the mother cannot tolerate them) and that communicating them would be equivalent to creating the terrible prospect of losing the mother's love. It is thus that the frustration, anger, and aggressiveness that circulate in any human relationship are split and repressed, producing a deep rupture in the developing personality.

It is above all in the area of desire, with its constellations of repression and prohibition, that a dangerous splitting between affect and sexuality can occur. This is possible in those whose aggressive components have been split; because these elements have been repressed, they could subsequently emerge in the form of sexual fantasy or perversion. It can happen that the need to safeguard the gratifying experience with the "good" mother and one's own love object from these aggressive components (or those simply experienced as such) renders necessary a splitting of the internal image of femininity—either the good mother, who then becomes the good wife, or the courtesan, the dark object of desire who will become the repository of projections veined with sadism and a morbid eroticism.

In any case, I believe that problems of sexuality must be approached with due caution, as it is an area in which making a distinction between what is permissible and what is not, between what is normal and what is deviation, is practically impossible. Moreover, even those who consider themselves capable of making that distinction must come to terms with the question of responsibility, which is ultimately also a question of freedom. But is there anyone who can honestly claim to be in control of his own sexual life? Despite the infinity of rules and "instructions for use" conditioning the sexual act, no one can presume to have mastered it, since if anything it is the sexual act that has for centuries mastered us. As to the choice of love *object,* even that is not in the final analysis a free choice. It is doubtful that even our sexual fantasies are free, since the various cultural codes imposing their particular iconography, models, and variations result in our producing certain fantasies and only those, in the same way that we fall in love, conditioned by specific aesthetic, literary, and cultural canons. In other words, neither the sexual act nor the love object is free of cultural coercion.

That which we desire, the way in which we desire it, the means we use to obtain it, seduce it, and make it ours, cannot

191

exclude social, cultural, aesthetic, and linguistic factors belonging to the place and time of which we are the products. And yet, there does remain something that is truly free in sexuality: the power of desire, apart from the object desired, eros "pure and simple." For this reason it is fearful and feared.

Whatever the time, place, or culture, desire disturbs the existing order; it asserts itself as something excessive, something de trop that destroys linearity. Any norm, code, or set of rules for comportment that has resisted over time, any moral system or institution that must be conserved, will be defended tenaciously against the eruption of destabilizing elements. As we know, every *novum* is initially a desire for change, an erotic straining in the direction of development. Eros is the god of transformation, of evolution, of life itself. That which moves the individual, rendering him intolerant of regimentation that suffocates personal freedom, is always desire.

David H. Lawrence, the dominant theme of whose quest was the need to place in discussion the closed world of ready-made and institutionalized reality, produced extraordinarily powerful passages on the force of desire and the need for endless renewal.

It is also interesting to note that Lawrence, in *Lady Chatterley's Lover* (1936), refers to libertinism as a form of "sexuality cultivated in the head," the roots of which are not in the fullness of desire, but in "squallid promiscuity."

It is a baseness, Lawrence points out, which does not belong naturally to man, but to which he falls prey because of an "idiotic" civilization that has never learned to respect the true current of desire. As a result, not having been educated to comprehend the true nature of their desire, men and women abandon themselves to a sort of prostitution. And to explain what he intends by the true nature of desire, he advances his erotic philosophy, which has been called the "erotic utopia" of Lawrence. That which exists, from the stone to the human being, possesses a dual nature: its being singular and unique and possessing solidity, and its expanding "beyond itself," moved by the winds of eros, in order to participate in the eternal dance of the cosmos. The tree, for example, participates in this dual movement, in order to conserve its wholeness and singularity despite the external agents that would undermine it, plunging its roots ever deeper toward the center of the earth, all the while surging and expanding toward the open space, in a motion of vertical attraction to the light of the sun. But the impulse to grow and the impulse to take root are potentials and forces that the tree can only fulfill and obey. In the same way, it is not the child who decides as regards his own development, and this can also be applied to adult human beings, although they may be unaware of it, convinced as they are that they are the agents of their own destiny and conduct their amorous exploits.

In the sphere of amorous comportment, the error into which man falls—being a prisoner of his own individualism—is that of attempting to absorb into his ego the desired object, reducing it to an object possessed: and this, once more citing Lawrence, is lasciviousness, disgusting anthropomorphic lust. It is a question of a compound error: first of all, that of considering oneself the subject of one's desire, believing that it is by means of an individual's will and capacity that he seduces and possesses the other, when in reality there is another source; the force of eros, not generated by the ego or its will, is simply part of the immense and mysterious current of desire circulating through the universe. It is this sin of pride that produces the second part of the error, which is considering the other purely as the object of one's own desire, if not an instrument. The other is a prey, and flees from an ego so arrogant that desire is instead a power flowing from one to the other, each one completing the other. The cult of individualism has reduced man to such a state of egoism that he considers his fellow nothing more than an object to be consumed, the "enjoyment" of which provides the illusion of being the possessor of a unique capital: the ego. One is not pierced by desire; therefore, one no longer knows how to desire.

Desire, as implied by its etymology, is the expression of a loss of the usual points of reference: we are no longer able to orient ourselves; we no longer perceive any light, any north star to indicate the way. The other projects us beyond all the familiar roads, leading us "elsewhere," far from all that is familiar, to a dimension in which reality can no longer be interpreted with the usual criteria, because we ourselves are no longer what we were, no longer see in the same way or use the same words to communicate, no longer recognize ourselves. It is in this decentralization, in this troubling mutation of the ego, that we recognize the workings of desire, the violence of seduction, the authenticity of the love dimension. In this sense, Don Juan is incapable of loving—or, as Lawrence would have it, cannot desire. He is unable to abandon himself to passion and is limited to imitating its gestures. He is unable to abandon himself to the desire of the other, because he fears it would be fatal to do so. He fears losing himself, and thus remains closed to desire.

Eros always creates psychic movement, establishes new connections, places us in contact with the unexpected. Every transformation implies the risk of losing identity; love is always accompanied by a sense of dread. We are projected violently onto an unfamiliar horizon, where we are strangers to ourselves. Falling in love is inevitably accompanied by that very fear, and if that sacred dread is lacking, so is loving. That fear is more than justified, since the greatest suffering we can experience or inflict will always be the result of love: expectations, absence, betrayal, loss of the loved one. All this is part of the love condition, and he who has experienced the metamorphoses of love knows only too well how impossible it is to remain unwounded. Great effort is required, along with a stability of the ego, to bear the suffering and trials implied by the love relationship and permit that temporary eclipse of reason and that tempest of sentiment that can bring about true transformation.

Fourteen

A Particular Kind of Deceit

By night on my bed I sought him whom my soul
loveth; I sought him, but found him not.
—*The Song of Solomon*, Chapter 3, King James

Seduction, as we have seen, is a profoundly different experience for seducer and victim: the one "extorting love" and the one giving it. However, the reader might at this point wonder why so much attention has been given to the former, while the latter has been practically ignored. Is it not, he might ask, the very fault we attribute to Don Juan and all past and present libertines: that is, considering the victim simply an interchangeable "object," no more than a cipher, a trophy of the seducer? The answer to that question is that, from the psychoanalytical point of view—which is the one that interests us here—the seduced coincides with the "one in love"; he who is taken by love is always the one seduced. And the literature produced on the experience of falling in love is legion and includes eminent authors such as Stendhal, Proust, and Roland Barthes, to name but a few.

The experience of the seduced, or the enamored, is ecstatic, one of extreme joy and extreme suffering. And the subsequent expectation, solitude, hope, memory, and fear of losing the loved one are extremely painful. For partaking of so sublime an experience is fatal and produces the torment of doubt, jealousy, and the anxiety that the other will be carried off, because we are undeserving and do not merit him as we may have merited reaching other goals or objectives, often through toil and sacrifice. It is a precious gift, happened by chance, and therefore might just as arbitrarily be taken away from us. Like every enamored's one, the solitude of the seduced is charged with anxiety and torment: the expectation of the other is haunted by phantasms, the place of waiting becomes unreal; it is a state perceived by the one experiencing it in a completely different way than those around him, exiled as he is in a twilight area, far removed from the daily bustle, concrete order, and the discourse of others. Barthes wrote that the identity of the enamored is inevitably one of *he who waits:* no matter what he does, what task he undertakes in order to shake off the desire and the memory of the other, he will fail to get away from himself. If it is not his thoughts that are haunted by the other, it will be his physical languor that conjures up that person to the sound of a fugitive sigh or the wild beating of a heart. Thus, once more, he will be plunged into the depths of his own sentiment, where the other becomes increasingly present as his absence is protracted because, while the identity of the seduced is one who waits, the identity of the seducer is one who is too often *absent.* For the seduced there is nothing but an immutable time of devotion, of hope, and of the fear of being less loved than loving. As he waits, he carries on a conversation with the absent partner, and this anomalous love discourse—in a certain sense, analogous to the mystical discourse—has the effect of rendering the object of desire ever present. From this singular distortion emerges that suspended time in which the lover lives, a suspension of magical creation, illusion, hallucination. Although the object of desire is absent, in the imagination he is still present, called up, longed for, anticipated, imagined in a hypothetical, shared future, or recalled in the moments shared—all of which are propitiatory rituals, magic confirmations of the authenticity of what is being experienced and at the same time exorcisms of the fear that everything could vanish or turn out to be nothing but a dream.

In this illusion that permits the one who loves to manipulate the absence of the loved one and to fill it with images of him, there is a dangerous oscillation between meaning and the lack of meaning. Knowing that the other passes his time in complete freedom and—what is worse—that he may not even be aware of the anxiety and torment imprisoning the other relegates the one who loves to an unbearable solitude. The other, he thinks, may never have really considered, never loved him, and he struggles against this possibility. And here we have the inflexible logic of the love delirium, the atrocious conclusion that "if the other has never loved me, I have never existed." It is at that point that the amorous subject experiences the anguish of abandonment and, in a masochistic dialectic, reaches the point of believing that loss and death had been present and victorious from the very beginning. Subsequent to this tragic conclusion, the one who loves attempts to shake off that state of solitude and waiting, and it is from this death passage that he attempts to defend himself and the cherished image, so as not to plunge into the desperation of vain expectation and an imagined presence.

Illusion and truth, memory and forgetfulness are woven together, creating a complex web inevitably containing those emotional references that constitute lovesickness and at the same time the initiation to love. This initiatory aspect, the precept and education and the psychic reality that the love experience can represent for us, its disciples, is important because love, as Kahlil Gibran wrote, prunes us in order to render us more fertile:

> For even as love crowns you so shall he crucify you. Even as he is for your growth so is he for your pruning, . . .

It conceals in its plumed wings a blade to wound us where we are most virginal, most unconscious, in order to render us more human.

The very particular disturbance characterizing the love dimension is a shifting of an internal, centripetal force, an interiorization of the experience. Every event, every gesture, every encounter are objects for reflection, interrogation, fear. The absence of the other, his distance, wraps the soul in a mantle of solitude in which to plumb its own depths, know itself, and thus become permeable to the most subtle nuances of sentiment. But it also renders the soul docile, grateful for the joys that love provides, capable of reconsidering its ideal claims, exalting instead the daily experiences of life. Obviously, solitude and waiting imply suffering, but a union for self-realization necessitates suffering, requires the "destructive-constructive" aspect of the creativity of eros (Hillman 1979, 108). Eros is violent—of this there can be no doubt. Thus, the experience of being dependent on another, our need of the other's giving himself and loving us in order to confer meaning to our existence, could be defined as an extreme experience. And yet, this violent estrangement, this anguished realization that in order to exist we need another human being to shed light on the authentic meaning of subjectivity, is beneficial. Man, imprisoned in his closed subjectivity, presuming to possess a capital called ego, has need to create an "us" and achieve the fullness of an encounter in order to realize his totality. We are incomplete beings who find realization only through relationship. Actually, the desire for the other is essentially the desire to break the bonds of finiteness, to become transcended in the other. It is the presence of the other that helps us understand our limited autonomy, and his absence that cruelly reveals the magnitude of our need for him. It is through the encounter that we discover the possibility of transcending our solitary condition, through it that the appearance of the other becomes the discovery of a priceless treasure. For these reasons, otherness is the measure of both the transcendence and the inadequacy of man. Thus we discover, through passionate desire for the other, that what frightens us is also what we yearn for most. We are frightened by the solitude into which we will be plunged the moment the desired object makes us aware of our boundless need for love. And nevertheless it is precisely this we yearn for, in order that the wound we are inevitably dealt can be dressed, and we can experience the inebriation of loving and being loved.

It is at this point that the analogies between the love of the enamored and the love of the seduced end. Although the same promise of gratification is present in both the seduction and the love relationship, in the former it remains suspended, expanding infinitely the space of desire. The relationship implies an unrelenting confrontation between two kinds of being *other,* during which the elation of that fusion gradually and inevitably is replaced by the stress of separation, by preferring to idealization a voyage that is more realistic but not for that reason less fascinating, by the discovery of what becomes possible to share— although reality will inevitably cut down to size and, at least partially, crush even this hope. Instead, the space of seduction is still on this side of the relationship, a potential space in which the other remains in the shadows, leaving the seduced in a total uncertainty, on the dangerous edge separating illusion from disenchantment. Denied the nourishment of the concrete satisfactions that feed a relationship, the seduced is forced to resort to the surrogates of fantasy, of daydreaming. The other is at the same time a real and an imaginary being, a fetish, a shifting object. And this uncertainty, this being and not being of the loved one, eventually also renders less certain the self-image of he who loves, placing in discussion his identity. This is because, as it inevitably must be with those who "fall in love," the power of seduction that certifies our existence is all in the hands of our seducer. Without knowing how or why this has occurred, the other has taken possession of our fate, and our very happiness or unhappiness hinges on his choices, his movements. All this becomes comprehensible only with maturity, but then is that not as it should be? Many years of analytical experience have taught me that the most vivacious individuals—those who carry the burden of their years lightly, without the body or the mind showing signs of the ravages of time—must conserve a particular type of self-deception or illusion as regards the matter of seduction, whether in the role of seducer or seduced. I might add that the second case would represent the more significant love experience, as it would imply that an internal predisposition, considerably fragile to begin with, has subsequently maintained a considerable permeability as regards emotional experience. All of these are, clearly, painful and difficult moments, but they are also essential to the existential passages of a lifetime.

However, as long as that fascination persists, it will be difficult to recognize to what extent the other—precisely due to his avoiding confrontation by remaining in the shadows—incarnates our phantasm, one of our powerful internal images which, like the characters of Luigi Pirandello in search of an author, asks to be "brought into the world," to what extent he incarnates those unconscious contents still awaiting elaboration. The fact itself that the other appears to us as the obstinate bearer of immovable difference renders him extraordinarily attractive. Difference is the appearance of the unknown, with all its disturbing/attractive aspects. What do we seek in the other, if not the possibility of exploring with him the hidden zones of our own being, the buried potential, the untapped truth of sentiment—in other words, that adventurous passage to self-knowledge that can be undertaken only in the company of another human being? What happens in seduction is that the other conjures up our internal images, those fleeting and elusive images of that "other" who we are to some extent but—once more citing Jung—we can never succeed in being fully.

But the problem does not end there. There is in man a categorical imperative, a spasmodic, even violent tendency and obsessive need to enter into relationships with other human beings. If initially this impulse would seem to have a specifically sexual connotation, upon closer examination it becomes clear that the desire for relationship is inherent to human nature, in that man's awareness of his own being in the world occurs precisely through relationship. We have seen how all profound affective content appears to us projected onto another person, who then becomes the numinous representation of all our expectations, illusions, and desires. The game of projections is inevitably present, unavoidable. However, this does not take anything from the validity of our relationships, which with the passing of time are partially liberated of this necessary aspect, put into another perspective and (depending on whether or not we succeed in integrating them into the existential context) either become deeper or are exhausted. But this territory is extraneous to the seductive game precisely because the other is and is not, appears and disappears, wounds us with the pangs of love and takes flight like Cupid, leaving us in anticipation of his return. However, it would be well to remember that knowing the rules of the game in seduction serves to no avail. The only thing that could help us avoid falling into the net is the diminishing of desire, but never that human quality called wisdom.

Passion increases with distance, with the eternal oscillation between presence and absence. We attempt to convince ourselves that we can control this divergence, all while knowing that we will be disappointed. Thus we accept disappointment as the price to be extracted for our becoming more human, and yet we are aware that, despite maturity, we will be seduced again, and once more *carried elsewhere,* beyond the laboriously acquired certainties, still needful of suffering for someone who makes us wait, for a job that does not materialize, for a nonexistent future—absolutely aware of the power of the illusion, mirage, and deceit of the senses. Every seduction is a promise, a half-opened door onto the unfamiliar, momentarily glimpsed, world of splendor—an expectation not only attenuated by desire and waiting, but intensified.

As a psychoanalyst, I have had years of being intimately in contact with that desperate, heartfelt cry at the moment of separation, that moment of desperate yearning for something that exists but that, the moment its authenticity and solidity is discovered, unfailingly appears to withdraw forever. At that point, we can only cling to the pure pretense that the world we inhabit will, sooner or later, become once more *our* world. Certainly, this desire and this expectation can—and very often does—render us victims of some mirage, seeing Paradise where there is only arid desert. But to err is human, in the noblest sense of the word. And it is therein that our most authentic humanity lies, because it is through error that we learn to know ourselves and to live. The fear of erring, ultimately, is the fear of living.

Bibliography

AA.VV. 1990. Fusionalità. Scritti di psicoanalisi clinica. Rome: Borla.

Adorno, T. 1951. *Minima Moralia.* Turin: Einaudi, 1954.

Agamben, G. 1977. Stanze. La Parola e il fantasma nella cultura occidentale (Stanzas: Word and Phantasm in Western Culture). Turin: Einaudi.

Alberoni, F. 1986. *Erotismo.* Milan: Garzanti.

Aleramo, S. 1991. *Dialogo con Psiche.* Palermo: Ed. Novecento.

Alighieri, Dante. *Inferno. La Divina Commedia* (Divine Comedy). Milan: Zanichelli, 1987.

Andreas-Salomé, L. 1900. Gedanken uber das Liebesproblem in Neue Deutsche Rundschau, vol. 2.

Argyle, M. 1975. *The Body and Its Language: Studies on Non-Verbal Communication* (Italian translation, 1978).

Argyle, M., Lalljec, M., and Cook, M. 1968. The effects of visibility on interaction in a dyad. In *Human Relations,* no. 21: 3–17.

Balint, M. 1932. Character analysis and new beginning. In *Primary Love and Psycho-analytic Technique.* London: The Hogarth Press and the Institute of Psycho-Analysis, 1952.

Barthes, R. 1977. *A Lover's Discourse. Fragments.* London: Jonathan Cape, 1979.

Bataille, G. 1951. L'Amour d'un etre mortel (The Love of an Immortal Being). In *Botteghe Oscure* VIII (November): 105–115.

———. 1961. *Les Larmes d'Eros* (The Tears of Eros). Paris: Societé Nouvelles des Editions Pauvert, 1969.

Baudrillard, J. 1979. *De la séduction* (Seduction). Paris: Editions Galilée.

———. 1987. *L'autre par lui-meme.* Paris: Editions Galilée.

Benjamin, J. 1988. *Legami d'amore*. Turin: Rosenberg and Sellier (Italian translation, 1991).

Bergmann, M. S. 1971. Psychoanalytic observations on the capacity of love. In J. B. McDevitt and C. F. Settlage, eds. *Separation-Individuation: Essays in Honor of Margaret S. Mahler*. New York: International University Press.

Bibring, E. 1954. Psychoanalysis and the dynamic psychotherapies. In *Journal of the American Psychoanalytic Association* 2.

Bolen, J. S. 1984. *Le dee dentro la donna. Una psicologia al femminile* (Goddesses in Everywoman: A New Psychology of Women). Rome: Astrolabio (Italian translation, 1991).

Bouhour, I. P. 1986. Pourrions-nous tutoyer? In *Etudes Freudiennes* 27.

Bucelli, D. 1993. L'Oggetto invisibile. Note sull'indifferenza e la meraviglia. In G. Antonelli, ed. *Forme del sapere in psicologia*. Milan: Bompiani.

Calasso, R. 1988. *Le nozze di Cadmo e Armonia* (The Marriage of Cadmus and Harmony). Milan: Adelphi.

Calvino, I. 1986. *Sotto il sole giaguaro* (Under the Jaguar Sun). Milan: Garzanti.

Campbell, J. 1967. *Myths to Live By*. New York: Viking Press.

Camporesi, P. 1989. *I balsami di Venere*. Milan: Garzanti.

Cantoni, R. 1976. Introduzione to S. Kierkegaard, *Don Giovanni. La musica di Mozart e l'eros* (The Music of Mozart and Eros). Milan: Mondadori (Italian version).

———. 1990. Introduzione to S. Kierkegaard, *Diario del seduttore* (Diary of a Seducer). Milan: Rizzoli (Italian version).

Cappellano, A. (André le Chapelain). 1980. *De Amore*. Milan: Guanda.

Carotenuto, A. 1970. Osservazioni su alcuni aspetti del transfert e del countrotransfert. In *Rivista di Psicologia Analitica* 1: 125–156.

———. 1972. Psicopatologia dell'analista. In *Rivista di Psicologia Analica* III/2.

———. 1980. *A Secret Symmetry: Sabina Spielrein Between Jung and Freud*. New York: Pantheon Books, 1982.

———. 1986. *Kant's Dove: The History of Transference in Psychoanalysis*. Wilmette, Ill.: Chiron Publications, 1990.

———. 1987a. *Eros and Pathos: Shades of Love and Suffering (Studies in Jungian Psychology)*. Toronto: Inner City Books, 1989.

———. 1987b. La terapia inquieta. In *Rivista di Psicologia Analitica* 36.

———. 1988. *The Difficult Art: A Critical Discourse on Psychotherapy*. Wilmette, Ill.: Chiron Publications, 1992.

———. 1991. *To Love, To Betray: Life as Betrayal*. Wilmette, Ill. Chiron Publications, 1996.

———. 1992. *Trattato di Psicologia Analitica*. Turin: UTET.

Cavalcanti, G. *Rime*. Turin: Einaudi, 1986.

Courtine, J. J., and Haroche, C. 1988. *Historie du visage. Exprimer et taire ses émotions. XVIᵉ—olé début XIX siècle*. Paris: Editions Rivages.

da Ponte, L. 1787. *Il dissoluto punito ossia il Don Giovanni*. Milan: Edizioni Ricordi, 1956.

David, C. 1971. *L'Etat amoreux*. Paris: Payot, 1972.

De Benedetti Gaddini, R. 1989. Cure materne, seduzione e controtransfert. In A. Saraval, ed. *La seduzione. Saggi psicoanalitici*. Milan: Raffaello Cortina.

Degrese, C., and Amory, P. 1989. *Il grande gioco della seduzione*. Milan: Lupetti and Co. (Italian translation, 1990).

De Marchi, L. 1991. *Poesia del desiderio*. Florence: La Nuova Italia.

Eibl-Ebesfeldt, I. 1970. *Amore e odio* (Love and Hate). *Per una storia naturale dei comportamenti elementary*. Milan: Adelphi (Italian translation, 1971).

Fairbairn, W. R. D. 1952. *Psychoanalytic Studies of the Personality*. London: Tavistock Publishers.

Ferenczi, S. 1909. Introjection and transference. In *Sex and Psychoanalysis: The Selected Papers of Sandor Ferenczi*, vol. I. New York: Basic Books, 1950.

———. 1933. Confusion of tongues between adults and the child. In *Final Contributions to the Problems and Methods of Psychoanalysis: The Selected Papers of Sandor Ferenczi*, vol. III. New York: Basic Books, 1955.

———. 1985. *Journal clinique* (Clinical Diary). Paris: Payot.

Fisher, H. E. 1992. *Anatomy of Love: The Natural History of*

Monogamy, Adultery and Divorce. Harcourt Brace Jo-vanovich, Inc., and Faber and Faber Ltd.

Flaubert, G. 1857. Madame Bovary. In *Oeuvres completes*. Paris: Société des Etudes littéraires francaises, Club de L'Honnete Homme, 1971.

Flournoy, O. 1986. La séduction réhabilitée ou la passion de l'enfant oedipien. In *Etudes Freudiennes* 27.

Follesa, P., ed. 1987. *Psicoanalisi: l'Eros*. Rome: Borla.

Fordham, M. 1957. Notes on transference. In *New Developments in Analytic Psychology*. London: Routledge and Kegan Paul.

Freud, A. 1936. The ego and the mechanisms of defence, vol. 2. London: The Hogarth Press, 1966.

Freud, S. 1901. Fragment of an analysis of a case of hysteria. In *SE*, vol. 7. London: The Hogarth Press, 1964.

_____. 1905. My views on the part played by sexuality: the aetiology of the neurosis. In *SE*, vol. 7. London: The Hogarth Press, 1964.

_____. 1910–17. Contributions to the psychology of love. In *SE*, vol. 11. London: The Hogarth Press, 1964.

_____. 1914a. Observations on transference-love. In *SE*, vol. 12. London: The Hogarth Press, 1964.

_____. 1914b. On narcissism: An introduction. In *SE*, vol. 14. London: The Hogarth Press, 1974.

_____. 1915–17. Introductory lectures on psychoanalysis. In *SE*, vols. 15 and 16. London: The Hogarth Press, 1963.

_____. 1919. The uncanny. In *SE*, vol. 17. London: The Hogarth Press, 1955.

_____. 1938a. Findings, ideas, problems. In *SE*, vol. 23. London: The Hogarth Press, 1974.

_____. 1938b. An outline of psycho-analysis. In *SE*, vol. 23. London: The Hogarth Press, 1974.

_____. 1985. *The Freud/Jung Letters (1887–1904)*. Cambridge, Mass.: The Belknap Press of Harvard University Press.

Galimberti, U. 1989. *Il gioco delle opinioni*. Milan: Feltrinelli.

Gargiulo, L. 1990. *Dalla selva alla rosa. Il testo e le trame della Divina Commedia dall'Inferno al Paradiso. Guida alla lettura per temi*. Rome: Signorelli.

Gill, M. M. 1954. Psychoanalysis and exploratory psychotherapy.

In *Journal of the American Psychoanalytical Association* 2: 771.

Goethe, J. W. 1809. *Elective Affinities*. Harmondsworth, Middlesex: 1986.

Goldoni, C. 1655. *Don Giovanni o la punizione del dissoluto*. Turin: Einaudi.

Graves, R. 1955. *The Greek Myths*. London: Penguin Books, 1960.

Green, A. 1980. *Narcissisme de vie, Narcissisme de morte*. Paris: Les Editions de Minuit.

Greenson, R. 1967. *The Technique and Practice of Psychoanalysis*. New York: International Universities Press, Inc.

Grinberg, L. 1981. *Psicoanalisis. Aspectos teoricos y clinicos*. Barcelona, Buenos Aires: Paidos.

Hall, E. T. 1959. *The Silent Language*. New York: Doubleday and Co., Inc.

———. 1966. *The Hidden Dimension*. New York: Doubleday and Co., Inc.

Harding, M. E. 1953. *Women's Mysteries*. New York: G. P. Putnam.

Havelock, E. 1906. Il simbolismo erotico. In *Psicologia del sesso*, vol. VI. Rome: Newton Compton, 1971.

———. 1933. *Psicologia del sesso* (The Psychology of Sex). *L'autoerotismo, la periodicità sessuale, il pudore*. Rome: Newton Compton, 1970.

Hesiod. *Teogonia in Opere*. Turin: UTET, 1977.

Hillman, J. 1972a. *An Essay on Pan*. Milan: Adelphi, 1977.

———. 1972b. *The Myth of Analysis*. Evanston, Ill.: Northwestern University Press.

———. 1975. *Re-visioning Psychology*. New York: Harper and Row.

———. 1979. *Puer wounds and Ulysses' scar*. In Puer Papers. Dallas: Spring Publications.

Hinde, R. A., ed. 1972. *La Communicazione non verbale* (Non-Verbal Communication). Bari: Laterza (Italian translation, 1974).

Inni Omerici. 1986. Milan: Mondadori.

Jacobi, J. 1944. *The Psychology of C. G. Jung: An Introduction*. New Haven, Conn.: Yale University Press, 1951.

Jung, C. G. 1912–52. Symbols of transformation. In *CW*, vol. 5. Princeton, N.J.: Princeton University Press, 1956.

———. 1914. Some crucial points in psychoanalysis: A correspondence between Dr. Jung and Dr. Loy. In *CW*, vol. 4. Princeton, N.J.: Princeton University Press, 1961.

———. 1934. The practical use of dream-analysis. In *CW*, vol. 16. Princeton, N.J.: Princeton University Press, 1956.

———. 1940. The psychology of the child archetype. Vol. 9, Tome I. Princeton, N.J.: Princeton University Press, 1959.

———. 1940–50. Concerning rebirth. In *CW*, vol. 9, Tome I. Princeton, N.J.: Princeton University Press, 1959.

———. 1946. The psychology of the transference. In *CW*, vol. 16. Princeton, N.J.: Princeton University Press, 1966.

Kaplan, L. *Female Perversion: The Temptations of Madame Bovary*. London: Pandora (an imprint of HarperCollins Publishers), 1991.

Kerényi, K., and Jung, C. G. 1940–41. *Essays on a Science of Mythology*. New York: Pantheon, 1950.

Kernberg, O. 1976. Impedimenti all 'innamorarsi e al restare innamorati. In B. Zanuso (a cura di) Capacita' d'amore: scritti di. M. S. Bergmann and O. F. Kernberg. Turin: Bollsti Boringhieri, 1993.

Kierkegaard, S. 1843. *Either-Or*. New Haven, Conn.: Yale University Press, 1944.

Klein, M. 1937. Love, guilt and reparation. In M. Klein and J. Riviere. *Love, Hate and Reparation*. London: The Hogarth Press, and the Institute of Psycho-Analysis, 1953.

Krutzenbichler, H. S., and Essers, H. 1991. *Muss denn Liebe Sunde sein? Uber das Begehren des Analytikers*. Freiburg: i.Br., Kore, Verlag Traute Hensch.

Lacan, J. 1975. *Le séminaire de Jacques Lacan. Livre I. Les écrites techniques de Freud (1953–54)*. Paris: Editions du Seuil.

Laing, R. D. *The Self and Others*. London: Tavistock Publications, 1960.

Laplanche, J., and Pontalis, J. B. 1985. *Fantasme originaire, Fantasmes des origines, Origines du fantasme*. Paris: Hachette.

Lawrence, D. H. 1936. *Lady Chatterley's Lover*. Hammondsworth, Middlesex: Penguin Books, 1961.

Levinas, E. 1949. Le Temps et l'Autre. In *Le Choix, le Monde, l'Existence. Cahiers du Collège Philosophique* 1.

Lilar, S. 1963. *Le Couple.* Paris: Editions Bernard Grasset.

Loewenstein, R. M. 1951. The problem of interpretation. In *The Psychoanalytic Quarterly* 20.

Lopez, D. 1987. *La via nella selva. La trasformazione delle passioni.* Milan: Raffaello Cortina.

López-Pedraza, R. 1977. *Hermes and His Children.* Zurich: Spring Publications.

Lowen, A. 1967. *The Betrayal of the Body.* New York: Macmillan.

Macchia, G. 1990. *Tra Don Giovanni e Don Rodrigo. Scenari secenteschi.* Milan: Adelphi.

———. 1991. *Vita avventure e morte di Don Giovanni.* Milan: Adelphi.

Maffesoli, M. 1988. *l'Ombra di Dioniso* (The Shadow of Dionysus). Milan: Garzanti.

Mann, H. 1905. *Professor Unrat order Das Ende Eines Tyrannen.*

Masciangelo, P. M. 1988. Su Freud per il dopo Freud. Una riflessione metapsicologica. In A. A. Semi, ed. *Trattato di psicoanalisi,* vol. I. Milan: Raffaello Cortina.

Masson, J. M. 1984. *The Assault on Truth.* Toronto: Farrar, Straus and Giroux.

Miller, G. 1951. *Language and Communication.* New York: McGraw-Hill.

Molière. 1665. *Don Juan.* Oxford: Oxford University Press, 1989.

Montagu, A. 1981. *Saremo bambini.* Como: Red (Italian translation, 1992).

Montefoschi, S. 1980. *Dialettica dell'inconscio.* Milan: Feltrinelli.

Moreno, M. M. 1980. *Antologia della mistica arabo-persiana.* Bari: Laterza.

Nelli, R. 1952. *l'amour et les mythes du coeur.* Paris: Hachette.

Neruda, P. 1960. *Cento sonetti d'amore.* Milan: Accademia Ed., 1973.

Nietzsche, F. 1888. *The Case of Wagner.* New York: Random House, Inc., 1967.

Olivenstein, C. 1988. *Le non-dit des emotions.* Editions Paris: Odile Jacob.

Otto, R. 1936. *The Idea of the Holy.* London: Pelican Books, 1959.

Parry, J. 1968. *The Psychology of Human Communication.* New York: American Elsevier Co.

Pavese, C. 1947. *Dialoghi con Leucò.* Milan: Mondadori, 1982.

Perry, J. P. 1976. *Roots of Renewal in Myth and Madness.* San Francisco, Washington, London: Jossey-Bass Publishers.

Person, S. E. 1993. Introduction. In S. E. Person, P. Fonagy, and A. Hagelin, eds. *On Freud's "Observations on Transference-Love."* New Haven, Conn.: Yale University Press.

Petrarch, F. *Rime e Trionfi.* 1953. Turin: UTET.

Petronio Andreatta, G. M. 1989. Don Giovanni e Casanova. In A. Saraval, ed. *La seduzione. Saggi Psicoanalitici.* Milan: Raffaello Cortina.

Pinkola Estes, C. 1992. *Women Who Run with the Wolves: Myths and Stories of the Wild Woman Archetype.* New York: Ballantine Books.

Plato. *Phaedrus.* London: Penguin Classics.

Plotinus. *Enneadi,* III 5, 3. Milan: Rusconi, 1992.

Racker, H. 1968. *Transference and Countertransference.* London: The Hogarth Press.

Rank, O. 1909. *The Myth of the Birth of the Hero.* New York: Robert Brunner, 1952.

———. 1922. *The Don Juan Legend,* David G. Winter, tr. Princeton, N.J.: Princeton University Press, 1975.

Robin, L. 1964. *La théorie platonicienne de l'Amour.* Paris: Presses Universitaires de France.

Rousset, J. 1978. *Le myth de Don Juan.* Paris: Librairie Armand Colin.

Sandler, J., and Freud, A. 1985. *The Analysis of Defense: The Ego and the Mechanisms of Defense Revisited.* New York: International Universities Press, Inc.

Sappho, Sappho: A New Translation. Berkeley, Calif.: University of California Press, 1958.

Saraval, A. 1987. Dall'amore de sé all'amore dell'altro. In D. Lopez. *La via nella selva. La trasformazione delle passioni.* Milan: Raffaello Cortina.

Schafer, R. 1983. *An Analytic Attitude.* New York: Basic Books.

Schopenhauer, A. 1844. *Metaphysik der geschlechtliche Liebe.*

Schwartz-Salant, N. 1984. Archetypal factors underlying sexual acting-out in the transference-countertransference process.

In M. Stein and N. Schwartz-Salant, eds. *Transference/ Countertransference*. Wilmette, Ill.: Chiron Clinical Series, Chiron Publications.

Searles, H. F. 1965. *Collected Papers on Schizophrenia and Related Subjects*. London: Mouton and Co.

Sebeok, T. A., Hayes, A. S., and Bateson, M. C., eds. 1964. *Approaches to Semiotics: Transactions of the Indiana University Conference on Paralinguistics and Kinesics*. London: Mouton and Co.

Simmel, G. 1909. Psychologie der Koketterie. In *Schriften zur Philosoèjoe imd Soziologie der Geschlechter*. Frankfurt am Main: Sirkamp, 1985.

Stein, C. 1986. De la séduction à la névrose de transfert ou la liberté obligee. In *Etudes Freudiennes* 27.

Stein, R. 1974. *Incest and Human Love*. Baltimore: Penguin Books.

Stendhal. 1822. *De l'Amour*. Paris: Mongie.

Stevens, R. 1975. *La comunicazione interpersonale. Codici segnali, interazioni*. Milan: Mondadori, 1979.

Taylor, C. 1982. Sexual intimacy between patient and analyst. In *Quadrant* 15: 47–54.

Ulanov, A. 1979. Follow-up treatment in cases of patient/therapist sex. In *Journal of the American Academy of Psychoanalysis* 7: 101–110.

Valletta, N. 1787. *Ciclata sul frascino volgarmente detto jettatura*.

Winnicott, D. 1971. *Playing and Reality*. London: Tavistock Publications.

Yourcenar, M. 1957. *Fires,* Dori Katz, tr., in collaboration with the author. London: Black Swan (Transworld Publishers Ltd.), 1985.

Zorilla, J. 1844. *Don Giovanni Tenorio. Dramma religioso fantastico in due parti*. Rome: Atlantica Ed., 1946.

Index